REBEL FROM BACK CREEK

JAMES BYRON DEAN (1931-1955)

REBEL FROM BACK CREEK

JAMES BYRON DEAN (1931-1955)

A GENEALOGICAL STUDY

BARBARA INMAN BEALL, Ph.D.

Aventine Press

Published by Aventine Press
55 E Emerson Street
Chula Vista, CA 91911
www.aventinepress.com

ISBN: 1-59330-767-5

Library of Congress Control Number: 2012937626

This book is dedicated to
"The Little Prince"
James Byron Dean (1931-1955)—
Who made this book possible—

And to my husband
Howard Lee Beall—
Who has put up with my obsession—

And to my friend
Susan Ann Anderson Huang (1943-2005)—
Who told me that I should write this book ten years ago!

"…I don't really know who I am…but it doesn't matter. There is no possibility for greatness in this world. We are all impaled on a crook of conditioning. A fish that is in the water has no choice that he is. Genius would have it that he swim in sand. We are fish and we drown. We remain in one world and wonder. The fortunate are taught to ask why. No one can answer."

James Dean
Summer 1955

"It is only with the heart that one can see rightly; what is essential is invisible to the eye."

Antoine De Saint-Exupery
"The Little Prince"

"For now we see through a glass darkly; but then face to face: now I know in part; but then shall I know even as I am known."

I Corinthians 13:12--KJV

Table of Contents

PROLOGUE

Painting of Marilyn Monroe and James Dean

--my birthday present in 2010. Howard bought it for me in an antique-collectible store in Georgetown, Colorado. Dated 2007—James Dean Foundation under authorization by CMG

"**C**an I ask you something?"

The student, a twenty-year-old male, approached me at the end of class, my course packet in his hand.

"Of course," I responded.

"Why did you choose him?"

My approach to teaching the research portion of the freshman composition course gradually transformed each semester, beginning with my dissertation of 1998 from a study of student resistance. The second semester of the freshman composition course had the highest drop-out rate of any course in the college curriculum, igniting a search for new ways to inspire students to complete the class. Incorporating research into college writing and doing so correctly is not the most exciting challenge for freshman students. Students sometimes encounter a task master for an instructor who approaches the course and grading with a greater emphasis on failure rather than on success. I remember one such encounter when my class was entering a room where the previous class was still departing. One of my former students, who bailed out of my class at the beginning of the previous semester, now stood before such an instructor, hoping he would accept his topic.

"No! You can't do that!" the instructor snarled.

"Why?" the young man asked.

"Because I don't want to read it, that's why!"

"Well, what about this topic?"

"I don't want to read about that either!"

"Well, what am I supposed to do?"

"Find a topic for your research paper, and I need to approve it!"

"Well, where am I supposed to find it?"

"That's your job! Now, I have to leave! And I expect you to have it approved by me on Thursday!"

The student glanced at me and his expression said everything—"Why didn't I finish your class?"

Research for my dissertation proved that unless students are excited about their research topics, they are not going to finish the class. And yes, it is true that as each semester passed, I discovered certain topics I did not want to read about any longer—cell phone usage, for example. I wanted to see students choose topics that (a) they couldn't find similar papers for on the Web; (b) would enhance their critical and creative thinking; (c) would empower them in making future decisions. By way of example, one semester I used a career theme in the class, in addition to two other themes students could choose from. In the career theme, students were encouraged to incorporate both primary and secondary research into the class and focus on a career of interest. One young man spent the semester studying the Highway Patrol. "CHIPS" was his favorite television program as a small boy, so he grew up planning to become a state highway patrolman. At the end of his project, he decided that becoming a state highway patrolman was the last thing he wanted to do. He wrote in his final self-assessment: "I don't know what I want to do. In fact, I'm going to take a year off from college and think about it. I want to thank you for this project because you saved me a lot of time and money in pursuing something I would end up not liking."

The other two themes consisted of a genealogical study and an ethnographic study where students spent the semester focusing on a group. The genealogical study yielded an interesting project. One of my students told me that she was of Scottish ancestry. As she pursued her Scottish line, she encountered a distant cousin who lived in Scotland. They began corresponding. Four years later, I ran into this same young woman on campus. She was about to graduate and her graduation present? She was going to Scotland to visit the distant cousin she met while doing her research project her freshman year!

By Winter 2000, I was looking for something else to include in the course. I worked as an adjunct faculty member for three colleges: two community colleges and one four-year institution. One of the community colleges focused entirely on online instruction. The syllabus was pre-designed and we were all doing the same thing. The other two schools allowed adjuncts to select their own textbooks and create their own syllabus. And by Winter 2000, I felt that my three-year focus on primary and secondary research needed a new injection. Students will always be students. I always wrote my own course packet and I discovered that some students passed not only the packet along to their friends, but their papers as well. I always had to stay one jump ahead of some of them! I was thinking about what I could implement into the course when a film catalog for teachers arrived in my mailbox. As I leafed through the pages, I began thinking, "Why not incorporate films in the freshman composition research class?"

Why not! The campus had spent a fortune on new media equipment in the classrooms and in most classes, that equipment remained idle. Why not put it to use?

Then my speculation quickly led me into a new concern: what films could I use in the course? I had already been yelled at because a previous textbook contained an essay using profanity—that complaint from a female student who didn't like my direction of the course at all and who withdrew without giving it a chance. My complaining friend was representative of a number of students who resisted any change to their perception of what the course should be. That group wanted to memorize, be assigned a traditional topic, and did not want to do collaborative work. How would freshman students respond to the implementation of films in the course, I wondered? After all, films are primary research, and watching the film with the group is an example of a social setting and interaction. But what film or films would I use?

Modern films were out of the question, so I started looking at the classical section of the catalog. I read through the descriptions, thinking about the depth and themes of the films and their possible use in the course. Then I spotted a familiar title and paused to study it for a minute before turning the page. But each time I flipped the page, something kept drawing me back to the familiar title I had just seen:

"Rebel Without A Cause."

What follows is the description from the cassette tape, a portion of which appeared in the catalog:

> "Jim Stark is another good kid gone bad – and no one knows why. Not his teachers or the cops who arrest him on drunk and disorderly charges. Not even his parents. To all, Jim – like thousands of other middle-class kids – is just another "Rebel Without a Cause.
>
> Legendary James Dean, in one of screen history's most influential roles, stars as Jim Stark, the new kid in town whose loneliness, frustration and anger mirrored the feelings of many postwar teens – and still reverberate 30 [56] years later. Hoping to find among his peers the love and understanding missing at home, he must prove himself in a violent world of ritualistic switchblade duels and over-the cliff 'chickie runs,' an influential sequence extolled by moviemaker Allan Arkush in 'American Film' as '...an absolute classic of car action that has never, ever been surpassed.'
>
> Natalie Wood and Sal Mineo (in his screen debut) both received Academy Award nominations for their achingly true performances as Jim's lonely, suddenly-one-night girl friend, Judy and insecure, tagalong friend Plato. Together, they and Dean bond to form an us-against-the world surrogate family.
>
> Director Nicholas Ray adds rich, kinetic visuals to this heartfelt but disturbing classic that introduced middle-class America to an enemy of its own making: its children. For in 'Rebel Without a Cause,' Dean became the archetypal rebel for every cause."[1]

James Dean! I remembered him. I was in sixth grade in Iowa the spring of 1955 when "East of Eden" appeared in local theatres. I had seen him in television shows: one—"The Dark, Dark Hours"—in which he appeared with future President Ronald Reagan—I distinctly recall.

1   *Rebel Without A Cause.* James Dean, Natalie Wood with Sal Mineo, Jim Backus, Ann Doran, Corey Allen, Dennis Hopper. Screenplay by Stewart Stern. Produced by David Weisbart. Directed by Nicholas Ray. Music by Leonard Rosenman. Copyright: 1955, Warner Bros. Pictures, Inc. Renewed 1983, Warner Bros, Inc. Package Artwork, Design & Summary 1986, Warner Home Video Inc.

I was in seventh grade in September 1955 when he was killed on a Friday in an auto accident near Cholame, California. I didn't hear about it until the next day after returning from our Saturday visit with my maternal grandparents in Marion, Iowa. I turned on the evening news. James Dean's picture was on the screen while the announcer told the story of his death. I remember my father entering the room. He asked me what happened. I responded by saying, "James Dean was killed yesterday." And, of course, I thought my dad wouldn't know anything about James Dean.

"He was related to your grandmother," he told me.

I don't remember responding. I just remember thinking that Grandma had a lot of cousins. Then I filed that remark away for a future time when I would undertake genealogical research.

My friends all talked about his death at school the following Monday. Some of them kept his picture in their lockers. One of my friends did that all the way through junior high and high school. I once asked her why she kept his picture there.

"I like him!" she told me.

There were those who loved him and who wanted to look like him. By eighth grade, Elvis Presley arrived on the scene, giving our conservative preacher some new kindling for the fire he was building. He heaped coals of fire on James Dean, Elvis, and any other entertainer who captured the attention of teens. But then, our whole generation was headed for "hell in a hand basket", according to the preacher.

Magazines carried articles about James Dean, and I remember reading some movie magazine articles at the local drug store. One magazine stands out vividly in my mind. It was a Look Magazine dated 1956 with a close-up cover shot of James Dean wearing a western hat. We didn't subscribe to "Look", but we did exchange our magazines with my aunt and uncle. Our "Lifes" went to their house and their "Looks" came to ours. So for about six months, James Dean lay on the top of our magazine rack, staring out at me each time I passed the rack. Then one day, it was my turn to burn the trash.

We could burn in an open-air container in those days. I was hauling the trash out the door when my mother told me, "Here! Take these magazines as well." As I headed down the yard toward the incinerator in the alley, I noticed James Dean riding on top of the stack, and he was the last item inside the barrel. I struck the match and stood there watching him burn. His eyes were the last to be consumed by the fire, and it was almost as though he was saying, "Later!"

"Later" came during the spring of my sophomore year of high school and my Driver's Education class.

Driver's education was taught in high schools in those days. We had to take the course the semester just before turning 16, the time when we could get a driver's license. First thing on the syllabus: we had to watch a horrible slide show called "Death on the Highway" produced by a group from Ft. Meyers, Florida called "The Suicide Club." We had to get our parents' signatures in order to watch the slide show, and we had to watch the slide show in order to take the course. I remember walking to the underground location of the driver's training room, dreading what lay ahead of us. My friend, Susie, had watched the show a few days previously and described what she had seen on our way home from school that afternoon.

"They even have James Dean!" she informed me.

As the horrible images appeared on the screen, we closed our eyes or looked away. And then about half way through the show, James Dean's image appeared.

It was the same photograph that I had burned about three years before.

"This is the actor James Dean, as you remember him," the voice said. "The next photo is also James Dean, and you will not recognize him."

The image appeared on the screen. I turned my head. And while the horrible image remained on the screen, the narrator told the story of his death.

Years later, I mentioned having seen that picture on an internet discussion board, and was attacked by a number of people who said it did not exist. My husband Howard verified that it did. He was taking driver's education the fall of 1955—his senior year--the same semester when James Dean died. He remembered seeing the same photograph! A number of my friends also recalled having seen it.

In an effort to prove I was not imagining things, I searched the Internet for information on the old driver's ed programs from the 1950s and 1960s. I stumbled across a filmmaker who was making a DVD called "Hell's Highway"[2] using photos from those old driver's ed programs. I contacted the people, telling them about the James Dean photo, and their contact person responded by saying, "I didn't know we had James Dean!" Then I described some of the pictures I remembered from the "Death on the Highway" slide show, and that's how I was able to identify the program I had actually seen. But what I saw was the original slide show. Photos from the slideshow were reproduced in 1971 as a film, but James Dean was no longer included. In fact, James Dean disappeared completely from the slide show three or four years after I saw the photo. It is possible his family learned about the picture and put a stop to its inclusion in the program.

I did not see "Rebel Without a Cause" until I started using it in class! I saw "Giant" in the early 1970s on television. Because of the law suit that kept "East of Eden" under wraps, I did not see that film for many years. In the winter of 2000, however, I sat staring at "Rebel" in a film catalog, wondering whether I could successfully use it in a class of college freshmen!

By Spring 2001, I embarked upon my experiment and chose three films to show in my classes. "Rebel Without A Cause" was one of them. I no longer remember the names of the other two. They were not successful. "Rebel" grabbed the attention of the audience and held the students captive. And something else happened during my showing of that film. After sitting through it several times, I found myself being drawn into it. And when the film ended and I no longer had a need

---

2   *Hell's Highway—The True story of Highway Safety Films* (2003). Actors: Richard Anderson, Sonny Bono, John F. Butler, Hans Conried, Earle Deems. Directors: Bret Wood, Richard Wayman. Writers: Bret Wood. Producers: Earle Deems, Bret Wood, Richard Wayman, Felicia Feaster, Tommy Gibbons. DVD Release Date: November 28, 2003.

to show it in class, I thought, "Oh drat!" But my interest in James Dean grew. After that semester, the theme of my course became "The Influence of the Media on Society." I used James Dean as a model for that influence and for one or two semesters, showed all three of his films. Students could take the topic of media influence and run any direction with it, designing their own research projects. Looking back on it now, the experiment was 98% successful: 100% successful among serious, creative students who loved the challenge and freedom to explore, and 0% successful among the linear thinkers who wanted to memorize, avoid collaborative work and primary research, and who wanted to be told what to do. And the linear group generally involved some higher-level authority who had no idea what was going on in the class and who was more concerned with the fact that some student had complained about it. Fortunately, such encounters with students were few and far between. Some higher-level authorities proved to be greater thorns.

By Spring 2003, I scaled back my use of film to one: "Rebel Without A Cause" and I rewrote the course packet to shrink that usage. A new dean had come to power at one of the schools. The original dean was a wonderful man who promoted harmony among faculty, staff and students. Then he retired. The woman who replaced him sat back and watched the situation the first two years and by the third year, began meddling with everyone. The school became a cesspool where bickering and blame replaced harmony, and everyone looked over their shoulders. The new dean did not like James Dean in my course packet, and she wanted him removed. I remember wishing May 2009 would arrive quickly—the semester I planned to retire—and did! But in Spring 2003, I completely revised the packet and submitted it to my students and to my supervisor for their feedback prior to using it.

And it was in the fall of 2003, that I had a twenty-year-old man questioning my use of James Dean in the course at all.

"Why him?" he asked. "Why not use someone else? Why not use someone more recent?"

INTRODUCTION

Deanfest Headquarters, Marion, Indiana. Photo taken during our second trip to Fairmount, Indiana May 18, 2005.

In Summer 1995, I traveled to Pennsylvania to take my written comprehensives and orals for my doctorate, something that required me to stay there for five weeks. Howard and I were heading back to Colorado and decided to route our return trip through Fort Wayne, Indiana. Friends in Colorado told us that if we really wanted to visit an excellent genealogical library, we needed to stop at the Allen County Public Library in Fort Wayne.

"They have everything!" we were told.

"We might as well stop on our way home," Howard said. "Who knows? This might be our only chance."

It was by no means a quick stop. Howard investigated the stacks, while I investigated some family names I had been working on. In those days, I focused on my mother's Spence line and in 1995, I was just beginning to penetrate that background.

After an hour or so of searching, we left Fort Wayne. We were heading for Cedar Rapids, Iowa, and we hoped to get as close to it as possible that day. Altogether, we spent six summers traveling between Colorado and Pennsylvania, and we learned quite early that we didn't want to get tangled up in Chicago area traffic. So we were always looking for ways to avoid that city.

"We can take Highway 69 south to Indianapolis. And then we can jut over from there." Howard said, as he studied the map.

Highway 69 was a new experience for us since we had never driven it. Prior to the trip, I had been searching for a third great grand aunt's background in Putnam County, Indiana. As I studied the map, I noticed that we would be jogging through there on the other side of Indianapolis.

"At least I can say I've been there," I said. "That family left Putnam in 1843 and moved on to Missouri."

We drove along in silence, until I noticed signs for a town up ahead.

"Fairmount," I said, aloud.

"What's it noted for?" Howard asked.

"I don't know. Something about antiques and a museum."

Just as we approached the Fairmount exit, I saw a huge sign.

Home of James Dean! James Dean Burial Site! Where Cool was Born!

I read all of that aloud as we passed the exit.

"He came from here?" I exclaimed.

"And he's buried here?" Howard asked.

"That's what the sign said. I thought he was buried somewhere in California."

As I glanced back at the exit, I remember thinking how strange it was that I kept running into that guy in different places along the road in recent years!

The first experience was eleven years previously in 1984 when we took our kids on our one and only trip to California. That was a spring break expedition which started in a snow storm and ended in another snow storm. California was warm and sunny, however.

We traveled the full length of the state and were on our way down the coast to Los Angeles. I remember stopping in Salinas—long time Steinbeck fan that I am. The road was closed at Paso Robles due to a rock slide. We were forced to take a detour through Cholame—and that's where we saw the sign.

"Oh, my!" I exclaimed. "This is where James Dean was killed!"

"Who's James Dean?" our son Brian asked from the back seat.

He was a young teenager at that time, and he had never heard of him.

"Kind of doing it backwards," I muttered, as we now drove down Highway 69 in Indiana.

"What do you mean?" Howard asked.

"Oh, we saw where he died eleven years ago. Now, I guess we are seeing the area where he grew up! Then pausing for a moment or two, I added, "I guess I knew that! Remember Peetie—my friend from school? She's from Marion, Indiana, and she said something about it last summer."

"James Dean?"

"Oh, it was at the beginning of the class. We had to go around the room and introduce ourselves. Then we had to say something unique about the place we were from. Peetie said, *'I'm Peetie, and I'm from Marion, Indiana, and I'm not related to James Dean!'* I asked her why she said that and she told me, 'Oh, he was from there, and people ask me that all the time!'"

By now, we were more than fifteen miles past the Fairmount exit.

"Too late to turn around now," Howard said. "If we travel through here next year, maybe we'll stop."

* * *

James Byron Dean was born February 8, 1931 in Marion, Grant County, Indiana. He died at the age of twenty-four in a car crash near Cholame, California on September 30, 1955.

The End!

The end for most people, that is, but not for James Dean!

A friend of mine has been compiling a list of books that have been written about James Dean. If all the books written about James Dean could be assembled in one room, they would probably fill a small library. They certainly cover a wide range of perspectives beginning with scholarly analyses to filthy trash!

This book, which will hopefully appear on my friend's list at some future date, has been a project of mine for many years. I suppose the initial seeds were sewn by my father shortly after James Dean's death in 1955: "He was related to your Grandmother." I didn't spend years thinking about that statement, but I certainly remembered it when I noticed similarities of features between James Dean's family members and some of mine! (Actually, I connect with James Dean on two different family lines making him both my fifth cousin once removed and eleventh cousin once removed. He is also Howard's eleventh cousin on one of his lines, a discovery I recently made. I joke about Howard's connection from time to time by saying, "So, maybe we can go back to Fairmount again?")

I started this manuscript about ten years ago, and then put it away, deciding that it wasn't time to complete it. I actually forgot about my earlier endeavor until rearranging my research notebooks for the book I put out in 2010: *The Sum Total—A Search for Levi Clay (1843-1917) and Jesse James (1847-1881)*[3]. This current book extends the thesis from my 2010 endeavor—that we are all more or less the sum total of our ancestors. I also believe that we have their memories.

This book has been divided into the following Sections and Chapters:

Section One--Rebels With a Cause: James Dean's Ancestors: Chapter 1—*The Early Deans* focuses exclusively on the Dean line; Chapter 2-- *The Puritan Dilemma: A Contest of Wills (an Overview)* provides a general discussion of the Puritans and their identities; Chapter 3-- *Man of His Own Undoing: Hatevil Nutter* examines one of James Dean's tenth-great-grandfathers and his treatment of the Quaker community; Chapter 4-- *Jesse, Frank and Jimmy: The Cole/Coale Connection* looks at James Dean's connection with Jesse and Frank James through the Cole/Coale line; Chapter 5-- *To The Tune of a Different Drummer: The Rev. Stephen Bachiler (Batchelor)* provides a thorough examination of James Dean's most influential tenth-great-grandfather, The Rev. Stephen Bachiler; Chapter 6—*Seeds of Dissent: The Husseys and the Wings* presents two family lines who descend from Stephen Bachiler: James Dean's Hussey line and the author's Wing line; Chapter 7—*From Cavaliers to the Amish: The Ancestors of Mildred Marie Wilson* focuses on the ancestors of James Dean's mother—Mildred Marie Wilson.

3   Beall, Barbara Inman, Ph.D. *The Sum Total: A Search for Levi Clay (1843-1917) and Jesse James (1847-1882)*. San Diego, CA: Aventine Press (2010).

REBEL FROM BACK CREEK

Section Two—From Penrod to the Madman: An Artist in Studio: Chapter 8—*On the Bank of Back Creek* looks at the region surrounding Fairmount, Indiana, where James Dean was raised; Chapter 9— *The Adventures of Penrod Schofield, Tom Sawyer and Huckleberry Finn* focuses on James Dean as a child; Chapter 10— *"Perfect for Longmont!"* looks exclusively at the 1949 Speech Contest in Longmont, Colorado; Chapter 11— *"Three Long Mountains and a Wood"* looks at James Dean's decision to become an actor as well as two significant people in his life: Rev. James DeWeerd and Bette McPherson; Chapter 12— *"The Road Not Taken"* focuses on his return to Santa Monica to live with his father and new stepmother, his stint at Santa Monica College, his short stint at UCLA and his decision to move to New York.

Section Three—The Creation of "James Dean": Chapter 13— *"New York! New York!"* looks at James Dean's early experiences in New York and some of the people he encountered; Chapter 14—*Filmography* lists the radio, television, Broadway, Off-Broadway and film performances of James Dean; Chapter 15—*Looking Through a Glass Darkly* profiles *See the Jaguar* and some of James Dean's television roles; Chapter 16—*The Immoralist* focuses specifically on James Dean's last Broadway play; Chapter 17—*East of Eden*: The Essence of Cal Trask discusses Steinbeck's novel and the movie version. It also examines the relationship between James Dean and Pier Angeli; Chapter 18—*Rebel Without a Cause*: In Search of Jim Stark looks at the overall variety of teen movies in the 1950s and the political situation involving the Kefauver Senate Committee. It provides a special focus on the Greek tragedy elements in the film; Chapter 19—*Giant*: The Enigma of Jett Rink profiles Glenn McCarthy, the prototype for Jett Rink's character. It also provides background material for Edna Ferber's novel and the making of the film, with a special emphasis on the town of Marfa and its citizens; Chapter 20—*"Death is My Neighbor"* discusses the death of James Dean.

The **Conclusion** provides an analysis of the character of James Dean. An **Epilogue** follows the Conclusion, which returns to the event in the Prologue. The **Photo Section** contains photographs from our first and second trips to Fairmount, Indiana in 2003 and 2005.

SECTION ONE
REBELS WITH A CAUSE: JAMES DEAN'S ANCESTORS

The Stephen Bachiler Chair

CHAPTER 1—THE EARLY DEANS

While growing up on the farm outside Fairmount, Indiana, James Dean was undoubtedly oblivious of his ancestral lines. He may have been aware of some of them, however, because he apparently told someone that the Winslows were on the Mayflower.[4] His Grandmother Dean was quoted as saying:

> "You might say we're a close-knit family...That's what comes from living in one place so long. The first Deans came from around Lexington, Kentucky and settled in Grant County about 1815. My family, the Woolens [sic], and Jimmy's mother's family, the Wilsons, got here about the same time."[5]

James Dean appears to have adapted well to his new situation in Indiana after spending several years of his early life with his parents in California. His mother died in 1940, and his father did not feel adequate in caring for the needs of his son. So it was decided that Jimmy would return to Fairmount, Indiana and live with his father's sister and her husband, Ortense and Marcus Winslow. Although a number of writers have criticized Winton for doing this, what he did was not unusual. Many families raised children from other groups because of a death or divorce in the family, or whenever the child was to week or too ill to travel with the family in case of a move. In James Dean's case, it is fortunate that he was sent back to Indiana. His father was drafted and served in the Army in World War II and would not have been able to take care of him.

For the most part, criticism against Winton has applied to the lack of contact with his son after being released from the Army. He had

---

4 David Dalton. *The Mutant King.* p.21.
5 David Dalton, *The Mutant King.* p. 21.

remarried, but his visits to Fairmount were infrequent. Undoubtedly, Winton's absence had a major impact on Jimmy's life and sent him searching for a series of mother and father figures. Shortly before James Dean's death, Winton and Jimmy started doing things together. They had a special place in Colorado where they liked to camp and fish, a place James Dean referred to as "truly God's country." And they were together in California the day of Jimmy's death.

According to David Dalton:

> *Jimmy enjoyed the routine of farm life even though when he first arrived he was anemic. "I don't know whether I was looking for a greater source of life and expression...or for blood." His chores were milking, collecting eggs, feeding the stock and harvesting. Marcus ran the farm on his own, except for occasional help during busy times, so Jimmy was a big help to him. By the end of his first year with the Winslows he could drive the tractor. He found the runt of a litter of pigs, bottle-fed it to keep it alive, and it became his pet. When Jimmy and his dog, Tuck, ran across the farmyard, the little pig would be squealing and oinking behind them, trying to catch up.[6]*

He delighted in teasing his cousin, Joan, whenever he could. I remember watching an interview in which she said that she and her friends would always go up to her bedroom after school where they would try on clothes, put on make-up, and talk about boys. It wouldn't be long before they heard the old staircase squeaking, and she knew right away who was spying on them. She would call for her mother, who would bring the mischievous Jimmy downstairs. But he didn't stay there very long. Finally, Ortense made him sit in the kitchen with her. Several years later when Joan married, Jimmy made certain he had the tin cans securely fastened to the rear bumper of the car. And about that time, Marcus Winslow Jr. (Markie) was born. Marcus Jr. was like a young brother to James Dean.

We stayed at the Loft Inn Bed & Breakfast just outside Fairmount when we were there in 2003. The Loft Inn is a working farm located just down the road from the Winslow farm and caddy-corner from

---

6   David Dalton. *The Mutant King.* p. 21.

the Park Cemetery.   Patryce Loftin, the owner, told me that her grandfather was James Dean's Sunday School teacher. One day her grandfather wanted to put up a new fence, so he hired Jimmy and his friends to put up the posts, and he paid them by the hour. Jimmy and several of his friends became more engaged in clod-fighting than in fence-post placement, and Jimmy succeeded in putting in one post. Someone told the grandfather that he should pay those boys by the fence post and not by the hour![7] Concerning his work habits on the farm, David Dalton quotes:

> "Getting healthy can be hazardous," Jimmy told Hedda Hopper, the columnist he cautiously grew friendly with later on in Hollywood. "You have to assume more responsibility. Now, this was a real farm I was on and I worked like crazy—as long as someone was watching me. The forty acres of oats was a huge stage and when the audience left I took a nap and things didn't get plowed or harrowed."[8]

He was a great story teller and delighted in holding an audience captive with some of his tales. According to Dalton:

> It was this joy of invention and absurdity of life which Jimmy loved and cultivated in himself. He was fond of telling tales and told a friend about a "goose necklace" he once made: "I remember one time when I found out that if you give a duck a piece of salt pork, it goes right through him in about ten seconds. So I got me some fishing line and tied a piece of pork to one end and fed it to a big drake. It passed on through and I gave it to another duck and then another, and before long I had the whole barnyard full of ducks all strung together like pearls on a string. You should have heard them quack![9]

James Dean came from a long line of storytellers, and they could all hold an audience captive.

* * *

7   Patryce Loftin, Personal Conversation: Fairmount, Indiana, May 20, 2003
8   David Dalton, *The Mutant King*, p. 21.
9   David Dalton, *The Mutant King,* p. 23.

In the 1990s, genealogist Richard E. Brenneman of Boston undertook a number of genealogical searches while looking for notable kin of several Hollywood celebrities and contributed to the "New England in Hollywood Series of the New England Historical and Genealogical Society *Nexus*. Brenneman wrote part three of the "New England in Hollywood" series on Marilyn Monroe's possible Rhode Island ancestry. He undertook much research on the Blythe family for the ancestor table of President Clinton in NEXUS 9(1992):204-9 and he has also published in *The American Genealogist*. In February 1993, his article "Notable Kin: New England in Hollywood, Part Four: The Ancestry of James Byron Dean (1931-1955)" appeared in Vol. X, No. 1 of the NEHGS *NEXUS*. In describing the ancestry of James Dean, Brenneman writes:

> *Dean's immediate ancestors were border-South families who migrated to Indiana from Kentucky (Dean, Wilson, Leisure), Pennsylvania or Ohio (Cree, Felton), Maryland/Delaware (Woollen, Oldfield), Virginia (Smithson), or North Carolina (Williams). Likely eighteenth-century immigrants included English Chamnesses, Scottish Tennells (and possibly Leisures), German Feltons and Eslers, and Irish Mansfields (and possibly Ryans). Since he was raised by his father's sister and her Winslow husband, he is sometimes thought to have Mayflower forebears, but no such descent has been found.*
>
> *Quaker ancestry is derived through Dean's great-great-grand-mother Betty (Williams) Smithson of Highland Co., Ohio, whose parents had moved there from Chatham Co., N.C. Betty's mother, Sarah (Hussey) Williams (1795-1834), who also migrated to Indiana, was a great-granddaughter of Christopher Hussey, a Nantucket native (b. 1706) who moved to New Castle Co., Delaware. Hussey's paternal grandparents were Stephen and Martha (Bunker) Hussey of Nantucket; great-or great-great-grandparents included Rev. Stephen Bachelder, the 'ur-father" of Hampton, N. H. and Dea. John Hall, "President of the Court" Thomas Roberts and Hatevil Nutter, all of Dover, N. H. Nantucket Husseys or Bunkers have been noted in previous columns as ancestors of U.S. Senator Samuel James Ervin, Jr., William Sidney Porter*

(O. Henry), Mrs. H. L. Hunt of Texas, and Mrs. Lucretia Coffin Mott (NEXUS 3[1986]:26-27,7 [1990]: 157,159), and of mystery writer Dame Agatha Christie (5[1988]: 169-70, 6[1989]:34. Rev. Stephen Bachelder was an ancestor of Presidents Nixon and Ford, serial killer Herman Webster Mudgett (NEXUS 5:21-22), and western novelist Louis Dearborn L'Amour (7:114-15). John Roberts and Abigail Nutter were great-great-great grandparents of the poet John Greenleaf Whittier(6:205-6). Like many Americans from Midwestern or border states, many descendants of Quakers, and many Southerners as well, James Dean was descended from both mid-Atlantic pioneers and Great Migration immigrants to New England.[10]

In his book *James Dean: The Biography*, Val Holley writes:

James Byron Dean was born in a house at Fourth and McClure streets in Marion, Indiana, on February 8, 1931. His parents, Winton and Mildred Wilson Dean had married a little more than six months earlier, on July 26, 1930. Winton Dean was a dental technician at the local veterans' hospital, and Mildred Dean worked in a drugstore. The small family would soon move to Fairmount, Winton Dean's hometown, and live at a variety of addresses there and in Marion over the next five years. James Byron would be his parents' only child.[11]

James Dean's father Winton was born in Fairmount, Indiana January 17, 1908. He was still living when Brenneman conducted his research, but he died two years later in 1995. His second wife was Ethel Case[12] whom he married in California in 1944. She was born September 22, 1914—her death certificate mentions Iowa--and she died in Florida in 1988. Winton and Ethel are buried together beside Jimmy in Park Cemetery. Some writers have indicated that Jimmy was not fond of his stepmother, Ethel. The only picture I have seen of her was taken in Marion, Indiana when Winton brought her back to meet his son.

10   Richard E. Brenneman, "The Ancestry of James Byron Dean (1931-1955), p. 28.
11   Val Holley, *James Dean: The Biography,* p. 16.
12   Val Holley, *James Dean: The Biography,* p. 31.

A summary of the Dean ancestry follows:

Winton was one of three children born to Charles Desco Dean (1879-1961) and Emma Woollen (1885-1961). Besides Winton, there were his sister Ortense Dean Winslow (1901-1991)—wife of Marcus Winsow (1900-1976), and a brother, Charles Nolan Dean (1914-2002).

Charles Desco Dean was the son of Calvin P. Dean (an auctioneer), who was born in Johnson County, Indiana August 31, 1849, and who died in Fairmount December 7, 1918, and Arminta Alice Cree, who was born in Madison County, Indiana March 25, 1854, and who died in Fairmount January 28, 1922.

Calvin P. Dean was the son of John Dean, who was born in Kentucky about 1810, and who died in Grant County, Indiana in February 1890, and Sarah Tennell, who was born in Kentucky September 28, 1815, and who died in Grant County, Indiana June 3, 1890

John Dean was the son of Thomas Dean, who was born about 1770, and who later resided in Bourbon County, Kentucky. He died near Nicholasville, Jessamine County, Kentucky about 1848.[13]

Brenneman does not take the Dean line back any further. Work since his initial investigation has connected these Bourbon County, Kentucky/Grant County, Indiana Deans with the Dean Family of Dorchester County, Maryland. Concerning the Dorchester County Deans, an earlier work by Leonard Wilson, *The Heraldry of the Deane Family* describes the early Deanes as being "of the landed gentry and a number of them held large estates, not only in Kent and Sussex, Hampshire, Northampton, Gloucester, Wilts and Devon prior to 1300 A.D."[14] Wilson goes on to state:

It has long been asserted that the Massachusetts Deanes and those of Maryland were kindred in blood and of the same original stock. B. J. Johnson, Inc., compilers of "Men of Mark in England" and "Makers of America" assert that certain Deanes of Massachusetts

13   Richard E. Brenneman, "The Ancestry of James Byron Dean (1931-1955), p. 29.
14   Leonard Wilson. *The Heraldry of the Deane Family*. London, 1938.

and Maryland were of the same Somersetshire family. This is confirmed by a statement in "New England Families" published by the American Historical Society. William Armstrong Crozier, Fellow of the Royal Society, England, states that John and Walter Deane of Massachusetts came from Somersetshire England, and gives the Coat-of-Arms, Crest, and Motto properly appertaining to them, which proves this branch to be in direct descent from Richard de Dene of London. It follows that the arms borne by them, recorded by Crozier and verified by independent English records, are those which properly appertain also to the Deane Family of Dorchester County, Maryland.

Richard de Dene was head of the ancient House in London during the reign of Edward III (1327-1377). Among his descendants was the Most Reverand, His grace, Henry Deane, Archbishop of Canterbury and Lord High Chancellor of England during the reign of Henry VIII. It is of record that the Deanes of Somersetshire are a branch of Richard de Dene's line. One of its lines also claims descent by marriage from the more ancient Danish line. John and Walter Deane, who settled in Taunton, Massachusetts in 1637, came from the vicinity of Taunton, Somersetshire, England. William Henry Deane, founder of the Maryland Deane (Dean) family, and whose son, William Richard Deane, died in Dorchester County in 1699, was also a descendant of the Deane families of Somersetshire and Dorset, a well known British family of ship builders and mariners.[15]

Several members of the Dorchester County Dean families eventually left Maryland to relocate to other areas. Thomas Dean [1770-1848], James Dean's third great-grandfather, appears to have settled in Hampshire County, Virginia, where he married Keziah Bunnell about 1797. One of his brothers, Nathan Dean (1767-1831) relocated first to Washington and Greene Counties, Pennsylvania, where he was living in 1795. By 1797 he had relocated to Kentucky. Nathan established his family in Harrodsburg in Mercer County and by 1815 relocated to Harrison County, Indiana. He and his family members are buried in the Reep Cemetery there. Thomas first joined his brother in

15   Leonard Wilson, *The Heraldry of the Deane Family*, 1938.

Harrodsburg, and then settled in Jessamine County, Kentucky. From there, he moved to Bourbon County and then to the area where Grant County, Indiana is today. His wife was probably Keziah Bunnell (1770-1847), who died in Howard County, Indiana (west of Grant County), and who is buried in a cemetery in Howard County. After her death, Thomas returned to Jessamine County, Kentucky, where he died about 1848. Thomas's full name may have been Thomas James Dean or James Thomas Dean. The name "James Dean" appears on a number of Keziah Bunnell's records. [Note: A number of family trees on Ancestry.com have connected Keziah Bunnell with an earlier Thomas Dean. That earlier Thomas Dean did not go to Kentucky or to Indiana.]

James Dean's grandmother, Emma Woollen Dean, once mentioned that the Dean, Woollen and Wilson families moved from Kentucky to Indiana about the same period of time. Her early Woollen ancestors were in Dorchester County, Maryland quite early, and her earliest Woollen ancestor was Edmond/Edward Woollen. He was born in England about 1642, and he died in Dorchester County, Maryland ante May 17, 1699. His wife, Jane Pollard, was born on Taylor's Island in Maryland about 1680. She died there January 13, 1731.[16] It is entirely possible that the early Woollens and Deans knew one another in Dorchester County and may have intermarried on several occasions.

Two big incentives promoted migration to Kentucky. One, the Westsylvania movement in Western Pennsylvania and in what is today West Virginia, petitioned for statehood in that area at the end of the Revolutionary War. Congress ignored the petition and as a result, residents supporting the petition began protesting on its behalf. They were finally told that if they didn't stop protesting, they would be cited for treason. Many of those protesters relocated to Kentucky and to North Carolina.

The next big incentive arose from The Whiskey Rebellion of 1791-1794. This protest arose over an excise tax imposed by the Federal Government in 1791. According to the Early America Website:

---

16   Richard E. Brenneman, "The Ancestry of James Byron Dean (1931-1955), p. 30.

The tariff effectively eliminated any profit by the farmers from the sale or barter of an important cash crop and became the lightning rod for a wide variety of grievances by settlers of the region [primarily, Alleghany, Fayette, Washington and Westmoreland Counties, Pennsylvania]...

The rebel farmers continued their attacks, rioting in river towns and roughing up tax collectors until the so-called "insurrection" flared into the open in July of 1794, when a federal marshal was attacked in Alleghany County, Pennsylvania. Almost at the same time, several hundred men attacked the residence of the regional inspector, burning his home, barn and several outbuildings. Pittsburgh was another scene of disorderly enraged mobs.

On August 7, 1794, President Washington issued a proclamation calling out the militia and ordering the disaffected westerners to return to their homes. Washington's army of approximately 13,000—as large as the one who defeated the British—was under command of General Henry Lee, the then-Governor of Virginia and father of Robert E. Lee.[17]

This was the first use of martial law in the new country. It was also the first test of power of the new federal government. The article concludes:

In the end, a dozen or so men were arrested, sent to Philadelphia to trial and released after pardons by Washington.[18]

A number of people who were unhappy with the situation in Western Pennsylvania and in what is today West Virginia relocated to Kentucky. The Deans moved to Kentucky mid-to-late 1790s and can be found of record there on the 1800 Census.

---

17   The Whiskey Rebellion. The Early America Website. Accessed September 6, 2011. Available online at http://www.earlyamerica.com/earlyamerica/milestones/whiskey/.
18   The Whiskey Rebellion. http://www.earlyamerica.com/earlyamerica/milestones/whiskey/

CHAPTER 2—THE PURITAN DILEMMA: A CONTEST OF WILLS (AN OVERVIEW)

"James Dean was not a Puritan!" someone once said in an interview.

Maybe not, but the seeds of Puritanism spread throughout his heritage dating back to the very beginning of the movement.

No one knows the identity of the first Puritan. Puritans existed long before anyone ever heard the word. [The word was first used as a pejorative in 1564.[19]] As William Haller notes in his *The Rise of Puritanism*, "Chaucer met one on the road to Canterbury and drew his portrait. No better and no very different picture of the kind of man we shall be dealing with in these pages was ever drawn by any of the numerous pens which attempted the task two centuries later. The parson, Chaucer says, was a learned man, devoted to teaching and caring for his people. He was poor, but 'he coude in litel thing had suffisaunce.' When sufficiently provoked, he rebuked the obstinate whether of high or low estate, but his real business was to lead men to heaven by fair words and good example."[20] Puritanism as a movement, however, rose during the time of Elizabeth and her handling of the religious problem in England. The reformers (Puritans) were Calvinists, yet as Haller notes, "...but we shall fail to understand Puritanism if we conceive of English Calvinism in too narrow or rigid a sense."[21]

---

19   Ezra Hoyt Byington, *The Puritan in England and New England*, p. Xxxiii
20   William Haller, *The Rise of Puritanism, p. 3.*
21   William Haller, *The Rise of Puritanism*, p. 3.

Clearly, Elizabeth I, her successor James I, and his successor Charles I had their "hands full" with these people. Elizabeth was not the type of ruler who would allow preachers to "bark" at her.[22] However, she was not able to dispose of the problem as she wished. Puritanism was not "harried out of the land." Instead, its implementation was merely delayed—a delay that proved fatal to Presbyterianism (a philosophy that avowed separation from the Church of England)—and opened the door to congregationalism (a philosophy that avowed association with the Church of England while at the same time, disagreeing with some of its tenets.)

Probably the biggest division between Anglicanism and Puritanism was between "witty" versus "spiritual" preaching. The Anglicans focused on a "wisdom of words" while the Puritans focused on "the word of wisdom."[23] Puritans detested the Anglican method of citing sources other than the Bible. However, "the preachers, if they wished to survive, had to find means to stir imaginations, induce emotional excitement, wring the hearts of sinners, win souls to the Lord, in other words make themselves understood and felt."[24]

In 1633 William Laud, Archbishop of Canterbury under Charles I, attempted to reform the people from the pulpit. His main goal was to get the Puritans under control by destroying Puritanism and thereby, returning the Puritans to the Anglican stronghold. Laud's efforts failed and his persecutions elevated martyrs. His actions against the Puritans paved the way for the expanded settlement of New England and establishment of the Puritan oligarchy there. A casual observer might believe that these migrating Puritans would treat dissenters in a "kindlier and gentler" fashion in light of their own sufferings in England. Such was not the case. In the end, Puritan abuses against dissenters ended their utopian dream of a Puritan-controlled church state and changed their new world forever.

When the Winthrop fleet arrived in Massachusetts, the colony had already been settled for ten years by a group of pilgrims consisting of religious and non-religious people. Not all of the early settlers

22   William Haller, *The Rise of Puritanism,* p. 13.
23   William Haller, *The Rise of Puritanism, p. 23.*
24   William Haller, *"The Rise of Puritanism,* p. 23.

fled to America for religious freedom. Many of them were profi-
teers who were there to seek a fortune. The two earliest colonies in
the area were Plymouth Colony (the Old Colony) and the Colony of
Massachusetts Bay. The two colonies were settled at different times
by different classes of people. In his *The Puritan in England and New
England,* Ezra Hoyt Byington states:

> ...*The Pilgrims came from their life in Holland, where the influ-
> ence of William the Silent had given a free and tolerant spirit to
> the earnest Protestants who had stood heroically against the
> armies of Spain. They could not forget the country where they
> had found refuge from persecutions. They were the disciples of
> Robert Browne, and they had founded a separatist Church in the
> new settlement. The Puritans were fresh from the great national
> contest for their rights as Englishmen under Magna Charta, in the
> times of Charles I and Bishop Laud. They brought with them the
> principles of Sir John Eliot, John Hampden, and John Pryn. They
> had a great dread of Popery, and they believed the Church of
> England was relapsing into the superstitions of Romanism.*[25]

The Pilgrims, primarily separatists, did not want to have any connection with the established Church of England. The Puritans, on the other hand, while they objected to many of the practices of the Church
of England, did not want to separate from the church.

The question of class distinction is also important here. While the
Pilgrims were primarily people of humble means or as Governor
Bradford notes, "They were not acquainted with trades, nor traffic,
but had been used to a plain country life, and the innocent trade of
husbandry." They were also described as "north country peasants"
whose English family origins were and still are, unknown."[26] Their
leaders (Governor Carver, Governor Bradford, Governor Winslow,
Elder Brewster) came from "sound English stock", but the average
Pilgrim came from a very simple background.[27] The Puritans, on
the other hand, "were, for the most part, persons in comfortable
circumstances in life, of good education, and with good social

---

25   Ezra Hoyt Byington, *The Puritan in England and New England,* p. 85.
26   Ezra Hoyt Byington, *The Puritan in England and New England,* p. 89.
27   Ezra Hoyt Byington. *The Puritan in England and New England.* p. 90

connections in England."[28] To further this explanation, the Pilgrims came to Massachusetts not from England, but from Holland. They were already exiles. By contrast, the Puritans came to Massachusetts directly from England. Of the Pilgrim goals, Byington states: "They were especially anxious to find a place where they could bring up their children to good habits, and where they would be likely to use the English language and to keep their connection with the English nation. They had also very much at heart the conversion of the Indians to the Christian faith."[29]

The Puritans had a different agenda:

...They came here as representatives of the Puritan party,--a party which included at that time a majority of the English people. It does not appear from their history that religious motives had less influence with the Puritans than with the Pilgrims. But the Puritans had, in addition to their religious interests, certain political plans which they never lost sight of. There were great statesmen among them, and great theologians. That portion of this party which settled Massachusetts was in sympathy with the great Puritan leaders in England. They regarded themselves as the pioneers of a movement which was likely to transfer a large part of the nation to the New World...It was not their purpose to open their Colony to people of different views from their own for the reason that they were yet weak and comparatively few in number, and they could not tell what would be the result of opening their doors to all comers. They were going into the wilderness to enjoy peace and freedom; and they did not dare run the risk of losing the objects for which they had expatriated themselves by admitting people of all faiths and of all political views. They would found a Puritan state for the oppressed Puritans; and they claimed the right to send away any persons who seemed to them likely to disturb the peace and unity of the Colony.[30]

Less difference is found between the two groups in the area of legislation:

28   Ezra Hoyt Byington. *The Puritan in England and New England.* p. 90
29   Ezra Hoyt Byington. *The Puritan in England and New England.* p. 91.
30   Ezra Hoyt Byington. *The Puritan in England and New England. pp 92-93.*

The Pilgrims had profited by the larger and more tolerant spirit of the Dutch Republic. In both colonies the people claimed the rights and liberties of Englishmen. In both, after a few years, the people were taxed for the support of the regular ministers, just as they had been in England. Punishments which would now be considered harsh and cruel, such as the use of the stocks, the pillory, and the whipping-post, were used in both colonies.

The laws of Plymouth against the Quakers were as severe as those of Massachusetts. Meetings of the Quakers for public worship were forbidden by the laws of the Colony of Plymouth, and all who attended such meetings were liable to a fine of ten shillings, and all who spoke at such meetings were liable to a fine of forty shillings. Men in the Plymouth Colony were disfranchised because they were Quakers, and also because they had harbored Quakers in their houses. The law provided that the people called Quakers could be arrested, sent to the House of Correction, put in the stocks or in the cage, their books could be seized, and their horses also; they could be banished, and by a late law, they could be put to death. The last law, however, was never executed in Plymouth Colony...[31]

While Quakers were fined, imprisoned, disfranchised and even whipped in Plymouth Colony (not for religious practices, but for "disturbing the peace"), Quakers were put to death in the Bay Colony, or else they were "run out of town", as were other nonconformists who challenged authority. It should be noted here that persecution/prosecution of the Quakers did not stop in Massachusetts. Although Roger Williams later welcomed such groups to Rhode Island, he proved his own intolerance of these people by challenging them to a debate to "prove their error." J. Moss Ives states in his *The Ark and the Dove: The Beginning of Civil and Religious Liberties in America*:

The Quakers were given sanctuary in Rhode Island, but it was not a peaceful sanctuary. Although he would allow no one else to molest the Quakers in the exercise of their religion, he [Roger Williams] molested them by a challenge to an acrimonious debate

---

31   Ezra Hoyt Byington. *The Puritan in England and New England.* p 110.

and disturbed the peace which they sought and had reason to believe they would have in this haven of refuge. He did not try to force his own opinions upon them by laws, but he did attempt to do so by words. He tried to make them see the errors of their way of thinking by a barrage of controversy that lasted four days and four nights. His challenge to George Fox, the Quaker leader, rings like a challenge to a prize fight. Accompanying the challenge were fourteen propositions which he boasted he would maintain in public 'against all comers.'

Williams' controversy with the Quakers throws more light on his true nature than does any other incident in his life. The debates began in the Quaker meeting house at Newport and lasted three days and three nights and they were adjourned to Providence, where they terminated after another day, with the usual result, producing no effect, as one biographer says, other "than to exasperate the friends of both parties and set them still more violently against the other."[32]

The source of William's controversy with the Quakers was their emphasis upon the self. "They preached not Jesus Christ but Themselves... Yeah, they preached the Lord Jesus Christ to be Themselves."[33] This statement, of course, was an exaggeration; however:

...precisely because of their [the Quakers] antiauthoritarian bent, it would seem, they found it crucial to root experience in sacred precedent, and they recorded the workings of their Inner Light in journals entitled "Jacob Found in a Desert Land", "Babyland the Great," "A Long Travel to Bethel," "Asking the Way to Zion," "Passing Through the Red Sea," "Jacob Wrestling with God," "Journey out of Aegypt into Canaan." To make the purpose of the convention explicit, they described these parallels as the artillery of the spirit directed against the self, the "cement whereby we are joined as to the Lord so to one another."[34]

---

32   J. Moss Ives, *The Ark and the Dove*, pp. 194-195.
33   Qtd in Sacvan Bercovitch, *The Puritan Origins of the American Self*, p. 26.
34   Sacvan Bercovitch, *The Puritan Origins of the American Self*, p. 29

Besides the Quakers and other nonconformist groups, the Puritans also had a great fear of witchcraft in their community. During the time of Elizabeth, the Puritan targets included "papists, Armenians and antinomians, to say nothing of witches, blasphemers and atheists."[35] In Massachusetts, "It was the common opinion in the time of the Puritans that there were many persons who had entered into a secret league with the Devil, in order to gain power to injure and destroy their fellow men."[36] According to Byington:

> It is not easy to tell just what was meant by a witch in the Levitical law. An eminent scholar who lived three hundred and fifty years ago translated the verse in Exodus: "Though shalt not suffer a poisoner to live." Our revised version reads, "Thou shalt not suffer a sorceress to live." The root word in the Hebrew seems to mean, one who prays,--one who worships,--and is limited in its use to idol worship. It is sometimes used to denote the magicians of Egypt, who withstood Moses. A careful study of the Old Testament would have shown the Puritans (who had some good Hebraists among them) that the witchcraft so often referred to in the older Scriptures was very unlike the witchcraft which seemed to have grown up during the Christian centuries.[37]

However, the New England Puritans were absolutely certain that the devil was alive and well among them, and they believed they needed to take every step to eradicate witches from New England shores. Approximately twenty-six or twenty-seven years after the Puritan settlements began in New England, the first case of witchcraft was tried, according to Governor Winthrop's Journal, under the date of March, 1646:

> One Windsor [was] arraigned and executed at Hartford, as a witch.[38]

James Dean's grandmother, Emma Woollen Dean's early New England ancestors fell into two categories. While they were Puritans in the

---

35   William Haller, "The Rise of Puritanism, p. 20.
36   Ezra Hoyt Byington. The Puritan in England and New England, p 336.
37   Ezra Hoyt Byington. The Puritan in England and New England,.p 341
38   Ezra Hoyt Byington. The Puritan in England and New England, p 347.

beginning, a large number of them joined the Society of Friends, and they were not quiet about it!

The balance of the chapters in this section will focus on several ancestors who figure prominently in the early battles: James Dean's tenth great-grandfather, Hateville Nutter, who died in Dover, New Hampshire 1674-1675, and his son-in-law, John Roberts (1629-1694), who was James Dean's ninth great-grandfather; James Dean's connection with Jesse, Frank, and Susan James through the Cole/Coale line; and, James Dean's most influential ancestor, The Rev. Stephen Bachiler (1561-1656) and several of Bachiler's Hussey and Wing descendants. The last chapter in this section is devoted to his mother's ancestry.

CHAPTER 3—A MAN OF HIS OWN UNDOING: HATEVIL NUTTER

Birth:	*1603, England*
Death:	*1675*
	Dover
	Strafford County
	New Hampshire, USA

Hatevil was born between 1598-1603 in Fillongley, Warwickshire, England.
He married Ann before 1629, probably at St. Mary and All Saints Parish Church in Fillongley.
We believe they had at least five children together.
Hatevil died before June 25, 1675 in Dover.

"Hatevil Nutter, an elder and preacher, was born in 1603: he was one of a company induced to leave England with Captain Wiggin in 1635, and to help found Dover Neck, N. H., a "compact town" which never went farther than "High Street & Dirty Lane"; he received lots of land, in different localities. In 1643, he received a grant of land between Lamprill and Oyster River, which was laid out to his son Anthony in 1662; he also gave the 'Welchman's Cave," to Antony, to go afterward to Antony's son, John Nutter.

"The Elder was rich, and respectable, disliked the Quakers, and died in a good old age, about 71 yrs. old; his wife Anne ------- mentions in will. Antony: MARY (WINGET): and Abigail (Roberts)."

SOURCE: "Family Records of Branches of the Hanaford, Thompson, Huckins, Prescott, Smith, Neal, Haley, Lock, Swift, Plumer, Leavitt,

Wilson, Green and Allied Families" by *Mary Elizabeth Neal Hanaford; Published Rockford, Illinois; 1915; p. 277*[39]

***

A tenth-great-grandfather of James Dean, Hatevil Nutter was born in England between 1567-1603, and he died in Dover, New Hampshire between December 29, 1674 and June 30-1675.[40] (He also distantly connects with my husband Howard on Howard's Nutter line, but it is not a direct connection). Hatevil Nutter's wife was Ann Ayers, who died after December 29, 1674.[41] An elder in the Puritan Church, Nutter's main mission in life was to stamp out all dissension and to eradicate anything he considered out of step with the focus and agenda of the church. His son-in-law, John Roberts, who was born in England and who married Hatevil's daughter, Abigail, was his right arm. [Note: Roberts' father Thomas Roberts was a member of the Fishmongers Co. of London, "President of the Court" (thus his some-time designation "Gov."). John Roberts and Abigail Nutter were James Dean's ninth-great-grandparents.[42]

Hatevil Nutter's wrath centered upon three Quaker women who were upsetting services conducted by a Congregationalist minister, John Reyner, and who were bedeviling him at home.[43]

39   Harlene Soper Brown, Find-A-Grave Memorial #37858010, Record Added June 3, 2009. Find-a-Grave.com Website. Accessed September 5, 2011. Available at http://www.findagrave.com [Original Source: : "Family Records of Branches of the Hanaford, Thompson, Huckins, Prescott, Smith, Neal, Haley, Lock, Swift, Plumer, Leavitt, Wilson, Green and Allied Families" by Mary Elizabeth Neal Hanaford; Published Rockford, Illinois; 1915; p. 277]
40   Richard E. Brenneman, "The Ancestry of James Byron Dean (1931-1955), p. 31.
41   Richard E. Brenneman, "The Ancestry of James Byron Dean (1931-1955), p. 31.
42   Richard E. Brenneman, "The Ancestry of James Byron Dean (1931-1955), p. 31,
43   Boyce Thompson, Jr. "Hatevil Nutter was a Cruel Religious Hypocrite," Thompson Family History Website. Posted   April 15, 2011. Accessed September 4, 2011. Available at http://thompsongenealogy.com/2011/04/hatevil-nutter-was-a-cruel-religious-hypocrite/

According to the Thompson Website:

> For six weeks in 1662, the women had held meetings and ser-
> vices at various homes around town. The Quaker women [Nutter
> reasoned] had the liberty to go elsewhere, but they failed to
> exercise that liberty. Instead, they tried to spread their beliefs in
> Dover, preaching against professional ministers, restrictions on
> individual conscience, and the established customs of church-
> ruled settlements. Something had to be done.[44]

An article from the Dover, New Hampshire Public Library called "The
Whipping of the Quaker Women" describes what happened:

> In 1662 three young Quaker women from England came to
> Dover. True to their faith, they preached against professional
> ministers, restrictions on individual conscience, and the estab-
> lished customs of the church-ruled settlement. They openly
> argued with Dover's powerful Congregational minister John
> Reyner. For six weeks the Quaker women held meetings and
> services at various dwellings around Dover. Finally, one of the
> elders of the First Church, Hatevil Nutter, had had enough. A
> petition by the inhabitants of Dover was presented "humbly
> craving relief against the spreading & the wicked errors of the
> Quakers among them". Captain Richard Walderne (Waldron),
> crown magistrate, issued the following order: "To the consta-
> bles of Dover, Hampton, Salisbury, Newbury, Rowley, Ipswich,
> Wenham, Linn, Boston, Roxbury, Dedham, and until these vaga-
> bond Quakers are carried out of this jurisdiction, you, and ev-
> ery one of you are required in the name of the King's Majesty's
> name, to take these vagabond Quakers, Ann Coleman, Mary
> Tompkins, and Alice Ambrose, and make them fast to the cart's
> tail, and driving the cart through your several towns, to whip
> their naked backs, not exceeding ten stripes apiece on each of
> them, in each town; and so to convey them from constable
> to constable, till they are out of this jurisdiction". Walderne's

---

44   Boyce Thompson, Jr. "Hatevil Nutter was a Cruel Religious
Hypocrite,"   http://thompsongenealogy.com/2011/04/
hatevil-nutter-was-a-cruel-religious-hypocrite/

punishment was severe, calling for whippings in at least eleven towns, and requiring travel over eighty miles in bitterly cold weather.

On a frigid winter day, constables John and Thomas Roberts of Dover seized the three women. George Bishop recorded the following account of events. "Deputy Waldron caused these women to be stripped naked from the middle upwards, and tied to a cart, and after awhile cruelly whipped them, whilst the priest stood and looked and laughed at it." Sewall's History of the Quakers continues " The women thus being whipped at Dover, were carried to Hampton and there delivered to the constable...The constable the next morning would have whipped them before day, but they refused , saying they were not ashamed of their sufferings. Then he would have whipped them with their clothes on, when he had tied them to the cart. But they said, 'set us free, or do according to thine order. He then spoke to a woman to take off their clothes. But she said she would not for all the world. Why, said he, then I'll do it myself.. So he stripped them, and then stood trembling whip in hand, and so he did the execution. Then he carried them to Salisbury through the dirt and the snow half the leg deep; and here they were whipped again. Indeed their bodies were so torn, that if Providence had not watched over them, they might have been in danger of their lives." In Salisbury, Walter Barefoot convinced the constable to swear him in as a deputy. Barefoot received the women and the warrant, and put a stop to the persecution. Dr. Barefoot dressed their wounds and returned them to the Maine side of the Piscataqua River.[45]

The Thompson Family History site is explicit about treatment of the Quaker women:

---

45   "The Whipping of the Quaker Women." From the Dover, New Hampshire Website: http://www.dover.lib.nh.us/Dover%20History/whipping_of_the_quaker_women%20new.htm. Transcribed by Amelia Reimer, April 29, 2001. Posted on the Rootsweb Website. Accessed September 4, 2011. Available at: http://archiver.rootsweb.ancestry.com/th/read/HATEVIL/2001-04/0988579425

The medieval-style punishment was severe, even by Colonial standards. The order called for whippings in at least 11 towns. It would require travel over 80 miles in bitterly cold weather. The first stop was Dover, to which Nutter had come from England 30 years before. The women were seized on a frigid winter day by constables John and Thomas Roberts. George Bishop recorded the events:

"Deputy Waldrom caused these women to be stripped naked from the middle upwards, and tied to a cart, and after awhile cruelly whipped them, whilst the priest stood and looked and laughed at it."

Hatevil thought it was a real laugh-riot as well. According to Sewell.... "All this whipping of the Quaker women, by the Constables (in front of the meeting-house) was in the presence of one Hate-Evil Nutwell (Nutter), a Ruling Elder, who stirred up the Constables (John and Thomas Roberts) to this wicked action, and so proved that he bore a wrong name (Hate Evil)."[46]

Noting that justice eventually prevailed, the Thompson website states:

Barefoot had the support of the town's people, who were guided by the influential Major Robert Pike, one of the leaders of the lower Merrimac valley. According to history books, Pike stood far in advance of his time. He advocated religious freedom and opposed ecclesiastical authority. He even courageously wrote to the court at Salem, objecting to the witchcraft trials.

Eventually, much to Nutter's chagrin, the Quaker women returned to Dover and established a church. More than a third of Dover's citizens eventually became Quakers.[47]

---

46   Boyce Thompson, Jr. "Hatevil Nutter was a Cruel Religious Hypocrite," http://thompsongenealogy.com/2011/04/hatevil-nutter-was-a-cruel-religious-hypocrite/
47   Boyce Thompson, Jr. "Hatevil Nutter was a Cruel Religious Hypocrite," http://thompsongenealogy.com/2011/04/hatevil-nutter-was-a-cruel-religious-hypocrite/

The Thompson Website also provides some biographical data concerning Hatevil Nutter:

> *Hatevil was part owner of a sawmill at Lamprey River, and he owned a ship yard on the shore of the Fore River. He helped organize the First Church in November 1638 and served in various official capacities during his lifetime.*
>
> *"His house stood on the east side of High Street, about 15 or 20 rods from the north corner of the meeting house-lot," reads the history of Dover. "An old pear tree stands (1923) in the hollow, which was part of the cellar."*
>
> *Nutter was by no means alone in his hatred of Quakers. Laws were passed during his time imposing fines on the master of any vessel who brought a Quaker into the colony. Quakers who managed to set foot in the Colonies were supposed to be sent immediately to a house of correction, where they would receive 20 stripes and be confined to hard labor.*
>
> *A later act levied a 40-shilling fine against anyone who harbored a Quaker for one hour. After the first conviction, the offender, if a man, would lose one ear; and upon the third conviction, the other ear. Offending women would be whipped each time. After four convictions, offenders–men and women alike–would have their tongue bored through with a hot iron.*
>
> *Many Quakers came to America to escape religious persecution in Europe. They found it in new forms once they arrived.[48]*

A number of Hatevil Nutter's descendants became members of the Society of Friends. His great-granddaughter, Abigail Hall (b. Piscataqua. New Hampshire February 24, 1679/80) married Batchelor Hussey (b. Nantucket Feb 18, 1684/5)[49], a Quaker minister. The Husseys were James Dean's seventh-great- grandparents!

---

48   Boyce Thompson, Jr. "Hatevil Nutter was a Cruel Religious Hypocrite," http://thompsongenealogy.com/2011/04/hatevil-nutter-was-a-cruel-religious-hypocrite/
49   Richard E. Brenneman, "The Ancestry of James Byron Dean (1931-1955), p. 30.

The poet, John Greenleaf Whittier, a fourth-great-grandson of Hatevil Nutter and Ann Ayers and third-great-grandson of John Roberts and Abigail Nutter immortalized the suffering of the Quaker women in a poem:

How They Drove the Quaker Women from Dover

The tossing spray of Cochecho's falls
Hardened to ice on its icy walls,
As through Dover town, in the chill gray dawn,
Three women passed, at the cart tail drawn,
Bared to the waist, for the north wind's grip
And keener sting of the constables whip
The blood that followed each hissing blow
Froze as it sprinkled the winter snow.
Priest and ruler, boy and maiden
followed the dismal cavalcade;
And from door and window, open thrown,
Looked and wondered, gaffer and crone.[50]

---

[50]   "The Whipping of the Quaker Women." Dover, New Hampshire article transcribed by Amelia Reimer and posted at http://archiver.rootsweb.ancestry.com/th/read/HATEVIL/2001-04/0988579425

CHAPTER 4—THE JAMES GANG: JESSE, FRANK, AND JIMMY (THE COLE/COALE CONNECTION)

Late one Sunday afternoon in the mid-1950s, my family clustered around our television set in order to watch a program that had become a ritual. Hosted by Walter Cronkite, You Are There focused on a different historical event each week. This particular episode—The Capture of Jesse James—dramatized the killing of the outlaw by another gang member named Bob Ford on April 3, 1882 in a house in St. Joseph, Missouri.[51] The part of Jesse James was played by the actor John Kerr while a young rising star by the name of James Dean appeared as Bob Ford. I was around ten years old at the time and only remember the shooting in the program...[52]

My Forward last year while writing *The Sum Total—A Search for Levi Clay (1843-1917) and Jesse James (1847-1882)* and while recalling the experience of watching that old show! It was also while writing the book that I discovered Howard's connection with Jesse, Frank, and Susan James through his mother's Dorsey line. (As I recall, they were sixth cousins once removed, in addition to being connected again on several other lines.) And somewhere along the line, I recalled reading

---

51   You are There: The Capture of Jesse James. Director: Sidney Lumet. Release date: 8 February 1953. Narrator: Walter Cronkite: Cast: James Dean as Bob Ford: John Kerr as Jesse James. CBS Television Network Information available at IMDb website. Accessed September 25, 2010. Available at http://www.imdb.com/title/tt0751918/.

52   Barbara Inman Beall. Forward to *The Sum Total: A Search for Levi Clay (1843-1917) and Jesse James (1847-1882)*.p. 5.

that James Dean was also a distant cousin of the James brothers and sister through his grandmother Emma J. Woollen Dean's Cole line. When I wrote *The Sum Total* last year, I didn't know how Zerelda Cole (the mother of the James boys) connected with Emma's line. I also didn't know whether any of these Coles connected with the Quaker preacher William Coale, who was in Maryland in the 1600s.

That was then. In Summer 2011, I found the connection!

James Dean, Jesse, Frank and Susan James all connect to John Cole, Sr. (1669-1748) and Johanna Garrett (1669-1715). John Cole, Sr. and Johanna Garrett were James Dean's eighth-great-grandparents. They were also Jesse, Frank, and Susan James' fourth-great-grandparents. [James Dean descends from John and Johanna's son, Joseph Cole(1686-1748), and the James siblings descend from John and Johanna's son, John Cole, Jr. (1696-1757). It appears that James Dean was a fifth cousin four times removed of Jesse, Frank and Susan James.]

John Cole , Sr.(1669-1748) was the son of Thomas Cole, who was born in 1633 in Devonshire, England and who died in Maryland in 1705, and Hannah Galloway, who was born in 1633 and who died in 1669 in Anne Arundel County, Maryland. Thomas Cole was the son of the Quaker preacher, William Coale, who was born in England in 1598 and who died in St. Mary's, Maryland in 1669. It appears that while James Dean's branch of the family remained in the Society of Friends, the James branch of the family did not. That may have been the reason why John Cole, Jr. (1691-1757), ancestor of the James branch, left Maryland for New England and eventually relocated to Pennsylvania and Virginia before settling in Kentucky. James Dean's Cole line eventually relocated to North Carolina.

It is important here to note the family of Johanna Garrett (1669-1715), the wife of John Cole, Sr. Johanna was the daughter of Dennis Garrett, who died in Baltimore, Maryland in 1691, and Barbara Stone. They were the ninth-great-grandparents of James Dean and the fifth-great-grandparents of Jesse, Frank and Susan James.

The Garretts were prominent in Baltimore and appear to have been members of the Society of Friends. According to *Baltimore Families:*

> **Dennis Garrett** *was born in 1650.*) *He was living before 1685. He died on Sep 2 1691 in Baltimore Co. MD. Murdered by Capt. John Oldton (Odham?), who hit him on the head with a sword worth 20 shillings on July 31, 1691; Garrett died on Sep 2. Oldton was tried for murder, sentenced to death, pardoned by the King, and later became Commander of the Baltimore County Rangers.* [53]

The records are not clear as to why Capt. Oldton, or Odham, murdered Dennis Garrett. Garrett's son-in-law, John Cole, Sr. witnessed the attack and was a witness at the trial. Apparently Garrett was struck in front of family members. A more detailed account follows:

> **Dennis Garrett** *was born in 1650 Baltimore Co, MD. He married Barbara (?) in 1668 Baltimore Co, MD. Dennis Garrett died on 2 September 1691 Baltimore Co, MD; Lee Garlock (quoting from the Caples Family book) states in NGC msg 3/10/94 (COL-1) that Dennis Garrett was murdered by Capt. John Oldton in 1691 at "The Garrison", a fort built at the head of a branch of Jones Falls Creek for the purpose of guarding frontier villages against Indian raids. Oldton was found guilty and condemned to be hanged, but received a royal pardon in time to save his life.* [54]

[It is sad to note that several of James Dean's ancestors died violently: Dennis Garrett (on his father's side), who was murdered; Isaac Slaughter (on his mother's side), who was hit by a train; Mary E. Esler/ Eastes (on his mother's side), who died in a house fire. The latter two individuals will be discussed in a later chapter.]

---

53   Robert William Barnes, *Baltimore County Families, 1659-1757.* (1989)
54   "Dennis Garrett," EDLER, FISHER, REDSECKER, WALD and Related Families. *Notes on some of the ancestors and relatives of Karl & Barbara Edler, Bets & Bruce Wald and Martha & Jim Redsecker.* Person Page 96. Accessed September 14, 2011. Available at: http://www.edlers.org/notes/ p96.htm

The James Gang

In 1997, Phillip W. Steele researched the ancestry of the James brothers and sister in his *Jesse and Frank James: The Family History*. According to Steele:

> *The lineage of Zerelda Cole James extends from John Cole, a native of Pennsylvania. He married a girl named Susanna. John died in Culpepper County, Virginia in 1757 and his wife in 1761. A son, Richard Cole, Sr. was born to John and Susanna in Pennsylvania in 1729. Richard Cole, Sr. settled lands near Midway, Kentucky. He married first Ann Hubbard in 1762 and second Emsey Margaret James on July 21, 1795 in Woodford County, Kentucky. Richard Cole owned a farm and tavern known as the Black Horse Tavern on the old Frankfort-Lexington Road. This tavern became a popular stopping place for travelers and politicians of the day. Henry Clay and John Jordan Crittenden, who served as Kentucky's governor for two years and later as a member of President Fillmore's cabinet, often visited and campaigned around Cole's popular tavern. This tavern has been recently restored.*

> *As a result of the raw whiskey served and often rowdy atmosphere of Cole's Tavern, the religious community of the region began referring to the tavern's location as Sodom. Richard Cole, Sr. died at Midway, Kentucky on November 21, 1814.*[55]

The father of Richard Cole, Sr.--John Cole, Jr.-- was born in Baltimore, Maryland in 1691. He relocated to New England, where he married Susanna Elizabeth Goodwin in Hartford Connecticut in 1713. Susanna was from Somerset County, Pennsylvania. The Coles relocated to Pennsylvania after their marriage, and that's where their son, Richard Cole, Sr. was born in 1729. They eventually relocated to Culpepper County Virginia, where John died in 1757, and where his wife also died in 1761.

---

55   Phillip W. Steele. *Jesse and Frank James: The Family History*. Gretna: Pelican Publishing Co., 1997. pp. 39-40.

Zerelda Cole, the mother of the James brothers and sister, had a double-connection with John Cole, Sr. and Johanna Garrett through a "cousin" marriage on that line, as is noted in Steele:

Richard [Cole, Sr.'s] children were as follows:

John Cole; married Nancy Hines

Richard Cole Jr.

b.: April 23, 1763; d. July 9, 1839; married Sally Yates.

Rachael Cole

b.: 1760; d: 1840; married Willa Jett

Betsy Cole; married: Mr. Snape

Agnes Cole

Sallie Cole; married Benjamin Graves

Alsey Alice Cole

b. June 20, 1769; d. July 7, 1813; married Anthony Lindsay, Jr.

Lucy Cole; married Jonathan Cropper.[56]

As Steele notes, "James Cole [the son of Richard Cole, Jr. and Sally Yates] married his first cousin, Sallie Lindsay, the daughter of Anthony Lindsay and Alsey Cole."[57] James Cole and Sallie Lindsay were the parents of Zerelda Cole James. And according to Steele:

James Cole died February 27, 1827 after falling from a horse. Zerelda was two years of age at the time of her father's death and her brother, Jesse Richard, only one. After her husband's death, Sallie and her two children resided with her father-in-law, Richard Cole, at the Black Horse Tavern until he died in 1839. After Richard's death, Sallie married Robert Thomason, a widower with

---

56   Phillip W. Steele, *Jesse and Frank James: The Family History*, pp. 40-41.
57   Phillip W. Steele, *Jesse and Frank James: The Family History*, pp. 41-42.

six children, and the family, with the exception of Zerelda, moved to Clay County, Missouri.

Zerelda despised Thomason, according to family history, and chose to stay in Kentucky. She resided with her uncle, James M. Lindsay, in Stamping Ground (Scott County, Kentucky) while attending school at the nearby Georgetown Catholic Convent.

After marrying Robert James on December 28 1841, she moved with her husband to Clay County, Missouri. While staying with her mother and step-father, the Thomasons, and while Robert finished seminary work at Georgetown College [Note: he became a Baptist preacher] her first child, Frank, was born in 1843. Robert returned, acquired a farm in 1845, and, after the birth of his son Jesse and daughter Susan, left for California, where he died in 1850.[58]

Concerning Jesse James and the public's obsession with him, which still exists today, I will quote from my own study of the man:

Jesse James was a man who loved the limelight. Had he lived and not followed a life of crime, he probably would have made an excellent showman, or a preacher, or an actor. He would have commanded center stage in the civil world. Instead, he commanded it on a stage of his own theatre as an outlaw. And the public could not get enough of him.

Reams of dime novels were snapped up by a thirsty public. Newspaper accounts, both positive and negative, filled the pages of the nation's presses. Headlines loudly proclaimed his activities. And he was the topic of many table discussions. Soon people began talking about personal encounters with the man, and that only fed the flames. People spoke of his generosity in helping poor widows pay off their mortgages. Whenever he stayed at someone's home, he generously paid for the meal. People spoke of his politeness and courtesy. And because he was so widely proclaimed, people wanted to be Jesse James.

---

58   Phillip W. Steele, *Jesse and Frank James: The Family History*, pp. 42-43.

In 1995, the body of Jesse James was exhumed from the grave in Kearney, Missouri hopefully for one last and final time to settle the J. Frank Dalton claim from Texas that Dalton was the real Jesse James. DNA testing was to be performed not only on Jesse's body, but on the body of J. Frank Dalton as well. The body buried in Kearney, carried a 99.7% proof that it was indeed the body of Jesse James. There is no proof on the other side since the wrong body was exhumed in Texas.[59]

Two rebels distantly related: one, the Last Rebel of the Civil War[60], and the other, a Rebel Without a Cause. But as Robertus Love noted in his *The Rise and Fall of Jesse James*, "Every man is a sort of modified sum total of his ancestors."[61]

***

James Dean's Cole Line

Unlike his brother John, Joseph Cole (1686-1748) remained in Baltimore, and also remained with the Society of Friends. Joseph Cole was James Dean's seventh-great-grandfather. He married Susanna Darwell (1696-1720), James Dean's seventh-great-grandmother. Their daughter, Sarah Cole(1718-1773) married Anthony Chamness (1713-1777), and the Chamnesses relocated to Cane Creek in Chatham County, North Carolina. The Chamnesses, like the Coles, appear to have come from Baltimore, Maryland. A summary of Richard Benneman's research follows:

> *The daughter of Anthony Chamness and Sarah Cole, Martha Chamness(who was born in Frederick Maryland 11/11 mo. 1746, married Stephen Hussey (1739-1762). Their son, Christopher*

---

59   Barbara Inman Beall, *The Sum Total—A Search for Levi Clay (1843-1917) and Jesse James (1847-1882),* pp. 266-267.

60   T. J. Stiles, *Jesse James: Last Rebel of the Civil War.* Vintage: (October 28, 2003)

61   Robertus Love (1925). *The Rise and Fall of Jesse James.* Qtd. In Barbara Inman Beall, *The sum Total—A Search for Levi Clay (1843-1917) and Jesse James (1847-1882),* preface.

Hussey (1770-1851) married Sarah Brown, who died about 1813. And their daughter, Sarah Hussey (1795-1834) married Isaac Williams (1784-aft 1860). The Williams' daughter, Betty Williams (1813-1895) married David Smithson (1800-1826.) And their daughter, Adeline Smithson (1855-1891) married Edward Woollen (1847-1935). They were the parents of James Dean's paternal grandmother, Emma J. Woollen Dean.[62]

The connection between Jesse James and James Dean was made years ago after the *You Are There* documentary. I remember reading an article where someone asked James Dean whether he would like to make a movie about the outlaw. He wasn't all that interested, he answered. He was more interested in Billy the Kid because he felt that Billy was given a raw deal. The truth is that James Dean wanted to make a really great western movie. *Giant* was the closest he came to it.

---

62   Richard E. Brenneman, "Notable Kin—New England in Hollywood, Part Four: The Ancestry of James Byron Dean (1931-1955), pp. 29-30.

CHAPTER 5–TO THE TUNE OF A DIFFERENT DRUMMER: THE REV.STEPHEN BACHILER (BATCHELOR)

"*The contentions in Hampton were grown to a great height, the whole town was divided into two factions, one with Mr. Batcheller, their late pastor, and the other with Mr. Dalton, their teacher, both men very passionate, and wanting discretion and moderation. Their differences; were not in matters of opinion, but of practice. Mr. Dalton's party being the most of the church, and so freemen, had great advantage of the other, though a considerable party, and some of them of the church also, whereby they carried all affairs both in church and town according to their own minds, and not with that respect to their brethren and neighbors which had been fit. Divers meetings had been both of magistrates and elders, and parties had been reconciled, but brake out presently again, each side being apt to take fire upon any provocation. Whereupon Mr. Batchelor was advised to remove. ***And at this court there came petition against petition both from Hampton and Exeter; whereupon the court ordered two or three magistrates to be sent to Hampton with full power to hear and determine all differences there.*"[63]

* * *

James Dean's tenth great-grandfather, the Rev. Stephen Bachiler, has been called the "Ur" father of Hampton, New Hampshire. He

---

63   *John Winthrop Diary, July 15, 1644.* The Journal of John Winthrop, 1630-1649: Abridged Edition (John Harvard Library) by John Winthrop, James Savage, Richard Dunn and Laetitia Yaendle (Jan 1, 1997)

connects with James Dean through the Hussey line. He also is my eleventh-great-grandfather on the Wing line.

No portrait exists of the mysterious Rev. Stephen Bachiler (1561-1656). Most of his possessions were burned in a fire during his stay in Hampton. However, a written description of Stephen Bachiler has been handed down via *The History of Hampton, N.H.* by Joseph Dow:

> *Mr. Bachiler was a tall and sinewy man, with prominent features. Especially his nose, a very dark complexion, coarse black hair in his younger days, white in age, mouth large and firm, eyes as black as sloes, features long rather than broad, a strong clear voice, rather slow of motion and speech, simple in dress, obstinate and tenacious of his opinions to a marked degree, a powerful preacher drawing largely from scripture, impress the hearers with uncommon power and sanctity of his sermons, strong in his friendships and in his hates.[64]*

While Stephen Bachiler's physical features become readily distinguishable in many of his descendants, they are not the only characteristics handed down through his lines. Bachiler was a passionate man with a fierce temper, per the following:

> *...We are talking about a man who, because of his temperament, his outstanding need for independence and freedom, more often than not, was received with animosity and jealousy. Rev. Bachiler had enemies in high places...[65]*

The Case Against Reverend Stephen Bachiler also notes that "Rev. Bachiler tended to be outspoken, independent, and somewhat of a rebel...often refusing to follow the orders of the General Court of the Massachusetts Bay Colony. (Timothy) Dalton was more of a conformist...not as outspoken or independent as Rev. Bachiler...and from that point it seems as though they were in contention."[66]

---

64   Joseph Dow, *History of the Town of Hampton, New Hampshire 1638-1988.*(1988)
65   *The Case Against Reverend Stephen Bachiler.* Online. Accessed Spring 2002. Available at http://members.aol.com/Lynnash911/guilty.html
66   *The Case Against Reverend Stephen Bachiler.* Online. Accessed Spring 2002. Available at http://members.aol.com/Lynnash911/guilty.html

According to the Hon. Charles E. Batchelder in his 1892 *Rev Stephen Bachiler*, it is impossible to know whether any relationship existed between Stephen Bachiler and the other New England families by that surname. The seven immigrant families include:

1. Alexander of Portsmouth, N. H.

2. Rev. Stephen of Lynn, Mass., and Hampton, N. H.

3. Henry of Ipswich, Mass.

4. Joseph of Salem, Mass.

5. William of Charlestown, Mass.

6. John of Watertown, Dedham and Reading, Mass.[67]

Batchelder states that as of 1892, there were living descendants of the Bachiler name from four of these immigrants: Rev. Stephen, Joseph and John of Salem, and John of Reading. Batchelder continues:

> *The word "bachelor" has long been a sore puzzle to etymologists, says Lower, in his work on English Surnames. That the name "Bachelor", however spelled, is the same as the word "bachelor," meaning an unmarried man or a college graduate, is unquestioned, but many derivations have been given by different authors to account for the meaning of the word, some most fanciful and even grotesque, others with more probability of correctness. Knights bachelors were the most ancient, though the lowest order, of knighthood in England.*

> *It is said in a note to Chitty's Blackstone that the most probable derivation of "bachelor" is from "bas" and "chevalier", an inferior knight.*

> *The derivation of the word is given in Webster's Dictionary as from the old French, "bachiler," meaning "a young man." A common derivation given is from "baccalureus, "having reference to the chaplet of laurel berries with which the new bachelor of arts*

---

67   Hon. Charles, E. Batchelder, "Rev. Stephen Bachiler", *NEGHR* Jan, April, July, Oct, 1892

was crowned. The earliest mention of the name indicates that it was given originally to mark the condition of its possessor as an unmarried man or as a young man, when there was an elder person of the same Christian name living in the neighborhood. The English Registers of the thirteenth and fourteenth centuries, where we first meet the name, use the French prefix "le". Thus we find Jordanus le Bacheler, Gilbert le Bacheler, that is, Jordan the bachelor, Gilbert the bachelor. We may be reasonably sure that the names Jordan and Gilbert were then so common in a particular neighborhood that it was necessary to indicate by some addition to the Jordan or Gilbert that there was an elder or married person of the same name in the immediate neighborhood. If "Bachelor" meant simply an unmarried man it was not proper or fitting at the death of Jordan le Bacheler in 1297, for he left surviving him a wife, Alice, and a son, John. It is therefore, probable that the word "Bachelor" was used at that time much like junior, meaning simply "the younger," and though at first given to an unmarried man was not dropped upon marriage, as it was a convenient and not inappropriate designation of the younger, whether single or married. At a later period the "le", being superfluous, was dropped, and in 1433 we find John Bachelor returned in the commissioners' list of the gentry of Norfolk, England, though John ye Baschealer died at Kesale in Suffolk Feb. 1, 1552.[68]

According to family legend, three brothers with the surname "Bachiler" served under William the Conqueror. After the Battle of Hastings, they were rewarded with grants of land in Wiltshire. Batchelder notes, "For sign manual they were given a shield upon which were three boar's heads, united by three links, a spear above them *couchant*. There was no crest, indicating that they were private soldiers."[69]

Before 1600, the family name is found in Kent, Surrey, Sussex, Wilts, Hampshire, Bucks, Middlesex, Norfolk and Suffolk—all counties locat-

68   Hon. Charles E. Batchelder, "Rev. Stephen Bachiler", *NEGHR* Jan, April, July, Oct, 1892
69   Hon. Charles E. Batchelder. "Rev. Stephen Bachiler," *NEGHR* Jan, April, July, Oct,1892

ed in the southeastern part of England. The name is very infrequent north of London. The earliest mention of the name is in Surrey, and probably "Surrey or Sussex was the earliest home of the Bachilers."[70]

In 1898, another Stephen Bachiler descendant, Victor Channing Sanborn, wrote, "...the Channel Islands were the home of a Bachiler family of French extraction. Probably this French family, migrating to Southampton and forming an important part of the French Protestant church there, was the ancestral line of Stephen Bachiler. Certain it is that his lifelong connection was with Hampshire, and he was allied to the Le Mercier and Praulx families of Jersey and Southampton."[71]

While Stephen Bachiler's actual birthplace has been in doubt for years, World Family Tree at Ancestry.com states that he was born in 1561 at Wherwell, Hampshire, England. His parents have been identified as Philip Bachiler (Phillipe de Bachiler), born 1535, and his mother has been suggested as Anne Flanders (although some sources list her as Anne of Flanders).[72] George F. Sanborn, founder and genealogist of the Sanborn Family Association, investigated Stephen Bachiller's parentage and when he could find no proof of the Philip/Ann connection, rejected the claim. Eleanor Campbell Shoen made the following presentation at the Solomon and Naomi Cox Reunion, May 22, 1999:

> The village of Wherwell stretches along the westerly bank of the Test Stream (called a troutful stream), in Hampshire, three and one half miles from Andover. Wherwell Abbey was the home of three, possibly four English Queens renowned for their extraordinary beauty. In 986, Wherwell abbey was founded for The Benedictine Nuns in penitence for bloodshed by Aelfrida, in which she was concerned. Aelfrida was the wife of Edmund the Magnificent, King of England. She was our ancestress.[73]

---

70   Hon. Charles E. Batchelder. "Rev. Stephen Bachilder." *NEGHR* Jan, April, July, Oct, 1892
71   Victor Channing Sanborn, "Rev. Stephen Bachiler" from *Batchelder, Batcheller Genealogy* by Frederick Clifton Pierce, 1898.
72   Stephen Bachiler. World Family Tree at Ancestry.com. Last accessed May 15, 2011. Available at http://www.ancestry.com
73   Eleanor Campbell Schoen. "Our Fascinating Ancestor, Stephen Bachiler." Presentation May 22, 1999. Accessed September 15, 2011. Available at http://www.hampton.lib.nh.us/hampton/biog/bachilerschoen.htm

Stephen Bachiler matriculated at St. John's College, Oxford November 17, 1581. He received his B. A. February 3, 1586 and became the Vicar at Wherwell July 17 1587, until he was deposed 1604. However, in 1614, he is still of record there. Prior to his appointment as Vicar, he was a chaplain to Lord Delaware. According to Victor Sanborn:

> ...The college of that time was vastly different from the St. John's of today, with its peaceful gardens, smooth lawns and ancient cedars. The good Sir Thomas, since its foundation, had lost much of his money, and his college was very poor. Not for some years did it receive new foundations and added wealth. But, poor or rich, it was a part of that seat of learning, the great University of Oxford, at that time a very hive of Puritanism. The Regius Professor of Divinity was Lawrence Humphrey, an ardent Lutheran, who was disciplined by Archbishop Grindal for refusing to wear the churchly vestments. John Harmer, the Earl of Leicester's favorite and one of Queen Elizabeth's scholars, was Regius Professor of Greek. The unfortunate Thomas Kingsmill, another Puritan, was head professor in Hebrew. Edward Cradocke was Margaret Professor of Divinity, and the most renowned scholar of the day, an Oxford man, John Rainoldes, was the head and front of the Puritan arm of the church, and the spokesman of the Puritan party. Rainoldes is called by quaint Anthony Wood "a living library and a third university." He declined a bishopric, preferring to remain the President of Corpus Christi College, and from his Oxford study sent forth a mass of treatises in favor of the advanced doctrines. It was he who mainly represented Puritanism at the Hampton Court conference of 1604, and it was at his suggestion and by his aid that the well-meaning but pedantic King James undertook that translation of the Bible which is today mainly used.[74]

Bachiler's name appears sporadically on English records. In 1596 he was named as an overseer in the will of William Spencer of Cheriton, a rich Hampshire squire, who married one of his parishioners. However, church affairs were in complete disarray in England at this period of

---

74   Victor C. Sanborn, "Stephen Bachiller: An Unforgiven Puritan" (1917). Accessed September 15, 2011. Available at: http://www.hampton.lib.nh.us/hampton/biog/bachilerunforgiven.htm

time. The Church officials were corrupt and engaged in the same type of behavior that brought about the Protestant Reformation. According to Victor Sanborn:

> ...The death of the great Puritan prelate Grindal in 1583 sum-moned to the primacy John Whitgift, whose "cold mediocrity," as the elder Disraeli called it, was no match for the fiery arguments of the Martin Mar Prelate controversy. In the century and a half which had succeeded the dissolution of the monasteries and es-tablishment of a Protestant church in England, the same material abuses which had prevailed in the older church showed them-selves in the reformed episcopacy. The prelates waxed rich, while the people were overridden. The clergy was corrupt and the rites of the church were abused. Of a sudden pamphlet ridiculing these abuses ran like wildfire over the land. Whether the first "Mar Prelate" monograph was written by John Penry, by Barrow, or by Job Throckmorton will perhaps never be known, and does not now especially matter. The attack was so sudden, the knife went so deep into the vitals of the establishment, that the surprised and angry bishops retaliated in similar rude and currilous pam-phlets, and by fines, imprisonments, and persecutions attempted in vain to check the growing wrath of the people towards the prel-ates. The first categorical answer to the Mar Prelate pamphlets was written by Thomas Cooper, the same bishop of Winchester who had a year before ordained Bachiler vicar of Wherwell. But the established church was forced to attack both Romish priests and Puritan non-conformists, which weakened the force of at-tempts against either, and popular sympathy was far greater for the Puritan revolt against the establishment. The last years of Elizabeth's reign were marked by persecutions of recusants and reformers, with numberless imprisonments and executions. The faction grew steadily, and when in 1603 James of Scotland came to the throne great was the rejoicing among them, for it seemed that a Scotch King of England augured well for the victory of Presbyter versus Prelate.[75]

---

75   Victor C. Sanborn, "Stephen Bachiler: An Unforgiven Puritan" (1917). Accessed September 15, 2011. Available at: http://www.hampton.lib.nh.us/ hampton/biog/bachilerunforgiven.htm

Stephen Bachiler remained firmly entrenched on the side of the Puritans. He was one of few Vicars who signed a petition to King James, "which greeted the Scotch monarch on his coming to the English throne, --a petition which urged the King to reform the crying abuses of the established church, and besought him to allow the Puritan pastors to continue their 'prophesyings and preachings' undeterred by the persecutions of their bishops."[76] Puritan expectations failed, however. The following year (May 1605) Archbishop Bancroft, via ecclesiastical court, instructed Thomas Bilson, Bishop of Winchester, to dismiss all non-conforming clergymen. In August 1604, Stephen Bachiler was ejected from Wherwell and was also excommunicated from the church.

The balance of Bachiler's life in England is indeed fragmentary. Adam Winthrop (father of John Winthrop, the Massachusetts Governor) notes that he "suffered much at the hands of the Bishops", and family tradition claims that he fled to Holland with a band of separatists from Scrooby. In 1620, this band of separatists formed the settlement at Plymouth Colony (Massachusetts) and a number of them went to America on the *Mayflower*. Victor Sanborn continues:

> *Bachiler was at 45, in the prime of his powers. We may imagine that, fitted by scholarship and by the turn of his mind, he was an ardent, able controversialist. We know that many of his parishioners followed him from the church at Wherwell to his ministrations under Puritan auspices at the adjoining hamlet of Newton Stacy. In 1604 Henry Shipton, a wealthy tanner of Shawe, across the border in Berkshire, leaves him a small legacy, and in 1616 Edmund Alleyn of Hatfield Peverell, a rich Essex squire, bequeaths him a similar sum. In 1610 Bachiler's son Stephen was entered at Magdalen College in Oxford, the family college of the Wests, Lords Delaware. In 1621 the diary of Adam Winthrop, father of the Massachusetts Governor, says that he had "Mr. Bachiler the preacher" to dine with him. That he was not without means is shown by the Hampshire land records, which recited, between*

---

76   Victor C. Sanborn, "Stephen Bachiler: An Unforgiven Puritan" (1917). Accessed September 15, 2011. Available at: http://www.hampton.lib.nh.us/hampton/biog/bachilerunforgiven.htm

1622 and 1630, his purchase and sale of small properties in Newton Stacy. A petition of Sir Robert Payne, Sheriff of Hampshire in 1632, states that several of his tenants, "having been formerly misled by Stephen Bachiler, a Notorious incomformist, demolished a chapel at Newton Stacy, and executed many things in contempt of the canons and the bishop.[77]

Bachiler spent a score of years in England. By the time he was seventy, his children were all grown and married: "one son became a chaplain in an English regiment in Holland, and one a merchant in Southampton; one daughter married John Wing, an English Puritan minister at Flushing and The Hague; and another Christopher Hussey, perhaps a relative of the mayor of Winchester of the same name, who married a daughter of the Hampshire Puritan prebendary Renniger; a third daughter married a Hampshire Samborne, probably connected with James Samborne, the Winchester scholar and Oxford graduate, Puritan vicar of Andover and rector of Upper Clatford, neighboring villages to Wherwell."[78]

[NOTE: John Wing and Deborah Bachiler were my tenth –great-grandparents. Capt. Christopher Hussey and Theodate Bachiler were James Dean's ninth –great-grandparents.]

When the English Puritans received another blow in 1625, many of them began looking at the Plymouth Colony enterprise in America, including Stephen Bachiler. Most men of his age would decide to "quit the fight" and spend their twilight years in peace. This was not true of Stephen Bachiler. He thought he saw an Arcadia of religious freedom in America. Victor Sanborn explains what happened next:

In 1630 a small band of London merchants, perhaps friends of Bachiler's son Nathaniel, formed a colonizing company, called the "Company of Husbandmen" and obtained from Sir Ferdinando

---

77   Victor Sanborn, "Stephen Bachiler: An Unforgiven Puritan" (1917). Accessed September 15, 2011. Available at: http://www.hampton.lib.nh.us/hampton/biog/bachilerunforgiven.htm
78   Victor Sanborn, "Stephen Bachiler: An Unforgiven Puritan" (1917). Accessed September 15, 2011. Available at: http://www.hampton.lib.nh.us/hampton/biog/bachilerunforgiven.htm

Gorges, the great enemy to New England Puritanism, a patent to some 1600 square miles in his province of New England south of the river Sagadahock. This Company of Husbandmen sent to America in the fall of 1630 a small ship called the "Plough," with a meager band of colonists to settle on their new patent, probably about where the present city of Portland stands. The grant from Gorges seems to have conflicted with other grants, and the original patent is lost, so that we cannot exactly locate the land, which the Husbandmen thought embraced the seacoast from Cape Porpoise to Cape Elizabeth.[79]

This shipload arrived six months after the Winthrop fleet founded the Bay Colony and probably landed during the hard winter of 1631. The settlers were extremely disappointed with what they saw: a sterile and forbidding landscape; bare settlements except a few scattered fishing stages; and, of course, supplies were extremely limited. It is unknown whether Bachiler was an original member of the company for their records have not survived. He may have been since a letter from the London managers, dated March 1631-2 and sent to the colonists, speaks as though he had been interested in the Company's work for some time. The letter asks the colonists to remember their duty to return thanks to God who *"hath filled the heart of our reverend pastor so full of zeal, of love and persuading and exhorting—yea and as much as in him lieth—constraining all that love him to join together with us. And seeing the Company is not able to bear his charge over, he hath strained himself to provide provision for himself and his family, and hath done his utmost endeavor to help over as many as he possibly can, for your further strength and encouragement."*[80]

The Plough Company spent another year working in England to secure more colonists and to enlarge their resources. None of these men were rich, but as Sanborn notes, "all were bound together by some mystical religious fellowship, the exact significance of which

---

79   Victor Sanborn, "Stephen Bachiler: An Unforgiven Puritan" (1917). Accessed September 15, 2011. Available at: http://www.hampton.lib.nh.us/ hampton/biog/bachilerunforgiven.htm
80   Mass. Hist. Soc. Coll., 4 Series, vol. VII, pp. 91-4, notes

has been lost in the ensuing centuries of oblivion."[81] Bachiler and his kinsmen appear to have kept the company alive. The Company itself consisted of John Dye, Grace Hardwin and Thomas Jude, who were three London merchants of limited education and narrow resources. The first ship included John Crispe, Bryan Binckes and John Carman, who appear to have had some sort of connection with the company. A second shipment of goods and colonists went out March 1632 in the form of two ships, the *Whale* and the *William & Francis*. Bachiler was aboard the *William & Francis*, which indicates that he returned to England in order to bring over more colonists (if he were in fact already in Massachusetts). Those accompanying him included his third wife, Helena (Mason), his widowed daughter, Deborah Wing, and her three sons, Daniel, John and Stephen along with three Sanborne grandsons (Stephen, John and William) per the following:

> *"Ship: William and Francis". Mr. ??? Thomas, Master. Left London 9 March 1632. Arrived New England 5 June 1632, with about sixty passengers (per John Winthrop, Journal I, pp. 80, 81) Rev. Stephen Bachiler of Newton Stacy, County Hampshire, England; Mrs. Helen Bachiler; John Sanborn, William Sanborn, Stephen Sanborn. (No mention of Deborah and her three sons. Perhaps they were listed separately or came on another ship.[82]*

Other names of those accompanying Bachiler include Edward Winslow (returning from England to Plymouth), Rev. Thomas Weld (the libeler of Mrs. Hutchinson) and about sixty passengers in all— in the *Whale* were thirty passengers and sixty-eight cows—Captain Graves being shipmaster.[83]

The crossing was extremely difficult and lasted eighty-eight days. The cargo Stephen Bachiler brought follows:

---

81   Victor Sanborn, "Stephen Bachiler: An Unforgiven Puritan" (1917) Accessed September 15, 2011. Available at: http://www.hampton.lib.nh.us/hampton/biog/bachilerunforgiven.htm

82   Charles E. Banks. *Planters of the Commonwealth—Passengers and Ships*, P. 96.

83   F. B. Sanborn, *The Hard Case of the Founder of Old Hampton*. Accessed September 15, 2011. Available at http://www.hampton.lib.nh.us/hampton/biog/bachilerhardcase.htm

Four hogsheads of pease, twelve yards of cloth, two hundred yards of list, oaken furniture, and a collection box.[84]

His relative, Richard Dummer, who was also from Hampshire, captained the *Whale*. Dummer was not a member of the Company, but he apparently had the financial status the project needed. Dummer's exact relationship to Stephen Bachiler is unknown.[85] The name flourishes in Hampshire, and I have found it on records with the Mudges/Mudgetts, Deans, and Dillinghams there. Stephen Bachiler addressed Dummer as his cousin in a letter written to his son, Nathaniel Bachiler. And Richard Dummer's first wife was Stephen Bachiler's step-daughter (daughter of Rev. Thomas and Helena Mason—Frances Mason Dummer.) After Bachiler's return to England for the settlers, the original members of the *Plough* drifted down the coast, looking for a better location. Winthrop's diary of July 6, 1631 records their arrival at Watertown as follows: "A small ship of 60 tons arrived at Natascot, Mr. Graves master. She brought ten passengers from London. They came with a patent for Sagadehock, but not liking the place they came hither. Their ship drew ten feet and went up to Watertown but she ran on ground twice by the way."[86]

Victor Sanborn concludes:

The Husbandmen, with their vague and mysterious religious tenets, were with some reason looked on askance by the compact and intolerant colony of Endicott and Dudley. They had failed in their enterprise, and had come from the neighborhood of those fishing settlements along the north coast, whose rude and lawless members were in bad odor with the magistrates. It is doubtful, however, if they deserved the opprobrium which has clung to

---

84   Eleanor Campbell Schoen, "Our Fascinating Ancestor, Stephen Bachiler." Accessed September 15, 2011. Available at http://www.hampton.lib.nh.us/hampton/biog/bachilerschoen.htm
85   In *The Hard Case of the Founder of Old Hampton*, F. B. Sanborn states that Dummer was Bachiler's cousin. He married Bachiler's step-daughter, Frances, who was the daughter of Helena Mason, Bachiler's third wife.
86   *The Winthrop Diary, vol. 1, p. 65.* The Journal of John Winthrop, 1630-1649: Abridged Edition (John Harvard Library) by John Winthrop, James Savage, Richard Dunn and Laetitia Yaendle (Jan 1, 1997)

them because of a note added later by Winthrop or some other hand—"They most of them proved familists and vanished away." The offensive term of Familist, with its hint of free love tendencies, was applied to many of the settlers who resented and differed from the arbitrary standards of the Massachusetts colony.[87]

By June 1632 when Bachiler and Dummer arrived, the venture was already doomed. The band was already in disarray; the Company of Husbandmen was practically dead. Its assets were seized by the Massachusetts Court; its members had already scattered. Some returned to England, while others fled to Virginia. As a result, Maine became a dependency of the Bay Colony, even though Bachiler fought to keep it independent.

Richard Dummer was the only one who received a profit from the failed Company. Bachiler disposed of his small estate in Hampshire to provide funds for the colony. Some of his children and grandchildren were among the colonists. Stephen Bachiler found himself "at 71 stranded in Newtown without a settlement or a pastorate, and equipped with a moderate sum of money, a library of fair size, and a somewhat legendary coat of arms, which the fanciful herald, Sylvanus Morgan, says did 'appertain to Stephen Bachiler, the first pastor of the church of Ligonia in New England.'"[88]

Sanborn disputes Lynn historians Lewis and Newhall in their claim that Bachiler and his colony immediately established a church there. According to Sanborn, "Bachiler's own letter to Winthrop shows his first sojourn was at Newtown, now Cambridge."[89] Sanborn contends that "the handful of colonists left of the Plough Company set up their first tabernacle, and listened to the prophesyings of Master Bachiler.

---

87   Victor Sanborn, "Stephen Bachiler: An Unforgiven Puritan" (1917) Accessed September 15, 2011. Available at: http://www.hampton.lib.nh.us/ hampton/biog/bachilerunforgiven.htm

88   Victor Sanborn, "The Unforgiven Puritan: Rev. Stephen Bachiler." (1917). Accessed September 15, 2011. Available at: http://www.hampton. lib.nh.us/hampton/biog/bachilerunforgiven.htm

89   Victor Sanborn. "The Unforgiven Puritan: Rev. Stephen Bachiler." (1917) Accessed September 15, 2011. Available at: http://www.hampton. lib.nh.us/hampton/biog/bachilerunforgiven.htm

The arbitrary general Court of Winthrop's colony promptly suppressed the influence of these doctrines, which were perhaps more tolerant, and thus more acceptable to many of the newly arriving colonists not yet firmly bound to the compact and narrow limits of the oligarchy. Bachiler and his adherents had not joined the church covenant by taking the 'freeman's oath." The Court on Oct. 6, 1632, ordered that "Mr. Batchel'r is required to forbeare exercising his gifts as a pastor or teacher publiquely in our patent, unless it be to those he brought with him, for his contempt of authority and till some scandles be removed.[90] He probably relocated to Lynn after this and established his church there, and continued to preach at that location for three years. And his life was anything but peaceful. He undoubtedly rattled a few nerves when he chose to baptize his grandson first in place of the child who had been presented to him. (His grandson was the first child—Stephen (James Dean's 8th great-grandfather)--of Capt. Christopher and Theodate Bachiler Hussey.) Thomas Newhall had presented his child for baptism—the town's first born white child--and Bachiler responded by saying, "I will baptize my own child first!" After that, everything fell apart. There was no peace for Stephen Bachiler.

Bachiler's independent ideas came under scrutiny by the Puritan oligarchy. The oligarchs knew about his ideas, and they didn't like them. They especially didn't like his refusal to yield to the dictates of others (meaning "the oligarchs", of course). For this very reason, he was allowed only to preach to the congregation he brought with him and to take in no others. The records mention certain "scandles" on Bachiler's record, but at that period of time in Massachusetts, preaching outside the dictates of the oligarchs was considered scandalous. After five months, the sanctions were removed, and he was then free to establish a church in Massachusetts. He preached in Massachusetts Bay, including Ipswich, Yarmouth and Newberry. He was granted fifty acres of land in Ipswich; however, he stayed there only a short time. He settled in Yarmouth during 1637-8, which was about one hundred miles from Ipswich. He was seventy-six years of age at the time, and

90   Victor Sanborn. "The Unforgiven Puritan: Rev. Stephen Bachiler." (1917) Accessed September 15, 2011. Available at: http://www.hampton.lib.nh.us/hampton/biog/bachilerunforgiven.htm

he walked the entire distance during the worst of weather.

By 1638, Bachiler received a grant of land and soon after this, he was given the liberty to begin a plantation at Winnacunnet by the General Court of Massachusetts. He had the name changed to Hampton. Thereafter, he sold his land in Newberry and was granted three hundred acres of land for a farm, in addition to his house-lot in 1639. Sometime during his stay in Hampton, his house burned and he lost his great library, valued at two hundred pounds.

The church Stephen Bachiler organized at Hampton is now the oldest Congregational Society in New Hampshire. It is also the second oldest continuous church fellowship in the United States. It was here that many of his problems began in 1638 and continued to 1644. The conflict initially arose between Stephen Bachiler (the minister) and his teacher (Timothy Dalton). The conflict resulted in Bachiler's second excommunication.

Basically, Stephen Bachiler wanted the freedom to exercise his own conscience. He probably sympathized with Roger Williams, Sir Henry Vane, Rev. John Wheelwright, and Mrs. Anne Hutchinson, but the extent of his sympathy is unknown. These people were put down in Massachusetts with a rigorous hand: Williams was banished to Rhode Island in1640; Wheelright and his followers were disarmed—all their weapons were taken away, and they withdrew first to Exeter, and then to one of the many Maine colonies. Stephen Bachiler's independent spirit and nonconformity rubbed against Timothy Dalton's conformist position. In modern terms, the "sparks flew."

Dalton was a much younger man. He came from Suffolk, England in 1639, bringing parishioners with him and was made a colleague of Stephen Bachiler under the title of "Teacher" in Bachiler's Hampton church. By 1641, the battle raged. Charges of immorality were made by Dalton against the pastor (who was eighty years old at the time). Dalton accused Bachiler of proposing adultery with one of the female parishioners. John Winthrop (who kept a record of all gossip in his journal, and who appears to have thrived in doing so) reports November 12, 1641:

*After this, Mr. Bachiler went on a very variable course, sometimes
seeming very penitent, soon after again excusing himself, and
casting blame upon others, especially his fellow-elder, Mr.
Dalton (who indeed had not carried himself so well in this cause as became him, and was brought to see his failing, and acknowledge
it to the elders of the other churches, who had taken much pains
about this matter). He was off and on for a long time, and when
he seemed most penitent, so as the church were ready to have
received him again, he would fall back again, and as it were, re-
pent of his repentance. In this time his house and nearly all his
substance was consumed by fire. When he had continued excommunicated near two years, and much agitation had been about
the matter, and the church being divided, so as he could not be
received in,--at length the matter was referred to some magistrates and elders, and by their mediation he was released of his
excommunication, but not received to his pastor's office.[91]*

Bachiler denied the charge, which was in itself highly improbable;
but Dalton persisted and secured Bachiler's excommunication from
the Church. Reportedly, the church forgave his offense (whatever it
may have been) before excommunicating him. Bachiler was never
prosecuted for this offense, and no names were mentioned in the
records. Stephen Bachiler may well have had a roving eye—especially
since his third wife Helen Mason, was really "grave" (as she has been
described.) Perhaps Dalton noticed Bachiler's gaze upon the unidentified woman and "seized the moment." Whatever happened was no
doubt blown out of proportion.

It is also important to note here that Dalton's wife Ruth was one of
Bachiler's relatives—her exact connection is unknown at this time.
She may have been another cousin. Dalton was a relative of John
Winthrop, who had a keen dislike for Stephen Bachiler). According to
Philip Mason Marston:

*Soon after the arrival of Dalton the differences between the two
clergymen came to an open break and there occurred the inci-*

91   *The Winthrop Diary, 12 Nov 1641.* The Journal of John Winthrop,
1630-1649: Abridged Edition (John Harvard Library) by John Winthrop,
James Savage, Richard Dunn and Laetitia Yaendle (Jan 1, 1997)

dent which has most frequently been used to defame Bachiler's character. The alleged proposal to commit adultery was noted in his Journal by Winthrop under date of November 12, 1641. He wrote that Bachiler was about eighty years old at the time and was then married to a "lusty comely woman", that he denied the charges at first and "complained to the magistrates" concerning the slander against him but that he later confessed his guilt and was excommunicated from the church for a period of two years before being received back in again but without being restored to the office of pastor. The Reverend William Hubbard of Ipswich, Massachusetts, writing probably before 1682 and possibly having consulted the manuscript of Winthrop's Journal gives a similar but shorter account and describes Bachiler's second wife as "grave" rather than "lusty".[92],[93]

Sometime during this controversy, Bachiler's house burned, and he lost all his books and papers. Bachiler contended that Dalton was out for revenge. (I don't know whether he blamed Dalton for his house fire). In his letter to Winthrop, Bachiler hoped to get a trial so that he could publicly defend himself against the charges in the courtroom. However, and as F. B. Sanborn notes:

This was just after Massachusetts had paternally taken the four New Hampshire towns under her government, and the Lords Brethren did not want any more public wrangling than was unavoidable in that part of their Mosaic despotism. They had trouble enough from the free-spoken settlers in Maine and New Hampshire, who were not too well pleased to be "trotting after the Bay Horse."

At this point we have an important testimony to the high character of Mr. Bachiler from a source naturally hostile to him, --viz:

---

92   Helen Mason was Bachiler's 2nd or 3rd wife. Some historians claim Helen Weare was his 2nd wife and Helen Mason was his third. His first wife was Ann Bates, the mother of all his children.
.

93   Philip Mason Marston, *The Reverend Stephen Bachiler—Saint or Sinner?* Accessed September 15, 2011. Available at http://www.hampton. lib.nh.us/hampton/biog/bachilermarston.htm

the Church of England party in Maine, which was carrying on a controversy with the Puritan party, --the latter headed by George Cleeve, an original Casco settler, though not of the Plough Colony, Rev. Robert Jordan, a son-in-law of John Winter, and an Oxford graduate, like Bachiler, was an Episcopal clergyman originally, and continued of the Cavalier party, like Gorges and the Trelawnys. Writing to the Parliament member, Trelawny, who had a colony in Maine, Jordan said, after mentioning the fact that Mr. Bachiler had been chosen umpire in the disputes between Trelawny and George Cleeve:

"Mr. Stephen Bachiler, the pastor of a church in the Massachusetts Bay, was, I must say, a grave, reverend, and a good man; but whether more inclined to justice or mercy, or whether carried aside by secret insinuations, I must refer to your own judgement. Sure I am that Cleeve is well nigh able to disable the wisest brain. [94]

Bachiler was denied his due process in court. But, true to his nature, he did not give up the fight. In 1650, Bachiler sued the town of Hampton for wages due him, and he actually won the case!

Bachiler's wife, Helen, died in 1647. He was replaced by his friend and successor, John Wheelright, who was brought in to reconcile differences between the Bachiler/Dalton adherents. In the spring of that year, Bachiler removed from Hampton and conveyed all remaining property in Hampton to his grandson, Lieut. John Sanborn, who in turn gave bond for the other three grandchildren in America: Nathaniel Bachiler, William Sanborn, and Stephen Sanborn.

But trouble had a way of following Stephen Bachiler. This time, her name was Mary Magdalen Bailey Beedle, and she was at least sixty years younger than Stephen.

He met her in Kittery, a "wild place", where settlers did not generally comply with the Puritan orthodoxy. It was a trading and fishing community where Stephen Bachiler undertook missionary service after

---

94   F. B. Sanborn, *The Hard Case of the Founder of Old Hampton* (1900) Accessed September 15, 2011. Available at http://www.hampton.lib.nh.us/ hampton/biog/bachilerhardcase.htm

James Parker threw up his hands in despair and removed to Barbados (another Puritan stronghold). F. B. Sanborn describes her as "one of Satan's shepherdesses—a widow and adventuress"[95] who charmed the aged Stephen Bachiler into her snare. She was undoubtedly charming and attractive, and Stephen Bachiler needed to hire someone to help him with his housework. Some writers suggest that she was the inspiration for Hester Prynne in Hawthorne's *Scarlet Letter.* In a letter written to John Winthrop May 3, 1647, Bachiler wrote that he had found a widow to have "some eye and care towards my family" and that this arrangement had met with the "approbation of the whole plantation of Strabury Banke." However, as Marston notes, "… there were rumors that he was already married to her 'or certainly shalbe', and that there were 'cast on her such aspertions without ground or proufe' that he did not see how he could possibly continue to live in the place."[96]

Mary Beedle was a widow with children who had mercenary motives. She coveted the title "Mistress Batchelor" and although he was eighty-eight years of age, she inveiled him into marriage as early as 1648. According to Charles Batchelder:

> *Shortly after his removal to Strawberry Bank, Mr. Bachiler's usual good judgment seems to have deserted him. He was a widower and obtained for a housekeeper a widow, whom he calls "an honest neighbour." He soon married her and the match turned out in every way unfortunate. She was an adulteress and her husband speedily discovered her character. His third marriage is usually said to have been contracted early in 1650, but as the town of Kittery granted her a lot, under the name of Mrs. Batcheller, on the 14th of February, 1648, the marriage must have taken place in 1647 to 1648, when he was eighty-six or eighty-seven years old. His wife, Mary, was evidently much younger than he. In May, 1650, he was fined ten pounds for not publishing his intention of*

---

95   F. B. Sanborn, *The Hard Case of the Founder of Old Hampton* (1900) Accessed September 15, 2011. Available at http://www.hampton.lib.nh.us/ hampton/biog/bachilerhardcase.htm

96   Philip Mason Marston, *The Reverend Stephen Bachiler—Saint or Sinner?* Accessed September 15, 2011. Available at http://www.hampton. lib.nh.us/hampton/biog/bachilermarston.htm

marriage according to law. In October of the same year one half of this fine was remitted.[97]

Mary was caught in adultery with George Rogers, a local character. George Rogers and Mrs. Batcheller were presented "upon vehement suspition of incontency for living in one house together "lieing in one rome" at the General Court at Gorgeana October 15, 1650. They were ordered to "be separated before the next court or to pay 40s"[98] Under date of Oct. 15, 1651, York Court Records show the following:

> *We do present George Rogers and Mary Batcheller, the wife of Mr. Stephen Batcheller, minister, for adultery. It is ordered that Mrs. Batcheller, for her adultery, shall receive forty stripes save one, at the first town meeting held at Kittery, 6 weeks after her delivery, and be branded with the letter A.[99]*

Stephen Bachiler immediately filed for divorce from his faithless wife—who already had quite a history. She was thereafter sentenced for sexual irregularities in the Maine Courts 1651, 1652 and 1654. Mary Magdalene Bailey Beedle was the widow of Robert Beedle, a fisherman and farmer, by whom she had two children: a daughter, Elizabeth, and a son, Christopher. Apparently, George Rogers was the next door neighbor, and she didn't waste any time in becoming involved with him. She had at least one child, a daughter named Mary Magdalen, during her marriage to Stephen Bachiler, but the child wasn't his. In June 1654, the court ordered Thomas Hanscom, who was thirty-one-years of age, "not to live with Mary Batchiler"—so she had quickly lost her affection for George Rogers. It is ironic to note that after her divorce from Stephen Bachiler was finally granted, she married Thomas Turner and became a respectable, successful, church-going woman, who was active in community affairs!

When Stephen Bachiler initially filed for divorce from this woman, he received an astonishing ruling from the Court:

97   Charles E. Batchelder, "Rev. Stephen Bachiler" (1892)
98   Court Record qtd. In Charles E. Batchelder, "Rev. Stephen Bachiler" (1892).
99   Court Record qtd. In Charles E. Batchelder, "Rev. Stephen Bachiler" (1892)

That Mr. Batchelor and his wife shall live together as man and wife, as in this court they have publicly professed to do; and if either desert one another, then hereby the court doth order that the marshall shall apprehend both the said Mr. Batchelor and Mary, his wife, and bring them forthwith to Boston, there to be kept till the next Quarter Court of Assistants, that further consideration thereof may be had, both of them moving for a divorce: Provided notwithstanding, that if they put in 50 pounds each of them, for their appearance, that then they shall be under their bail to appear at the next court; and in case Mary Batchellor shall live out of the jurisdiction, without mutual consent for a time, then the clerk shall give notice to the magistrate at Boston of her absence, that further order may be taken therein.[100]

John Winthrop must have been delighted in making that ruling. Such a ruling was incomprehensible—but it is obvious that Bachiler's enemies planned to make the rest of his stay in America as uncomfortable as possible. And true to his nature, Stephen Bachiler did not abide by the ruling. His son-in-law, Capt. Christopher Hussey, secured his passage for England. According to F. B. Sanborn:

Upon leaving America, where he had been so ungratefully dealt with by all except his own kindred, he turned over the last remains of his American property to his son-in-law, Captain Christopher Hussey...as two of his old neighbors testified later:

"They did hear Mr. Bachiler say unto his son-in-law that in consideration the said Hussey had little or nothing from him with his daughter, which was then married to the said Hussey; as also that this said son Hussey and his wife had been helpful unto him both formerly and in fitting him for his voyage, and for other considerations; he did give to the said Hussey all his estate, consisting in cattle, household goods and debts, for which his gift aforesaid he also gave a deed in writing and delivered a copy thereof to the said Hussey.[101]

---

100   Old Norfolk County records (MS) 8th month, 1st-3rd day, 1651.
101   F. B. Sanborn, *The Hard Case of the Old Founder of Hampton.* Accessed September 15, 2011. Available at http://www.hampton.lib.nh.us/hampton/biog/bachilerhardcase.htm

After his departure for England, Mary Beedle filed for divorce.

Little is known about Stephen Bachiler's life after he returned to England in 1654. He appears to have spent his remaining years near London. His date of death has been erroneously recorded at 1660—a date that is still embraced by many. However, His date of burial was 31 October 1656 in the All Hallows Staining Church Cemetery, London England. For all the grief that he suffered, he lived to be ninety-five years old.

CHAPTER 6—SEEDS OF DISSENT: THE HUSSEYS AND THE WINGS

All of Stephen Bachiler's children were born by his first wife Ann Bates, the daughter of Vicar John Bates of Wherwell. And contrary to the thirteen or fourteen children sometimes listed as the children of Stephen Bachiler, he actually had only six: (1) Nathaniel (b. abt 1589); (2) Deborah (b. abt 1591); (3) Samuel (b. abt 1592); (4) Stephen (b. abt 1594); (5) Theodate (b. abt 1598); (6) Anna or Ann (b. abt. 1600). This chapter provides a short overview of four of these children— Nathaniel, Samuel, Stephen and Ann—and provides a more in-depth look at daughters Theodate and Deborah.

Nathaniel Bachiler (ca. 1589-1644/1645)

Nathaniel Bachiler was born in Southampton, Hampshire, England abt 1589 and was christened in Wherwell, Hampshire, England in 1590. He married Hester Mercer in Southampton in 1613. Nathaniel Bachiler was the direct ancestor of Daniel Webster, Herman Webster Mudgett, and Louis L'Amour]. Nathaniel died in Southampton in 1644/1645, and his wife then married Daniel du Comet, a merchant of Middleburgh, Zealand.[102]

Samuel Bachiler (b. abt 1592-1597—d. in 1640)

Samuel did not settle in Massachusetts. He is described in *Piscataqua Pioneers* as "a minister, late of Gorcum, Holland." According to Eleanor Campbell Schoen:

---

102   Frederick Clifton Pierce, *Batchelder,Batcheller Genealogy,* p. 42.

*...Samuel...was a minister in Sr. Charles Morgan's fighting regi-
ment in Holland. That same year Samuel was offered a pastorate in Flushing, but he declined. He preached "in the Armie" at
Danger-Leager, and to the English at Gorinchem and Amsterdam.
He wrote a book in 1625 of meditations on...Deuteronomy 23:9-
14: "When the host goeth forth against thine enemies, then keep
thee from every evil thing—for the Lord God walketh in the midst
of the camp to deliver thee, and to give up thine enemies before
thee; therefore shall thy camp be holy; that he seeth no unclean
thing in thee, and turn away from thee."*

*There is a three page preface to his book addressed "to all my
deare and loving countrymen in service to the states of the United
Provinces, the Honorable Officers, and all honest soldiers of the
English Nation residing in the Netherlands, and specially (as service bindeth me) to those of Gorcum in Holland.*[103]

Stephen Bachiler (b. abt 1594)

Stephen Bachiler's son, Stephen, entered Magdalen College in
Oxford (the family college of the Wests, Lords Delaware) in 1610.
He became a merchant in Southampton. He was also chaplain to Sir
Charles Morgan in Holland. The younger Stephen is also referred to as
"Deacon Stephen Bachiler." He remained in England.

Anna or Ann Bachiler (b. abt 1600)

Ann Bachiler's first husband was John Sanborn. [Ann Bachiler and
John Sanborn are direct ancestors of President Gerald R. Ford.]
According to *Batchelder/Bachiller Genealogy*:

*The husband of Anne Bachiler, bapt. 1600, was one of the
Hampshire Sambornes, descended from Nicholas, son of Walter
and Margaret (Drew) Samborne of Southcot in Berks, from whom
also descended the Sambornes of Timsbury in Somerset. It seems
probable that the connection between the American and English
Sambornes came somehow through Rev. James Samborne, son of*

103   Eleanor Campbell Schoen, *Our Fascinating Ancestor, Stephen Bachiler*
(1999) Accessed September 15, 2011. Available at http://www.hampton.lib.
nh.us/hampton/biog/bachilerschoen.htm

Rev. James and father of Rev. Thomas Samborne, who all lived in that part of Hampshire where the Bachilers came from, though in different parishes—at Weyhill, Grately, and Upper Clatford—or perhaps through Edward Samborne, an uncle of Rev. James of Grately and Clatford. Like Stephen Bachiler, the second Rev. James was an Oxford man, and settled within a few miles of Wherewell, where Bachiler was rector from 1587 to 1605. His patron, Sir Thomas Jervois, was a Puritan, like Bachiler; and his family was associated with Freefolk, very near to Kingsclere, the home of the Bachilers and to Newton Stacy where Stephen Bachiler lived from 1627 to 1631. But the exact connecting link between the husband of Anne Bachiler and the Timsbury Samborne family is yet to be discovered. All the Sanborns in America are descended from three brothers: John, William and Stephen, who came to America in 1632 with their grandfather, Rev. Stephen Bachiler, and were sons of an English Samborne who, about 1619, married Anne Bachiler. It has been supposed that the widow, Anne Samborne, came with her children, but no definite record of her life here has been discovered. Her will is not filed here, nor was she at Hampton with her father and sons in 1638. Very full records of the American Sanborns have been compiled. In 1855 an excellent beginning was made by Dr. Nathan Sanborn and this has been supplemented by genealogies in the histories of Hampton and of Sanbornton, NH and by Victor Channing Sanborn, of Chicago. No full account, however, has been given of the first generation in America...[104]

Ann's second marriage took place at Strood, Kent, England 20 Jan 1631/32, and her second husband was Henry Atkinson of London.

---

104   Frederick Clifton Pierce, *Batchelder,Batcheller Genealogy*, pp. 109-110.

Batchelor Hussey (1685-1737)

The Husseys

Theodate Bachiler (James Dean's ninth great-grandmother) was born about 1598 and died October 20, 1649 in Hampton, Rockingham Co., New Hampshire. On January 15, 1628, Theodate married James Dean's ninth great-grandfather, **Christopher Hussey**, son of John Hussey and Mary Wood (Woodin) in England. A family legend surrounds their marriage. Christopher was engaged to marry Theodate. Stephen Bachiler would agree to the marriage only if the couple agreed to migrate to America with him. Some records indicate that they were on *The William & Francis*; however, there is no evidence that they were aboard that ship. They may have gone ahead of *The William & Francis* because some records indicate that they were already residing in Lynn, Massachusetts when the Bachiler group arrived.

Apparently, Christopher was driven to Holland as a young man by religious persecution. It is reported that he met Theodate there. He is recorded as an original settler of Haverhill, Massachusetts, where he was an elected freeman May 14, 1634. The family was in Hampton, New Hampshire by 1639 where Christopher was a representative in 1658, 1659, 1660 and a selectman 1650, 1658, 1664 and 1669. He was town clerk from 1650 to 1653 and at one time, he was the "Kings Counselor" for New Hampshire. While he was one of the original purchasers of Nantucket, he never lived there. According to Hampton town records, Christopher Hussey was buried there March 8, 1686. After Theodate's death, Christopher Hussey married Ann, widow of Jeffrey Mingay , December 6, 1658. She died June 24, 1680. While Capt. Hussey was "inclined toward the Society of Friends", no record exists showing that he ever joined them. However, some records indicate that Theodate may have converted, as did a number of their children.

The children of Capt. Christopher Hussey and Theodate Bachiler follow:

(1) **Stephen Hussey** (James Dean's eighth great-grandfather), born 1632, Lynn, Massachusetts; died 1718 Nantucket, Massachusetts. Stephen married **Martha Bunker** (James Dean's eighth great-grandmother), daughter of George Bunker and Jane Godfrey. Stephen initially caused a commotion when his grandfather elected to baptize him ahead of the town's first born white child! Stephen grew up in Hampton, New Hampshire, where records show that he was in court April 1668 for disrupting the congregation on the Lord's Day and reviling Rev. Seabury Cotton. He was in court again in April 1669 and April 1670 for violating the not frequenting public ordinance. In April 1673, he failed to appear in court. At some period of time, he lived in Barbados, where he was convicted of rum running. He was a Quaker before there was a Society of Friends on Nantucket. He was a representative to the General Court, where he was known to be outspoken!

The children of Stephen Hussey and Martha Bunker were Puelia, who married Shubael Gorham; Abigail, who married Thomas Howes and Joseph Marshall; Sylvanus, who married Abigail Brown and Hepzibah Starbuck; **Batchelor Hussey** (James Dean's seventh great-grandfather) who married **Abigail Hall** (James Dean's seventh-great-grandmother and direct descendant of Hatevil Nutter.); Daniel; Mary, who married Jona Worth and Ebenezer Barnard; George, who married Elizabeth Starbuck; and Theodate, who married James Johnson.

According to family records, Batchelor Hussey argued with his brother, Sylvanus Hussey. The source and depth of the argument is unknown, but it was significant enough for Batchelor to leave Nantucket with his family and resettle in Biddleford, Maine. Batchelor was a Quaker minister.

Batchelor's son, **Christopher Hussey**(James Dean's sixth-great-grandfather) married **Ann Garretson** (James Dean's sixth-great-grandmother), daughter of Casparius Garretson and Ann Cox. He was a miller by trade and a Quaker, and he migrated to Adams County, Pennsylvania, where he married Ann. The family relocated to North Carolina in 1756 or 1760, and Christopher died there in 1774. Ann and her son Christopher returned to Pennsylvania in 1779 and by 1780, Ann was back in North Carolina. There is a story about the Christopher Hussey family that was handed down by one of their children, Naomi "Amy" Hussey Cox:

> *The Hussey home in Pennsylvania was a two-story house and the girls' bedroom was upstairs. The girls had a chamber pot in their bedroom for nocturnal use, but they disdained to use it unless absolutely necessary because they had to clean it after every use. They devised a "better way" when they "had to go." They simply went out on the upstairs verandah, raised their gowns and watered the shrubbery below. One night when the family was all asleep, little five-year-old Amy "had to go." She was following routine procedure when a great commotion exploded in the bushes below. She was startled to see an indignant, half-naked Indian run from his hiding place. The little girl went flying down the stairs screaming "Mama, Mama, I peed on an Indian!"[105]*

(2) **John Hussey**, born 1636, Lynn, Massachusetts. John married Rebecca Perkins September 21, 1659. This family migrated to New Castle, Delaware. [John Hussey and Rebecca Perkins are the direct ancestors of President Richard M. Nixon.] John died in 1706 or 1707 in New Castle, Delaware. Their son, also named John Hussey, married Ann Inskeep. And their son (also John) married Margaret Record. Record Hussey married Miriam Harry, and their daughter, Lydia, married Jacob Griffith. The line then winds down through the Griffiths, to the Milhouses, to the Nixons. (Richard Nixon's connection with Stephen Bachiler is on his mother's Milhouse line, through her Griffiths to the Husseys). These families were members of the Society of Friends.

(3) **Mary Hussey,** born 1637, had three marriages: Thomas Page, Henry Green and Capt. Henry Dow.

---

105   Naomi "Amy" Hussey Cox, Story told to her grandchildren. Date unknown. Qtd. In Schoen, Eleanor Campbell. "Our Fascinating Ancestor, Stephen Bachiler." Presentation May 22, 1999. Accessed September 15, 2011. Available at http://www.hampton.lib.nh.us/hampton/biog/bachiler-schoen.htm

(4) **Hulda Hussey**, born ca. 1643, married John Smith.

(5) **Theodate Hussey**, born August 20, 1640; died October 20, 1645

(6) **Joseph Hussey.** [I have no additional information on Joseph, other than his name.]

The Benjamin Franklin Kessler/Amanda Grace Wing Family
(ca 1890s)
Back Row: Iva (b. 6-12-1880 d. 3-30-1919), Jeanette (b.12-18-1870 d. after 1943), Effie (b. 3-25-1878, d. after 1943). William Douglas (b. 10-10-1866 d. 3-7-1941), Grace (b. 3-5-1875 d. unknown*), Alberta (Byrde) (b. 12-20-1868 d. after 1943) This is what is written on the back of the photo... Front Row: Julia (b. 4-10-1862 d. after 1943), Frank (b. 11-3-1886 d. 11-8-1963), Amanda Grace (mother) (b. 4-11-1844 d. 4-19-1915), John Edgar (b. 11-1-1884 d. 9-15-1939), Benjamin F. (father) (b. 2-12-1832 d. 11-11-1919), George Frederic (b. 10-30-1882 d. 11-2-1946), Josephine Spence (b. 1-7-1864 d. 7-8-1925) Several children died before this picture was taken: Clara May (b. 2-15-1861 d. 12-25-1875 of typhoid fever) Alfaretta (b. 2-16-1873 d. 9-8-1873 of bowel troubles) John F. (b. 2-20-1877 d. 3-27-1877 bled to death)

*Grace (1875-unknown) died about 1932. She was shot and killed by her third husband, A. J. Anderson, as she left the church service in the Joplin area. This information was provided by a direct descendant of A. J. Anderson via email about 1998 and a news account in The Carthage Banner.

The Wings

Deborah Bachiler (my tenth-great-grandmother) was born abt. 1591 and died January 31, 1692 in Yarmouth, Barnstable, Massachusetts. Deborah married **John Wing** (my tenth-great-grandfather), who was the first pastor of an English church in Middleburgh in Holland from 1620 onward. The Wings returned to England, however, where John died in 1630. According to The Wing Family of America Website, John Wing was a son of Mathew Wing, and was one of ten children. John Wing was baptized January 12, 1584, Banbury, Oxfordshire, England. His will was signed November 2, 1629 and proved August 4, 1630. He married Deborah Bachiler about 1609/10 in Wherwell, Hampshire, England. John graduated from Queens College Oxford with a B.A., February 12, 1603. He was minister to the merchant adventurer companies on the continent for many years. Some of his sermons have been reprinted and are available in many libraries.[106]

After John's death, Deborah left England with four of her five children. They were part of the "Plough Company", traveling with her father and many of her relatives. They sailed on *The William & Francis*, although Deborah and her children's names do not appear on the passenger list, arriving in Boston on a Thursday, June 5, 1632 after an eighty-eight day passage. The widow and her little family lived first in Saugus and when the "ten good men of Saugus" were given permission to start a new settlement on Cape Cod, she and the children went with them. After her children were married and settled, she passed her last days in the home of her son, John, in Yarmouth, Massachusetts. She did not remarry.

The five children of John and Deborah Bachiler Wing were:

(1) **Deborah Wing**, born abt 1611, England; died before 1680, England. Married before 1629, Edward Ford. No descendants have been found to date.

---

106   The Wing Family of America Website, Published by The Wing Family of America, Inc., Accessed October 10, 2011, Available at: http://www.wing-family.org/

(2) **John Wing**, born about 1613, probably in Yarmouth, England. A controversy continues concerning the identity of his first wife, but the prevailing opinion identifies her as Elizabeth Dillingham, daughter of Edward Dillingham and Ursula Carter. It appears that all of his children were by his first marriage: Susannah; Ephraim; Joseph, Ananias; Osea; and John. John's second marriage was to Miriam Dean, daughter of Stephen Dean (Deane) and Elizabeth Ring.

Stephen Dean (Deane) was among the "old-comers", who arrived in 1621 aboard *The Fortune*. His place of birth in England and his parentage are both unknown, but he was born about 1606 and he married Elizabeth Ring, daughter of William Ring and Mary Durant September 1627, in Plymouth, Massachusetts. They had three daughters and no sons: Susanna, who married (1) Stephen Snow—son of Nicholas Snow and Constance Hopkins; (2) Joseph Rogers—son of Joseph Rogers and Frances Watson. [Note: Joseph, husband of Frances, was a son of Thomas Rogers, who arrived in Plymouth aboard *The Mayflower*]; Elizabeth, who married William Twining, son of William Twining and Anne Doane; and Miriam, who had two marriages. Her first was to John Smith, son of John Smith and his wife Dorothy. And her second was to John Wing. Stephen Dean's widow, Elizabeth, married Josias Cooke, a tavern keeper, who was licensed to sell wine at Muaset June 7, 1648.

John Wing was a dissenter, but was not outspoken. According to *Batchelder/Bachiller Genealogy*:

An early record of the church shows only eleven male members, and neither in this nor in any subsequent notice of the business of the church does the name of John Wing, nor any of his family for many years appear. They had probably all been communicants at Saugus, and they were doubtless decidedly religious people, but inclined to greater freedom in worship and in ecclesiastical affairs. We shall see that this spirit soon took a direction which led a large portion of the family to forsake the church and the forms of worship established by the civil authority. Very little can be learned from the meager records of the town, the church or the general colony regarding the family history of John Wing.

He appears to have been a plain man of ordinary intelligence, never aspiring to political distinction, and only ambitious to cultivate his land and decently to bring up his family. In a few instances, however, his name occurs in the records of the general court as well qualified for public business. In 1641 he is allowed six acres for his share of the meadow lands held at first in common, but divided afterwards annually for use of the inhabitants in severalty. On another occasion he was concerned in the construction of a road connecting Sandwich with the earlier settlements. For some time the people had been obliged either to reduce their corn or meal by the slow and laborious Indian process by means of a mortar and pestle, or transport it all the way to Plymouth on their own shoulders or on the back of a horse or cow. Tradition points out the old Indian path by which the people on the Cape thus wearily conveyed their grist to and from Plymouth.[107]

(3) **Daniel Wing** (my ninth-great-grandfather) was born about 1617, probably in England, but he may have been born in The Netherlands or even in Germany. He died March 10, 1697/8, Sandwich, Massachusetts. His will was dated March 10 1698 and was proved April 5, 1698, Barnstable County, Massachusetts. His first wife was **Hannah Swift**, my ninth-great-grandmother. Daniel and Hannah were married 9 mo 5 dy 1642, Sandwich, Massachusetts. They were members of the Society of Friends. Hannah was born in England, and she died 10 mo 1 dy 1664/5. She was the daughter of William Swift and Joan Sisson. Daniel's second wife was Anna Ewer, daughter of Thomas Ewer and Sarah Learned (Larned). According to Wing Society records, Daniel had his estate confirmed to his children on December 3, 1658 in order to escape the fines of the court being levied due to his militant Quakersim. He was fined 10 pds. on June 5, 1658 for refusing to take the oath of "fidelitie". He was fined 20 shillings on December 3, 1658 for refusing to aid the marshal in execution of his office. He was fined 5 pds in October 1659, crime not stated. He was

107   Frederick Clifton Pierce, *Batchelder,Batcheller Genealogy,* p. 86.

fined 5 pds on June 8, 1660, once again over his refusing to aid the marshal in execution of his office. He was fined 5 pds Oct. 1659, crime not stated. He was fined 5 pds on June 8, 1660, once again over the oath of "fidelitie". This was when 5 pds would buy a house!

Children by his first marriage include Hannah, Lydia, Deborah, Samuel, Hepzibah, **John** (my eighth-great-grandfather), **Beulah** (my eighth-great-grandmother) [Note: I have a double descent from Daniel Wing , Deborah Bachiler and John Wing, and Stephen Bachiler], Deborah (a second daughter by that name), and Daniel. Children by his second wife include Experience, Bachelor, and Jashub.

When the Wings first settled in Massachusetts, Daniel and his brother John resided close to one another and perhaps, they were in the same house. On June 28, 1640, Andrew Hallet, being about to remove to Yarmouth, conveyed certain landed property to Daniel Wing, the instrument being witnessed by John Wing and Edward Dillingham. This was probably a farm in the immediate neighborhood. The Society of Friends made their first appearance at Sandwich in 1657. According to *Bachelder/Bachiller Genealogy*, "Daniel Wing, with three others, was arrested for tumultuous carriage at a meeting of Quakers and severely fined, though there is no evidence that a single Quaker, besides persons professed at that time any adherence to the new sect."[108]

It first appears that Daniel and his friends were merely tolerant of the new sect. But it wasn't long before they joined the Society. Quaker writers of that period say, "We have two strong places in this land, the one at Newport, and the other at Sandwich; almost the whole town of Sandwich is adhering towards them" and the records of the Monthly Meetings of Friends show that the Sandwich Monthly Meeting was the first established in America."[109] It should be noted that Daniel's first wife's mother, Joan Swift was actively involved in the Quaker movement. She was fined for "being att Quakers meetings" October 1660 in the

---

108   Frederick Clifton Pierce, *Batchelder,Batcheller Genealogy*, p. 89.
109   Frederick Clifton Pierce, *Batchelder,Batcheller Genealogy*, p. 89.

Plymouth Court. Daniel's son, **John**, married **Martha Spooner**. (They were my eighth-great-grandparents.) Their son, **John**, married **Experience Gifford** (my seventh-great-grandparents). Experience was the daughter of **William Gifford** and **Hannah** (my eighth-great-grandparents.) William's parents were **William Gifford and Patience Russell** (my ninth-great-grandparents.) This William Gifford was a member of the Society of Friends and his second wife, Mary Mills, has been described on the records as a "vagabond (traveling) Quaker missionary". None of these people remained quiet about their activities. Instead, they waved their passion in front of the Puritan oligarchs like a red flag!!!

(4) **Stephen Wing**, born abt 1621, The Netherlands. Stephen also joined the Society of Friends. He resided at Sandwich, Massachusetts. In 1646-7 he married Oseah, the daughter of Edward Dillingham, one of the nine associates to whom the town had been granted April 3, 1637. According to *Bachelder/Bachiller Genealogy*:

> *In accordance with the rigid laws of that period, and which were enforced against all, however high their position in society, some objections were made against him and a fine was laid upon him by the court at Plymouth, March 2, 1646-7, for the too early birth of his first child after marriage. He appears, however, to have been an earnest advocate of religion and of morality, for he was a strenuous supporter of religious meetings and of public order, yet he, with many others of that period, came in conflict with exclusiveness and intolerance to which both church and state were then committed. From the first the whole family of his father and his mother's father were inclined to a greater freedom in worship and life than the customs and laws of the colonies permitted. In this they had the sympathies of what seems to have been for many years a majority of the inhabitants of Sandwich...In 1657, when Nicholas Upsall visited Sandwich, there was a great commotion. Public proclamation was made that for every hour's entertainment of him "a severe fine was to be exacted." In spite of such a law, several families at that time not at all inclined to Quakerism, not only received him to their houses, but allowed him and others to hold meetings and attended upon them. Stephen, when*

*his brother Daniel began first with contending for tolerance, and
soon their sympathy with suffering was exchanged for conversion
to the faith of the sufferers. Severe fines were imposed upon him,
imprisonment was threatened if not absolutely inflicted upon
him, and even the town privileges of a freeman were withdrawn
from him and his friends because he declines for a time to take
the oath of fidelity which bound him to assist in the execution of
such laws.*[110]

(5) **Matthew Wing,** born abt 1627, Belgium or Holland (however,
some sources claim that he was born in Sandwich, Kent, England).
He also settled in Massachusetts and in 1644, married Joane
Newman of Malden. Matthew did not remain in Massachusetts
and by 1646, he was back in Kent, England. I can find the record
of only one child, John, who was born in 1646 or 1648, who apparently died in infancy. Matthew Wing died in England in 1680. I
have no further information about him.

* * *

James Dean's Hussey ancestors who relocated to North Carolina—
eventually intermarried with the Chamnesses, Coles, Williamses,
Smithsons and Woollens. The Woollens relocated to Grant County,
Indiana where his grandmother, Emma J. Woollen, married his grandfather, Charles Desco Dean.

My branch of the Wing family settled first in Saratoga Springs, New
York. In the late 1840s, my third great grandparents, Lettis Wing
(1806-1848) and Annaline Denton (1817-1894), settled in LaSalle
County, Illinois. Lettis died there in 1848. Annaline returned to New
York with her three children, one of them my second-great-grand-
mother, Amanda Grace Wing (1844-1915). By 1850, Annaline married
a widower named James Read (1807-1865), and the family relocated
once again to LaSalle County, Illinois. In 1860, Amanda Grace married
my second-great-grandfather, Benjamin Franklin Kessler (1832-1919).
And in 1867, the Kesslers relocated to Jasper County, Missouri, where
they spent the rest of their lives. They are buried in the Moss Springs

---

110   Frederick Clifton Pierce, *Batchelder,Batcheller Genealogy,* p. 93-94.

Cemetery in Jasper County, Missouri. Their daughter, Josephine Virginia Kessler (1865-1925), married Salathiel Monroe Spence (1854-1921) in Jasper County. They were my great-grandparents. They are also buried in the Moss Springs Cemetery.

James Dean's Woollen ancesters and allied families remained with The Society of Friends. Somewhere along the line, my branch of the Wing family became Methodist.

CHAPTER 7—FROM CAVALIERS TO THE AMISH/MENNONITES: THE ANCESTORS OF MILDRED MARIE WILSON

Several years ago, while doing a genealogical search on James Dean's background, I found several trees on Ancestry.com that connected Jimmy's mother Mildred Marie Wilson with his paternal grandmother, Emma Woollen. According to the charts, Jimmy's third great grandfather, **Jacob Wilson**, married **Sarah Hussey**, his third great grandmother on Emma Woollen's line. If such were the case, that would make Winton Dean and Mildred Wilson distant cousins.

While this connection sounds so tempting, to date, I have not found a marriage record for such an event. **Jacob Wilson** married **Mary Ann Polly Hughes** on April 11, 1806 in Bourbon County, Kentucky. **Sarah Hussey** married **Isaac Williams** in Highland County, Ohio on April 9, 1812. Isaac Williams and Sarah Hussey lived in North Carolina, Ohio and Indiana, and they remained married until Sarah Hussey's death. Isaac Williams died in Westfield, Hamilton County, Indiana post 1860, and Sarah Hussey died in Wayne County, Indiana in 1834. Isaac married Anna Cloud in Indiana in 1837, and they appear on the 1850 Census. Jacob Wilson died in Wayne County, Indiana post 1840 and **Mary Polly Hughes** died in the same county in 1827. Jacob may have remarried after Mary's death, but I do not have a record for a second marriage. I do not know the origin of the Jacob Wilson-Sarah Hussey marriage information, but I think it is more of a case of "wishful thinking" on the part of a researcher.

Mildred Marie Wilson was born in Grant County, Indiana September 15, 1910 to **John William Wilson** (1878-1966) and **Minnie Mary or**

Mae Slaughter (1883-1929).[111] Mildred was born in the country, and the family moved to Gas City at a later date. The Wilson family came from Kentucky and settled initially in Wayne County, Indiana prior to moving to Grant County. The Slaughters came from Ohio, settling first in White County, then Wayne and finally, Grant.[112] The following is a summary of the family:

James Dean's grandfather, **Isaac Slaughter**, was born in White County, Indiana March 31 1856 and died in Marion, Indiana November 15, 1911 when he was hit by a train.[113] His wife was **Sarah Leisure** (b.1867), and her second husband was John W. Brown.[114]

Jeremiah Slaughter is the earliest known ancestor on that line. He was born in Ohio between 1814 and 1815, and he was living in White County, Indiana in 1860. His wife was **Mary E. Esler** (or Eastes) who was born in Kentucky in 1838 and who died in Marion, Indiana January 1, 1903 in a kitchen fire.[115]

James Dean's grandparents on the Wilson line were **Levi D. Wilson** (1843-1920) and **Agnes Schmuck** (1849-1940). They were both born in Wayne County, Indiana and died in Grant County. Agnes Schmuck Wilson died in Marion.[116] Levi's father, **Alfred R. Wilson**, was born in Bourbon County, Kentucky November 29, 1815, and he was buried at Hackleman, Indiana July 13, 1895. His wife was **Eliza Felton**, who came from Ohio.[117]

Alfred R. Wilson was the son of **Jacob Wilson**, who was born in Perquimans, North Carolina September 27, 1784 and who died August 20, 1840 in Wayne County, Indiana and **Mary Ann Polly**

111   Richard E. Brenneman. "Notable Kin: New England in Hollywood, Part Four: The Ancestry of James Byron Dean (1931-1955)." NEHGS *NEXIS*, Vol. X, No. 1 (Feb. 1993), pp. 28-32.
112   Richard E. Brenneman, The Ancestry of James Byron Dean, p. 29.
113   Richard E. Brenneman, The Ancestry of James Byron Dean, p. 29.
114   Richard E. Brenneman, The Ancestry of James Byron Dean, p. 29
115   Richard E. Brenneman, The Ancestry of James Byron Dean, p. 29.
116   Richard E. Brenneman, The Ancestry of James Byron Dean, p. 29.
117   Richard E. Brenneman, The Ancestry of James Byron Dean, p. 29

Hughes, who was born in Virginia in 1786 and who died in Wayne County, Indiana in 1827[118] For a long time, I could not go beyond Jacob Wilson while searching Mildred's line. Recently, however, I was able to trace her Wilson ancestry back to **William Wilson** (1542-1615) by using the OneWorld Ancestral Trees at Ancestry. com and primary documentation to verify it.

[**Note:** Since initially writing this section, I have been able to progress on Jeremiah Slaughter's line. His father appears to have been **Jeremiah Slaughter**, who was born in Ulster, New York 27 Mar 1787 and who died 20 Aug 1871 in Republican, Jefferson , Indiana. Jeremiah's wife's name is unknown.]

A number of people have speculated (including Jimmy himself) that James Dean had Native American ancestry on his mother's line because of her dark hair and dark eyes and because of James Dean's prominent cheek bones. To date, no Native American ancestry has been found in either Winton Dean's or Mildred Wilson's families. Mildred Wilson's ancestors were Cavaliers of Virginia and Amish/Mennonites of Pennsylvania. Mildred descends from English, Scottish, Irish, French and German ancestry. For the most part, James Dean's facial bone structure came from his father Winton. And his large head came from his Stephen Bachiler heritage, along with a number of additional Bachiler attributes!!!

The Cavaliers

Mildred's Wilson line dates back to **William Wilson**, who was born in 1542 in Wellsbourne, Lincolnshire, England and who died May 15, 1615 in Windsor, Berkshire, England, and Elizabeth Woodhall, who was born in 1546 in Devonshire, England and who died in 1615 in Rochester, Kent, England. Their son, **Thomas Wilson**, born 1564, was an early Cavalier in Prince William, Virginia. His wife, **Isabella Bryce**, was from Scotland, and their son, **John Wilson**, was born and raised in Stirlingshire, Scotland. John's wife was **Catherine Rudd**, who

---

118   Jacob Wilson, OneWorld Ancestral Trees, Ancestry.com, Accessed October 9, 2011. Available at http://www.ancestry.com.

died in Surry County, Virginia in 1694. Apparently, John returned to Scotland after her death, and died there that same year. The Rudd family eventually intermarried with the Haskins family of Virginia, from whom I descend.

John and Catherine Rudd Wilson's son, **Robert Wilson**, was born in 1629 in Nansemond, Virginia, and he died December 21, 1696 in Perquimans, North Carolina. His wife was **Ann Blount**, the daughter of **Thomas Blount** (1612-1706) and **Ann Wilson** (1616-1716), thus connecting the prominent Blount line with the Wilson family.

The Blounts had a long history in England and an adventurous history in Southern Colonial America. Blount County, Tennessee acquired its name from this family. **Thomas Blount** was born in April 1612 at Sodington Manor, Sodington, Worcester, England, and he died March 28, 1706 at Kendrick's Creek, in North Carolina. **Ann Wilson** was born in 1616 in Worcestershire, England, and died in 1716 in Perquimans, North Carolina at the age of 100. As yet I have not been able to connect her with Mildred's main Wilson line, but I believe there must be a connection. Her father, **Robert Wilson**, was born in England in 1590. Thomas Blount's father—**Sir Walter Blount** (1577-1644)—and grandfather—**Sir George Blount** (1560-1610)—were both knights. Sir George Blount's parents were **Thomas Blount** (1496-1564) and **Jocosa (Joyce) Shirley** (1515-1560), thus connecting Mildred with the Shirley family of Virginia. (As yet, I have not computed Mildred's possible cousinship with **Myrabelle Shirley (Belle Starr)**, but it is possible that not only is James Dean a distant cousin of Jesse and Frank James, but of Belle Starr as well, albeit much more distantly.

Isaac Wilson (1668-1714), the son of Robert Wilson and Ann Blount, married **Ann Thigpen** (1668-1702), the daughter of **James Thigpen** (1627-1679) and **Elyn Travis** (1636-1689). Elyn was the daughter of the **Reverend John Travis** (b. 1623 in England, d. in England). While James Dean's paternal grandmother's line adopted Quakerism as their faith and his paternal grandfather's lines were for the most part Methodist, Mildred's Cavalier lines remained loyal to the Church of England. They eventually became Methodist.

The Cavaliers were wealthy, adventurous people, often from royal descent. Mildred Wilson Dean has been described as an imaginative young woman who delighted in fantasy and adventure with a flair for the dramatic--something she acquired from her ancestors and something she passed on to her son.

The Amish/Mennonites

Mildred's Amish/Mennonite ancestry comes through her paternal grandmother, **Agnes Schmuck**. Agnes was the daughter of **Eli Schmuck** (1821-1902) and **Margaret Felton** (1824-1882). Eli's parents were **Jacob Schmuck** (1803-1873) and **Catherine Hildebrand** (1785-1870). [Note: That age difference between Jacob and Catherine raises a question since Catherine appears to be 18 years older than her husband. However, it doesn't seem to be too far afield since James Dean was sometimes attracted to older women—something that will be discussed in a later chapter!] I have no further information on the Schmuck line. Mildred's Amish/Mennonite ancestors are on the Hildebrand line.

Catherine's parents were **Felix Hildebrand** (1749-1820) and **Mary Elizabeth Simon** (1746-1820), both of York, Pennsylvania. Her grandparents were **Johannes Hildebrand** (1725-1783) and **Barbara Glattfelder** (1725-1794). The Glattfelders came from Zurich, Switzerland, the route the Amish took after fleeing from Germany prior to relocating in America. The Glattfelders intermarried with the Gorius, Koch, Froehlichs, Ambergs and Raspbergers, and they settled in Lancaster, York, and Chester, Pennsylvania. Howard became acquainted with some of the Amish the summers we spent in Pennsylvania. They do not use electricity, do not drive cars, travel via horse and buggy and dress in nineteenth century clothes. Some of Mildred's ancestors may have been Mennonites, who are strict, but not as strict as the Amish.

It is a challenge to picture the Cavalier culture uniting with the Amish/Mennonites and combining them all in the same family. However, as families moved West, they left their "sophistication" behind while learning to tackle the wilderness. What is also of interest here is that the Wilsons settled predominantly in Perquimans County, North Carolina, remaining there through Jacob Wilson. My Spence, Perry, and Hunter ancestors lived in that area at the same period of time. I have discovered records showing they had business dealings with some of the Wilsons—no doubt some of Mildred's ancestors.

SECTION TWO
FROM PENROD TO THE MADMAN:
AN ARTIST IN STUDIO

The Winton Dean Family

CHAPTER 8—ON THE BANK OF BACK CREEK: THE NEW AQUARIAN

July 17, 1998

JAMES DEAN'S TOMBSTONE RECOVERED

James Dean is no longer a rebel without a tombstone. In what has to be one of the more unorthodox search-and-rescue operations, an off-duty sheriff's deputy found the screen legend's missing marker after ramming into it with his car, says the Associated Press.

Dean's lipstick-covered, rose-hued tombstone, which weighs about 400 pounds, was reported stolen on Tuesday from Park Cemetery in the late star's hometown of Fairmount, Ind.

According to the Associated Press, Tippecanoe County Sheriff's Deputy Aaron Gilman was driving on a deserted country road Thursday night when something suddenly tore out the transmission of his car. Turns out the culprit was the missing marker, which deputies promptly carted down to the county jail.

Someone from Dean's estate was scheduled to pick up the stone on Thursday, a fact that will bring a sigh of relief to the many fans who still make the trek to the "East of Eden" star's grave site each year. Dean, who died in a car crash in 1955 at the age of 24, still has a strong cult following, and many devotees leave Marlboro packs, notes, and flowers by the marker.

It isn't the first time Dean's final resting-place has been tampered with. Back in 1983, the original stone was stolen but was quickly recovered, only to be taken again a few months later. The tombstone stolen this week was a replacement of the original. It had been secured to the base with metal bars and glue, but chances are good more substantial measures will be taken to make sure it doesn't go missing again.[119]

James Dean did not live to see the hype and furor over him, but if interviewed about the theft of his tombstone, he might have said, "Well—then—there--now! Can't a guy get some sleep around here?"

As previously noted James Byron Dean arrived in the early morning hours February 8, 1931, and was born in a house known as the Green Gables Apartments located at 4th and McClure Street in Marion, Indiana. The house was eventually torn down to make way for a parking lot—something the town now regrets doing. His father Winton Dean, was a dental technician, whose his family had settled just outside Fairmount, Indiana for several generations. His mother Mildred Marie Wilson Dean came from nearby Gas City. There are several accounts as to where James Dean acquired his middle name. One suggests that since Lord Byron was his mother's favorite poet, she supplied the middle name. The other theory suggests that Winton chose the middle name from a close friend who worked in their neighborhood in Fairmount.[120]

Some biographers have compiled reams of paper about the nature of the Dean family, speculating about what may or may not have taken place. While on the one hand, Winton is described as a cold, distant man by some, he is pictured as warm-hearted and friendly by others. Mildred has been the focus of many writers. Some have found her to be dreamy and poetic while others have found her to be feisty and combative with Winton. More often than not, biographers have probed into what they perceive as her excessive doting on her son. Some writers have suggested that James Dean was born out of wedlock and that Winton was not the father. The fatherhood claim has been soundly rejected by both the Dean and Wilson families—and

119   "James Dean's Tombstone Recovered." Mr. Showbiz News Website. Dated July 17, 1998. Accessed 3/9/01. Available at http://mrshowbiz. go.com/archive/news/Todays_Stories/980717/dean071798.html
120   "Biography for James Dean." IMDb Website. Accessed March 5, 2001. Available at http://us.imdb.com/Bio?Dean,+James

rightfully so. Winton Dean was the father of James Dean. People need only to look at a photograph of the two of them together to recognize it!

Winton Dean and his family moved to Fairmount shortly after the birth of his son, where they lived in three homes within the town's limits and in a small home located at the north edge of the Winslow farm.[121] When James Dean was five years old, his father obtained a job as a dental technician at the Sawtelle Veteran's Hospital in Santa Monica, California. The family left Fairmount for Santa Monica. Some biographers have noted that Jimmy and his mother spent a lot of time at the movies. They also had a special wishing game that they played. Their lives were full of fun and frolic, but all of that ended in 1940 when Mildred was diagnosed with uterine cancer. Winton's mother--Emma Woollen Dean—realized how ill Mildred was after consulting with her own physician in Fairmount. She took a train to Santa Monica where she could be with the family. On July 14, 1940, Mildred Wilson Dean died at the age of 29. She is buried in the Grant Cemetery on the edge of Marion, Indiana.

It must have been a time of uncertainty for nine-year-old James Dean. After his mother's death, family members agreed that he would re-turn to Fairmount, Indiana with his grandmother, and he would live with Winton's sister, Ortense Dean Winslow, and her husband Marcus Winslow. Winton believed that Indiana would be the best place for Jimmy. Apparently, his mother Mildred had the same idea for him. According to Val Holley:

> A friend from Fairmount who visited the Deans in 1938 reported that Mildred said, "I don't want Jimmy to grow up out here. I've even been thinking about going back home to Indiana. Everything's so artificial here. I want my Jimmy to grow up where things are real and simple."[122]

---

121   Main Frame in James Dean Page. James Dean Artifacts Website. Accessed March 10, 2001. Available at http://www.jamesdeanartificats. com/frmain01.html
122   Val Holley, *James Dean: The Biography*, p. 18.

At the time of Jimmy's arrival in Fairmount, the Winslows had one daughter—Joan--who once noted in an interview: "He was nine and I was fourteen when he came to live with us. And we fought for position."[123]

So in Summer 1940, James Dean left California for the life of a farm boy on the bank of Back Creek in Grant County, Indiana—something that would direct the course of his life.

***

When Martin Boots and David Branson each donated thirty acres of land in 1831 for the site of Marion, they chose a location on the left bank of the swift, scenic river which the Miami Indians had named "Mississinewa," their word for "laughing waters." So rapid had been the tide of settlement that it followed by only 19 years the Battle of Mississinewa, 7 miles downstream, where U.S. troops and Indians had fought a bloody, pre-dawn encounter in 1812.[124]

..so notes the Grant County Indiana Website. When Grant County formed in 1831, the Dean, Winslow and other families had already been living in the area for some time. And when nine-year-old James Dean arrived there in 1940, he was adjusting to the new life thrust upon him by his mother's death, resettling in a totally new environment. David Dalton notes:

The mystery of James Dean lies not in his abrupt end, but in his origins. Jimmy was as ordinary a boy as ever came out of Grant County, and his frequent trips home, his allusions to Indiana and reveries of the farm where he grew up are the indications he left

123   "James Dean: A Portrait." WhiteStar Entertainment: A Division of KULTUR. Produced and Directed by Gary Legon. Produced & Edited by Sarah Legon. Written By Gary Legon and David Dalton. Music By Marc Governor. Narrated by Rip Torn. MCMXCV Estate Films Inc. An Estate Films, Inc. Production.
124   The History of Marion and Grant County, Indiana Website. Marion and Grant County Convention & Visitor's Bureau. Available online at http://www.grantcounty.com/discover-grant-county/history

behind, as if he subtly led us back here with his clues. The very opacity of Jimmy's life in Fairmount must persuade us that through his very lack of distinction he represents a typical outgrowth of an Indiana childhood. The sum and epitome of his region and town, from which he emerged after a long incubation."[125]

Back Creek was in Grant County long before the first settlers arrived, and has been a nuisance from time to time over the years. According Andy West of The Back Creek Web Spot: "It flows just more than nine miles (fifteen kilometers) from its sources in Madison County until it drains into the Missisinewa River just north of Jonesboro."[126] According to West, the creek flooded in 1913 (when it inundated the town of Fairmount) and again in the early 1990s. He describes its course:

> *The stream has its sources in Madison County within one square mile south of the county line, converging just south of the county line road and flowing north-by-northeast to Fairmount. Then it flows northward through Fairmount just west of Mill Street until it crosses Fourth Street, whereupon it flows east of Mill. It leaves town north of Eighth Street (State Road 26), flowing along first the wastewater treatment plant and then Park Cemetery, through which a tributary, Winslow Ditch, crosses before emptying into the creek.*

> *The creek then flows parallel to Sand Pike until it passes behind Back Creek Friends Church and across the Winslow farm where James Dean lived as a teen. Then after passing county road 700 South it turns northeast, crosses Sand Pike and flows along a largely wooded course to Jonesboro, where it passes through the town, along its park, and across State Road 22. Finally it hooks up with another tributary, Little Newby Ditch, and flows eastward to empty into the Mississinewa River.*[127]

---

125   David Dalton, *The Mutant King*, p. 27.
126   Andy West. The Back Creek Webspot (2010). Last Updated February 19, 2011. Accessed September 3, 2011. Available at http://www.andywest.org/fm/back_creek.html
127   Andy West, The Back Creek Webspot (2010). http://www.andywest.org/fm/back_creek.html

Howard and I first visited Fairmount in 2003, where we were taken on a tour by Phil Zeigler. Phil recounted the number of famous people who were born and raised in the area. Howard asked, "Why were so many famous people born here?" Phil responded by saying, "It's in the water!"

James Dean once wrote a poem about it, called "Old Creek":

> *I took a little drink from an ample stream*
>
> *I fear thereby result in fertile jest to her source*
>
> *Her current swift direct and crystal*
>
> *There is a want to be there and drink long*
>
> *Nature's plea, ovum, stem and pistil*
>
> *But there is more to streams*
>
> *Than the water to gorge on*
>
> *Plunge your face in a brook*
>
> *To wash the desire away*
>
> *A fool to drink*
>
> *To drink and not to taste.*[128]

Grant County was indeed the home of a number famous and infamous people:

> *Actor James Byron Dean was born in Marion; composer Cole Porter studied music here; Caleb B. Smith, Lincoln's secretary of the interior, served as a prosecuting attorney; Kenesaw Mountain Landis, first commissioner of organized baseball and U.S. Supreme Court Justice Willis Van Devanter practiced law here. Captain George*

---

128   James Dean, "The Creek," qtd. In Dalton, David, *James Dean: The Mutant King*, p. 217.

W. Steele, Jr., who crossed the Atlantic by air four years before Lindbergh did, was a Marion native.[129]

James Dean and Jim Davis (Garfield's creator) have been specifically identified with Fairmount and are represented in their local museum. Their images also appear on the Fairmount water tower! In addition to James Dean, the Grant County History Website states:

> *Famous natives of Fairmount also include: Jim Davis, creator of the comic strip, "Garfield;" CBS news correspondent, Phil Jones; Robert Sheets, former director of the National Hurricane Center; and Mary Jane Ward, author of The Snake Pit.[130]*

Fairmount also had a number of infamous people living in the area over the years, something that is recorded by David Dalton in *The Mutant King:*

> *A real-life outlaw, Jessie's brother Frank James, retired to Fairmount, and what was left of the Dalton Gang also hid out and settled in the town, guessing that the Kansas Rangers would never dream to look for them there. Bad guys don't always come from somewhere else though—the first train robbery ever pulled in the United States of America was perpetrated by a native Indiana gang, the Reno Boys, in 18[6]6.[131]*

I don't know why Frank James chose to settle in Fairmount, but as already noted, Jesse, Frank and Susan James were distant cousins of James Dean and his paternal grandmother, Emma Woollen Dean! Frank James' mother Zerelda Cole James Samuel may have told him that distant relatives resided in Grant County, Indiana. The James brothers were always looking for such places because they felt safe there! And, of course, Frank lived in Fairmount under an assumed

---

129   The History of Marion and Grant County, Indiana Website. Marion and Grant County Convention & Visitor's Bureau. Accessed September 4, 2011. Available online at http://www.grantcounty.com/discover-grant-county/history

130   The History of Marion and Grant County, Indiana Website. Marion and Grant County Convention & Visitor's Bureau. http://www.grantcounty. com/discover-grant-county/history

131   David Dalton. *James Dean: The Mutant King.* pp. 18-19.

name. If he encountered his distant cousins, he didn't make his identity known. And if they did know, they didn't broadcast it!

As with many places, Grant County history was not without turmoil.
According to Val Holley:

> *Indiana, with its great scenic beauty, long-standing tradition of*
> *excellence in education, and many native literary and political*
> *stars, certainly has its points. But it also has a dark past. Due to*
> *geographical factors, Indiana's principal settlement was not from*
> *the east, as with other Midwestern states, but from the south, so*
> *its attitudes were largely southern. Although Indianapolis had a*
> *bigger automobile industry than Detroit at the end of the nine-*
> *teenth century, Detroit would soon steal its thunder by welcoming*
> *Eastern European and southern blacks as auto plant workers—a*
> *step Indianapolis prohibited through commercial zoning restric-*
> *tions.*

> *During the widespread resurgence of the Ku Klux Klan in the*
> *1920s, it was not Georgia or Mississippi but Indiana that was*
> *the organization's banner state. It permeated every county and*
> *most of its small towns; Fairmount was no exception. Issues of*
> *the Fairmount News from the early 1920s are replete with ac-*
> *counts of surprise appearances by hooded Klan representatives at*
> *local church services. Usually these visitors delivered a monetary*
> *contribution and a letter to the minister commending the church's*
> *efforts to keep America white, and signed "Knights of the Ku Klux*
> *Klan, Fairmount, Indiana." [According to the Fairmount News of*
> *January 9, 1923, one of these letters stated, "We are convinced*
> *that the white race is the race chosen by God to accomplish His*
> *purposes and fulfill the destinies of this nation."]*[132]

Six months before James Dean was born, a lynching occurred in the
town of Marion, which is described in a Wikipedia entry:

> *A* lynching *occurred in Marion on August 7, 1930. A large mob*
> *estimated at 2,000 gathered at the county* jail *where three young*
> *black men were held on charges of killing a white man and*

---

132   Val Holley, *James Dean: The Biography,* p. 15.

raping his girlfriend. Before they could be tried, the three, Thomas Shipp, Abram Smith *and* James Cameron, *were dragged from the jail and severely beaten. Shipp and Smith were hanged, but Cameron was released when an unidentified man claimed that he had nothing to do with the crimes. In 1931 he was convicted as an accessory to murder and served four years before being paroled. James Cameron went on to serve as the Indiana State Director of Civil Liberties from 1942–1950 and founded three local chapters of the NAACP. He served as the first president of the Madison County, Indiana chapter. In 1988 he founded* America's Black Holocaust Museum *in* Milwaukee *to preserve the history of African Americans who had faced the terror and violence of lynching. In 1993, James Cameron received an official apology and a full pardon from the state of Indiana. Cameron later said, "Since the state of Indiana forgave me, I forgive the state of Indiana." In 2005, the U.S. Senate also officially apologized to Cameron and others. The event in Marion was notable as the last confirmed lynching of blacks in the* Northern United States.[133]

I believe it is fair to say that James Dean developed a love-hate relationship with his town and region, as is evidenced by a poem he wrote after living in New York for about a year:

My town likes industrial impotence

My town's small, loves its diffidence

My town thrives on dangerous bigotry

My town's big in the sense of idolatry

My town believes in God and his crew

My town hates the Catholic and Jew

My town's innocent, selfistic caper

My town's diligent, reads the newspaper

133   Marion, Indiana. The Wikipedia Website. Accessed Sept. 4, 2011. http://en.wikipedia.org/wiki/Marion,_Indiana

My town's sweet, I was born bare

My town is not what I am, I am here[134]

One wonders why someone with so many objections about a place would continually be drawn back to it, but as Val Holley explains:

> *James Dean refused to limit himself with strictures imposed by others. As an adult he was happy to count African-Americans among his friends; he was particularly interested in what they could teach him. Thus he would study dance with Katherine Dunham and bongos with Cyril Jackson, and enjoy the company of Eartha Kitt, Bill Gunn, Sammy Davis, Jr., Marietta Canty, and others.*
>
> *Nor was James Dean an anti-Semite; he could claim that most of his best friends were Jewish: Dizzy Sheridan, Barbara Glenn, Roy Schatt, David Diamond, Leonard Rosenman, James Sheldon, Norma Crane, Arlene Sachs, Bob Heller, Martin Landau. Race, creed or sexual preference had no bearing on Dean's estimation of others; he judged them on the basis of what he could learn from them.*
>
> *Another of Dean's virtues was his feeling for the underdog. Various experiences made him aware of his own separateness: being a de facto orphan and particularly his suspension from high school. Nicholas Ray, his director in Rebel Without a Cause, said Dean "would extend sudden affection to lonely and struggling people; he adopted "several." One such adoptee in Fairmount was Larry Lee Smith, who regarded Dean as a hero for being nice to him while his older brother, one of Dean's basketball teammates, always bullied him.[135]*

To this, he adds:

> *The remarkable thing about James Dean's Indiana background is that he rose above it. He threw off aspects that were limiting—*

---

134   James Dean, "My Town". Qtd. In Dalton, David, *The Mutant King*, p. 85.

135   Val Holley, *James Dean: The Biography*, p. 15.

racist and homophobic bigotry, small-mindedness—and retained only those that were charming and natural.[136]

Despite the characteristics he "rose above" or "shred from his life, James Dean returned to Fairmount for renewal whenever he was completely drained. Two friends, Dizzy Sheridan and Bill Bast, accompanied him there once, a journey remembered by Bill Bast in his 1957 biography *James Dean: A Biography*:

> *Fairmount, Indiana, is a peaceful, wholesome little farm town near Marion. The countryside is a level expanse of gently rolling fields of grain and corn, interspersed with occasional sycamore groves and quietly twisting streams. In the winter all is muffled under the soft layer of snow which hugs the fertile earth protectively; in the spring thaws the streams and rivers flow faster, accenting the rhythm of the land coming alive; in the summer the rich soil produces, and the verdure is so thick one can smell it; and in the fall, after a brief spectacle of magnificent color, the trees, the land lie ghostly barren, waiting silently for the long sleep to come...*

> *From the moment we arrived, the Winslows opened their home and hearts to us. Mom, as Jimmy called Ortense, saw to it that we had plenty of good food and clean, warm beds. With quiet joy and affection she attended to the needs and whims of her oldest son; that is what she considered Jimmy. The more he boasted of her cooking, the more loving care she put into the preparation of the meals. Marcus gave us the run of the farm, taking time and patience to show us around and explain the mysteries of farming.*

> *After all the years of seeing Jimmy alone and without a family, it was a wonderful thing to watch him touch again the gentle roots of his early years. He was back in his element again, and he loved it.*[137]

His birth sign was Aquarius. His ascendant sign was Scorpio-Rising. While Astrology is not an exact science, there are so many similarities

---

136   Val Holley, *James Dean: The Biography*, p. 14.
137   William Bast, *James Dean: A Biography*, pp. 78-79

between personality traits of those signs and James Dean that they cannot be overlooked. Approximately ten years ago, I recall reading an article on the internet written by an astrologist who labeled James Dean as her prime example of an Aquarian. Unfortunately, I no longer have that article. After conducting a recent internet search, I identified three articles I have combined into the chart below summarizing the traits inherent in Aquarian and Scorpio-Rising personalities: Jennifer Copley's Aquarius Personality Profile, Aquarius Personality Traits— Aquarius Personalities, and Scorpio-Rising Ascendant in Scorpio:

Major Traits of Aquarius with Scorpio Rising

Aquarius

Aquarius people are extremely open-minded, tolerant, extroverted, experimental and emotionally detached.[138]

Traits:

- Eccentric and Unpredictable
- Extroverted and Experimental
- A Love of Debate
- Technological Aptitude
- Generous and Bad with Money
- Humanitarian Leanings
- Tactless and Rebellious
- Independent and Friendly[139]

---

138   Jennifer Copley, Aquarius Personality Profile. Accessed September 5, 2011. Available at: http://jennifercopley.suite101.com/aquarius-personality-profile-a60945
139   Jennifer Copley, Aquarius Personality Profile: http://jennifercopley.suite101.com/aquarius-personality-profile-a60945

Likes:

- Fame
- Themselves
- Privacy
- Dreams
- Magic
- Change
- Eccentricity
- Surprises
- Living within their means[140]

Dislikes:

- Emotion
- Intimacy
- Show-offs
- Taken for granted
- Being 'pinned down'
- Violence
- Senseless extravagance[141]

---

140   Aquarius Personality Traits—Aquarius Personalities. Accessed September 5, 2011. Available at: http://www.aquarius.arollo.com/personality/
141   Aquarius Personality Traits—Aquarius Personalities. Accessed September 5, 2011. Available at: http://www.aquarius.arollo.com/personality/

Scorpio-Rising

You know if there is a Scorpio Rising nearby... you can feel their presence. They have an aura about them that lets others know they are not to be pushed about. They command respect, and with some, even fear. They can be loud or quiet, but their determination always shines through.

Traits:

- Scorpio Rising rarely goes unnoticed... most people either love them or hate them.

- Scorpio Ascendant likes their privacy to the point of appearing paranoid. They need to control their surroundings and can strategize to their benefit. They move with care and deliberation, relying on their inner sense to figure out their situation and what others may do.

- Scorpio Rising wants a partner who is down to earth and reliable.

- Scorpio Ascendant has the power to recover from economic, mental and physical problems that would be overwhelming for someone else. They have very strong defense mechanisms and don't like to make a decision unless they have all the pertinent facts. You won't learn much about Scorpio Rising's personal life until you've earned it. Once you've earned their trust, they are loyal friends... as long as you remain a loyal friend.

- Socially, Scorpio Ascendant is soft-spoken and quiet, unless they're catching up with an old friend. They are passionate and creative.

- Scorpio Rising will usually have a strong drive to succeed... whether it is to win a cooking competition or to become the CEO of a large corporation, if that is what they set their sights on, they will go all out for it. The intensity with which they can pursue their goals is rivaled only by their tenacity. They welcome competition.

- Scorpio Ascendant has a real stubborn streak, and it is difficult to get them to change their mind once it is made up. They are emotional creatures, but they are rather adept at hiding this vulnerability. They are good at observing details and can be shrewd when it comes to taking risks.

- Energetic and ambitious, Scorpio Rising seeks activities that are financially rewarding as well as challenging them physically or mentally. They are very resourceful and clever. In a crisis, Scorpio Ascendant will be cool, courageous and persistent. The worse the situation, the more quietly they work at the task of seeing it through to the end.

- Scorpio Rising is intuitive and sometimes psychic. This makes it imperative that they not give in to their sarcasm as it may strike deeper than they intend. They may have healing talents.[142]

Astrology is only one facet of a multi-dimensional approach in the study of any person, but it is amazing how many of these characteristics apply to James Dean. It is also important to note that seeds of dissension and inner conflict were sewn and nurtured on his behalf many years before his birth.

---

142   Scorpio-Rising Ascendant in Scorpio. Always Astrology Website. Accessed September 5, 2011. Available at: http://www.alwaysastrology. com/scorpio-rising.html

CHAPTER 9—THE ADVENTURES OF PENROD SCHOFIELD, TOM SAWYER, AND HUCKLEBERRY FINN

*P*enrod sat morosely upon the back fence and gazed with envy at Duke, his wistful dog.

A bitter soul dominated the various curved and angular surfaces known by a careless world as the face of Penrod Schofield. Except in solitude, that face was almost always cryptic and emotionless; for Penrod had come into his twelfth year wearing an expression carefully trained to be inscrutable. Since the world was sure to misunderstand everything, mere defensive instinct prompted him to give it as little as possible to lay hold upon. Nothing is more impenetrable than the face of a boy who has learned this, and Penrod's was habitually as fathomless as the depth of his hatred this morning for the literary activities of Mrs. Lora Rewbush--an almost universally respected fellow citizen, a lady of charitable and poetic inclinations, and one of his own mother's most inti-mate friends.

Mrs. Lora Rewbush had written something which she called "The Children's Pageant of the Table Round," and it was to be performed in public that very afternoon at the Women's Arts and Guild Hall for the benefit of the Coloured Infants' Betterment Society. And if any flavour of sweetness remained in the nature of Penrod Schofield after the dismal trials of the school-week just past, that problematic, infinitesimal remnant was made pungent acid by the imminence of his destiny to form a prominent feature of the spectacle, and to declaim the loathsome sentiments of a charac-ter named upon the programme the Child Sir Lancelot. After each rehearsal he had plotted escape, and only ten days earlier there had been a glimmer of light: Mrs. Lora Rewbush caught a very bad cold, and it was hoped it might develop into pneumonia; but she recovered so quickly that not even a rehearsal of the Children's Pageant was postponed. Darkness closed in. Penrod had rather vaguely debated plans for a self-mutilation such as would make his appearance as the Child Sir Lancelot inexpedient on public grounds; it was a heroic and attractive thought, but the results of some extremely sketchy preliminary experiments caused him to abandon it.

There was no escape; and at last his hour was hard upon him. Therefore he brooded on the fence and gazed with envy at his wistful Duke. The dog's name was undescriptive of his person, which was obviously the result of a singular series of mesalliances. He wore a grizzled moustache and indefinite whiskers; he was small and shabby, and looked like an old postman. Penrod envied Duke because he was sure Duke would never be compelled to be a Child Sir Lancelot. He thought a dog free and unshackled to go or come as the wind listeth. Penrod forgot the life he led Duke. There was a long soliloquy upon the fence, a plaintive monologue without words: the boy's thoughts were adjectives, but they were expressed by a running film of pictures in his mind's eye, morbidly prophetic of the hideosities before him. Finally he spoke aloud, with such spleen that Duke rose from his haunches and lifted one ear in keen anxiety.

"`I hight Sir Lancelot du Lake, the Child, Gentul-hearted, meek, and mild. What though I'm but a littul child, Gentul-hearted, meek, and----' oof!"

All of this except "oof" was a quotation from the Child Sir Lancelot, as conceived by Mrs. Lora Rewbush. Choking upon it, Penrod slid down from the fence, and with slow and thoughtful steps entered a one-storied wing of the stable, consisting of a single apartment, floored with cement and used as a storeroom for broken bric-a-brac, old paint-buckets, decayed garden-hose, worn- out carpets, dead furniture, and other condemned odds and ends not yet considered hopeless enough to be given away. In one corner stood a large box, a part of the building itself: it was eight feet high and open at the top, and it had been constructed as a sawdust magazine from which was drawn material for the horse's bed in a stall on the other side of the partition. The big box, so high and towerlike, so commodious, so suggestive, had ceased to fulfil its legitimate function; though, providentially, it had been at least half full of sawdust when the horse died. Two years had gone by since that passing; an interregnum in transportation during which Penrod's father was "thinking" (he explained sometimes) of an automobile. Meanwhile, the gifted and generous sawdust-box had served brilliantly in war and peace: it was Penrod's stronghold.

There was a partially defaced sign upon the front wall of the box; the donjon-keep had known mercantile impulses:

The O. K. RaBiT Co. PENROD ScHoFiELD AND CO. iNQuiRE FOR PRicEs

This was a venture of the preceding vacation, and had netted, at one time, an accrued and owed profit of $1.38. Prospects had been brightest on the very eve of cataclysm. The storeroom was locked and guarded, but twenty-seven rabbits and Belgian hares, old and young, had perished here on a single night--through no human agency, but in a foray of cats, the besiegers treacherously tunnelling up through the sawdust from the small aperture which opened into the stall beyond the partition. Commerce has its martyrs.[143]

So begin the misadventures of Penrod Schofield, a comical character created by Indiana writer Booth Tarkington from 1914 through 1917, and read by several generations of children.

James Dean was not one to shirk from the opportunity of appearing in a play or other dramatic event, but he was a Penrod Schofield, Tom Sawyer, and Huckleberry Finn rolled into one. In his book, *The James Dean Story*, Ron Martinetti states:

143   Booth Tarkington, "Chapter I: A Boy and His Dog," *Penrod*. Classic Reader Website. Accessed September 20, 2011. Available at http://www.classicreader.com/book/1207/1/

To Jimmy, waiting was a terrible waste of time; nor was the ability to sit still ever counted among his virtues. When he wasn't pestering Carter with endless questions about whatever machine the mechanic was then working on, he would occupy himself entertaining the other boys who usually crowded the shop. One of them remembers that Dean liked to stand at an imaginary public address system, pretending to call out a race. 'He'd get us all lined up,' he recalls, 'tell us what kind of weather it was, who got the jump, who crashed at the first turn, whose motorcycle was bursting into flames. Damned if he didn't make it sound so real, I had to look twice to make sure I wasn't really racing.'[144]

James Dean's flair for drama began with his mother Mildred. He had a special love for his mother, and also a special anger, as noted by Barbara Glenn, a former girl friend, in a later interview with David Dalton:

"Jimmy had a terrible anger for his mother. She died. He was a nine-year-old child saying how can you leave me? When he talked about her, it wasn't a twenty-one- or twenty-two-year-old. It was a child and he was deserted. He'd loved her desperately. He'd loved her desperately and she left him. I think it had a profound effect on him. And he expressed it in terms of his art."[145]

In describing James Dean's early artistic endeavors, David Dalton writes:

Jimmy recalled the parts he played for his mother in an interview with Hedda Hopper. It is a catalogue he did not care to elaborate on. 'When I was four or five my mother had me playing the violin—I was a blasted child prodigy. My family came to California and before it was over my mother had me tap-dancing. Not at the same time I was playing the violin. My mother died when I was eight and the violin was buried too."[146]

---

144   Ron Martinetti, *The James Dean Story*, p. 9.
145   David Dalton, *James Dean: The Mutant King*, p. 7.
146   David Dalton, *James Dean: The Mutant King*, pp. 7-8.

Of course, he had to endure a certain amount of teasing from other children when they saw him tap-dancing and carrying his violin. He engaged in a number of dust-ups over the matter. While he appears to have been a good-sized baby, he grew up to be quite small—something that irritated him immensely when he realized it. As an adult, he was no more than five feet eight inches tall (probably closer to five seven). (This is the reason he "slouched"—to camouflage his short size!) He was not afraid of getting hurt and when his honor had been in some way impuned, he rectified the situation with his fists. Someone once noted in a later interview that he was a good one to have on your side in a fight!

James Dean was a sensitive boy who learned to compensate for what he considered deficiencies. Extremely far-sighted, he had to wear eye glasses. His uncle, Marcus Winslow, once said:

> *"He smashed fifteen pair of eyeglasses in tryin' to be an athlete. Breakin' em as fast as I could get 'em...I was called into the principal's so many times I almost moved into her office."*[147]

He broke out his front teeth while performing acrobatics in the Winslow barn, requiring a bridge, and that bridge required frequent replacement as well. In an interview years later, Dizzy Sheridan, reported that bridge generally ended up in some unusual place: in someone's drink, down the back of someone's shirt, in someone's plate of food. Besides his sensitive nature, he was a great tease. But if someone ridiculed him, he could easily fly into a rage. One such encounter is described by Val Holley. It occurred while Jimmy was preparing for the Indiana State Speech Contest in high school:

> *Just before Christmas break, Dean recited "Madman" before his peers in advanced speech class and was heckled by David Fox, one of his basketball teammates. The two young men got into a brawl, for which Dean, but not Fox, was suspended from school for three days. [Brookshire—Adeline Nall, the teacher—speculates that the principal, who was new that year, hoped to establish his authority by suspending Dean.] Dean was not allowed to play in the basketball game against Sweetser High, which his*

---

147   David Dalton, *James Dean: The Mutant King*, p.47.

team barely won without him, forty-three to forty-two. Adding insult to injury, when he tried to buy a student ticket to watch, the ticket taker happened to be Raymond Elliott, the study hall disciplinarian, who told him he was not a student. And that was not the end of it. At season's end, the two teammates who edged Dean out as top season scorer had played eighteen games, while Dean, without the Sweetser game to his credit, had played only seventeen.[148]

Joe Hyams describes the Dave Fox encounter in his *James Dean: Little Boy Lost:*

Adeline Nall recalls that, from the start, Jimmy had a natural feeling for the mood contrasts required by the monologue, which opens with a scream and calls for the character to subtly drift from sanity to madness and back again.

One day in class, David Fox, a junior, began to make sarcastic remarks about Jimmy's reading. Despite Mrs. Nall's admonitions to David to quiet down, he continued heckling Jimmy.

"What're you trying to do, Dean?" Fox asked. "We know you're a great talent, a regular John Barrymore."

Jimmy's blue eyes blazed as he told Fox to shut up or he'd shut him up, but the taunting continued as the other students snickered.

After class everyone went to the playground where the two boys squared off and scuffled. Roland DuBois, the school principal, happened on the brawl and demanded to know who threw the first punch. Both boys were silent.

"You're both expelled," DuBois said with finality.

Then Jimmy spoke up. "I threw the first punch, sir." He was expelled from school but was soon reinstated"[149]

148   Val Holley, *James Dean: The Biography*, p. 24.
149   Joe, Hyams, *James Dean: Little Boy Lost*, p. 22.

In the 1949 Fairmount Yearbook, James Dean willed Dave Fox "my temper." He had a self-deprecating way about him, but he couldn't handle being ridiculed by others. His aunt once noted:

> *"Jimmy" had a bright mind but he didn't always apply himself in high school...He used to say, 'I'd rather not get good grades, than be called a sissy.' But his last year in high school he promised he'd make the honor role and he did."*[150]

According to Ron Martinetti , "Dean received two A's and two B's, one of which was in math, a subject he disliked. Only a lone C in U.S. Government marred his report card."[151]

Concerning his acceptance by other students, Val Holley writes:

> *Dean's separateness was not invisible to other people in Fairmount; he was not quite the "regular guy" that his uncle insisted he was. "We watched Jimmy with a little awe, but felt he was explosive and not part of the community," remembers Sue Hill, three years younger than Dean. "We were aware he marched to a different drummer than ninety-nine percent of Fairmount. Some people in town were glad to see him go to California." Hill's twin sister, Shirley, adds, "His dramatic ability awed us, but his artistic capability in oils and his basketball and baseball talents gave him peer acceptance and popularity in spite of his individuality...*

> *In the summer of 1948, the local Veterans of Foreign Wars sponsored weekend dances in a hall above Fairmount's dime store to give the local teens an alternative to driving into Marion, the county seat. "Once Jim came with an out-of-town girl," says Hill, "and they proceeded to make out like bandits. Well, the chaperones sent everyone home early and that was the last of those weekend dances."*

> *Another classmate, Barbara Leach, felt that "audacious" would be the single best word to describe Dean. "He was a little more*

---

150   Qtd. In Ron Martinetti, *The James Dean Story*, p. 14.
151   Ron Martinetti, *The James Dean Story,* p. 14.

daring" than her other peers, she said. Her earliest memory of
Dean (she moved to Fairmount just in time for their senior year)
was at a Halloween party in a barn. From up in the loft, Dean tried
to pour cider into the open mouths of the kids below."[152]

James Dean was often the dare devil. While a student at Fairmount
High School, he knew how to scale the rafters in the roof of the building, and he also knew where he could look down into the teacher's
lounge, as his speech teacher Adeline Nall once recalled in an interview. Teachers were not allowed to smoke in those days. If they did
smoke, they would keep it out of the sight of the public and never
do it in front of the students. Jimmy knew that his speech teacher
Adeline Nall was a closet smoker. He had done something that dis-
pleased her one day at school, so she was busy reading him the royal
riot act about it. He stood there looking at her with that look in his
eyes. Then he reached inside his shirt pocket, pulled out a cigarette
and casually handed it to her. She said, "I felt like popping him!"

Indeed he was an artist as well as a poet. Howard recognized this
when we toured the Fairmount Historical Museum in 2003, after visiting the spot behind Back Creek Friends Church on the bank of Back
Creek, which was shown to us by Phil Zeigler. It was here where Jimmy
liked to draw, write poetry and meditate—his special place where
he wanted to be alone. Jimmy was a doodler, and he had drawn a
grasshopper in the margin of a school paper, now on display in the
Fairmount Museum. Howard told me, "When I saw that grasshopper
and how detailed it was, I knew then that he had an amazing talent!"

James Dean's acting ability was well-known and admired in the community. When we were staying at the Loft Inn Bed & Breakfast in
Fairmount in 2003, Patryce Loftin described the one and only time
she recalled actually seeing James Dean. She was a toddler and he
was a teen-ager, but to her, he was a great big adult. It was approach-
ing Halloween, and her grandfather was planning a Halloween party
for the local children in one of the barns. He wanted to "scare the
kids", so he solicited the aid of young Jimmy. She said she can still
see them talking with each other, nodding, smiling and plotting. A

152   Val Holley, *James Dean: The Biography,* p. 16.

platform was erected in the barn with a trap door. Jimmy dressed as a ghost and hid beneath the platform until "the appropriate time." The kids were all enjoying the party, having a big time, when suddenly the lights went off, and a special light focused on the platform. Ghost Jimmy wiggled up and down through the trap door, making the most frightening sounds—and the kids all screamed in fright. She said, "I don't know how he was able to wiggle up and down through the hole like that, but he did, and he was certainly convincing!"[153]

Jimmy got his first school acting part in his sophomore year in *The Monkey Paw*. During his junior year, he got a good part in *An Apple from Coles County*. Then came *You Can't Take It with You* in his senior year. According to David Dalton:

> *Jimmy had his own grandfather, Charlie Dean in mind when he interpreted the part. His grandmother remembers him as a child mimicking her husband Charlie's every move, crossing and uncrossing his little arms as his Granddad did and marching behind him, every movement in tune. "It was more than a child's playful mocking," she said. "Even then, Jimmy seemed to be able to be another person!"[154]*

There was also *Goon With the Wind*, which David Dalton describes:

> *In October, the sign outside the gym that read "Quaker Power" had its big bold letters changed to orange and black for the annual Halloween festival. Inside the gym the audience of students and parents sat in the bleachers while the drama society presented "Goon with the Wind", a monster parody in which Jimmy had the starring role of Frankenstein, spending hours on his costume and make-up to get the right look. Like the 'gory odes' of the WCTU, Jimmy relished the chance to screech and howl, express his "pretended" anger and anguish at being trapped in an alien body in a strange land. As Fairmount's Frankenstein he could well portray the monster's dilemma—the creature that doesn't fit in anywhere. It's no surprise that teenagers thrive on monster sto-*

---

153   Loftin, Patryce, Personal Conversation, Fairmount, Indiana, May 20, 2003.

154   David Dalton, *James Dean: The Mutant King*, p. 41.

ries. No matter how scary they might be, monsters are fearless and can do whatever they want! Smash down the house, grab the girl, squash the mad scientist, swallow a supermarket and disappear without a trace![155]

Jimmy's aunt, Ortense Winslow, was a member of the local chapter of the WCTU (Women's Christian Temperance Union.) One of Howard's aunts belonged to that organization, and I remember going to the airport to pick her up one year when she flew from Florida to Cedar Rapids, Iowa to visit the family. When she stepped off the plane, she headed straight for the ticket counter and announced: "I don't approve of your airline. It is nothing more than a flying saloon!" In Fairmount, the WCTU met at the Back Creek Friends Church where a young James Dean did readings for them. David Dalton notes:

Ortense Winslow first encouraged Jimmy to get up on the stage when he was in the seventh grade by persuading him to do a reading for the Women's Christian Temperance Union. "I felt a need to prove myself and had the facility to do so," Jimmy told Hedda Hopper about the dramatic readings for the WCTU. "I was that tall, and instead of doing little poems I recited gory odes. This made me a straight little harpy in short pants. But I won all the medals the WCTU had to offer. I became pretty proficient and later I won the Indiana State dramatic contest reading 'The Madman.' The decision to act was never prompted. My whole life has been spent in dramatic display of expression.'[156]

Using a chair as a prop which he gripped tightly, his first reading follows:

Bars! Bars! Iron bars! No matter which way I look I see them always before me! Long, menacing, iron bars that mock and sneer at me, even in my sleep. At times I think I hear them shout: "You killed a man! You killed a man!" Then I shout back at them: "I didn't! I didn't! I tell you, I didn't!" But did I? My God above, did I—I who as a boy could not bear to inflict pain on anyone?[157]

155   David Dalton, *James Dean: The Mutant King*, pp.42-43.
156   David Dalton, *James Dean: The Mutant King*, pp. 33-34.
157   David Dalton, *James Dean: The Mutant King*, pp. 34.

Then came a night when a reading and a track meet conflicted with one another. According to David Dalton:

> *When the night of the reading finally came, it happened to be the same night of the junior high school track meet. Jimmy was torn between the two, but Ortense's insistence won. Just before his reading, the committee took Jimmy's "bars" away, since props weren't allowed, a technicality Mrs. Nall thought they would overlook. Jimmy began, faltered, gave up and stood there saying nothing until he was gently urged off the platform. "I was sure then of what I had known all along," Ortense said. "You couldn't make Jimmy Dean do things he didn't want to do."[158]*

---

158   David Dalton, *James Dean: The Mutant King*, pp. 34.

**The Old Longmont High School Building on
Main Street, Longmont, Colorado.**
*Photo taken October 2008 when we were driving through Longmont.
The high school relocated to another facility years ago. Currently,
this building is the Adult Education Center for the St. Vrain Valley
School District. It previously served as the location for a charter
school. The dolls are characters on my Historical Footprints 2010
Website: Travels with Jim—a Mattel James Dean doll and a Mattel
Portuguese Princess Doll: http://www.historical-footprints-2010.com*

CHAPTER 10—"PERFECT FOR LONG-MONT!"

Approximately ten years ago, Howard was standing at the coffee cart in the lobby of the Veteran's Hospital in Denver, Colorado and struck up a conversation with the volunteer. She told him her home was in Longmont—that she was born and raised there, and he remembered a conversation with me earlier in the week.

Howard: "Did you graduate from Longmont High School?"

The Volunteer: "Yes, I certainly did!"

Howard: Did you go to the old high school building on Main Street?"

The Volunteer: "Yes, I certainly did!"

Howard: "And do you remember the speech contest in 1949?

The Volunteer: "I was there!"

Howard: "So, you remember James Dean?"

The Volunteer: "Ohhhh, yes!"

Howard: "My wife would love to talk with you!"

The Volunteer: ""Well, I'll tell you something! For years, my brother-in-law's claim to fame was that he beat out James Dean at the 1949 Speech Contest in Longmont! He talked about it for years!"

The building that once housed Longmont High School still stands on the upper portion of Main Street, the high school having moved to a new facility years ago. It is not abandoned, however, and is still in excellent shape. Approximately six years ago, it was home to a charter school. Today, it is the Adult Education Center for the St. Vrain Valley School District. Since we only live a half-hour's drive south of Longmont, I passed that building many times before learning about its connection with the speech contest. In the words of Ron Martinetti:

> Longmont is a small, quiet town nestled high in the Rocky Mountains, but it opened its doors gladly to the contestants who poured in from around the country. Students and their faculty representatives boarded with local families, and the town arranged picnics and square dances to help entertain its young guests. For a solid week everyone had a ball; Dean's hosts even allowed him use of the family car.[159]

James Dean and another Fairmount student won the state competition of the National Forensic League held in Peru, Indiana in the spring of 1949—a competition in which he woke up the judges with his blood-curdling scream as "The Madman." His win entitled him to enter the national competition scheduled to be held at Longmont High School in Longmont, Colorado in April. His aunt and uncle were completely surprised at this announcement. He had apparently said nothing to them about going to Colorado. The school raised the funds to send Jimmy and Adeline (Brookshire) Nall to Colorado by train. That would put them in Union Station in Denver, which is currently undergoing substantial remodeling. Now owned by the Regional Transportation District, the new owners want to restore the depot to its look in the 1940s-1950s. From there, Jimmy and Adeline Nall would take a train to Longmont, which is no longer has passenger train service. The old train depot in Longmont is currently a liquor store! Val Holley describes James Dean's departure from Fairmount:

> On the morning of April 27, the Fairmount High student body gave Dean a send-off on the school grounds, planned by the principal, who had forgiven him for punching David Fox. The band played, the cheerleaders led a yell, and Dean choked up. "He bawled," said Joyce John. "In fact, we all got rather dewy-eyed."

159   Ron Martinetti, The James Dean Story, p. 15. [Note: Longmont is actually in the foothills of the Rocky Mountains on the eastern side, known as The Front Range.]

From the school, a caravan of cars trailing streamers took Dean to the Marion depot, where he and Adeline Brookshire, chaperone as well as coach, boarded a train to Chicago. Dean cried for the second time that morning as he recounted the send-off for Brookshire.

In Chicago, Brookshire, Dean, and the other Indiana winners and coaches boarded the Denver Zephyr. Brookshire was a closet smoker and, while ostensibly in the powder room, would slip out to the car's rear platform for an unobserved cigarette. Forty years later she learned from the Fort Wayne contestant that Dean was resorting to the same subterfuge so Brookshire would not observe his smoking. When it came time to sleep, a porter brought pillows, but Dean thrashed about restlessly, keeping Brookshire awake in the adjacent seat. Finally he repaired with Lester Tucker, coach of the Howe Military Academy contestants, to the glass-domed observation coach on the upper deck, leaving Brookshire in peace.[160]

Students arrived in Longmont, Colorado from all over the country for the contest. Host families let the students stay in their homes. I have yet to discover the name of the host family for James Dean, and that is probably something that will never be known. He borrowed the host family's car and went exploring with some other students. I have no idea how far they drove, but in 1949, Longmont was fairly isolated in the country. When we first moved to Colorado in 1980, Longmont telephone calls incurred a long-distance charge. Today, it is part of the metropolitan area. When Adeline Nall called the host's home to check on her charge, she was told by the host that he had borrowed the car. She wanted to meet with him about his performance. Jimmy's independence went into play from the beginning.

According to Joe Hyams:

Although competitors were supposed to appear in suits and ties, Jimmy insisted on wearing an open shirt and jeans on the theory that he couldn't act crazy all dressed up. Also the entries were

160   Val Holley, *James Dean: The Biography,* p. 25.

supposed to be no more than ten minutes, and despite Mrs. Nall's insistence Jimmy refused to cut his monologue down to less than twelve.[161]

David Dalton describes his performance in detail:

He was out of Fairmount and away from its confines, beyond the reach of Jonesboro Pike, which had been the border of the known world. Nothing is so sure to breed monsters as confinement, and the scream he let out that day was the wild cry of the "thing that grows on the green side of the heart," a shattering of all the layers of varnish that a small town will lay on you:

"Aaaarrraaaaeeeedayyyyyhhhaa!"

The judges flinched. He used the scream to wake them up, then began his recitation.

"Yes! A Madman's!...the blood hissing and tingling through my veins, till the cold dew of fear stood in large drops upon my skin, and my knees knocked together with fright! Ho! Ho! It's a fine thing to be mad! To be peeped at like a wild lion through the iron bars—and to roll and twine among the straw, transported with such brave music. Hurrah for the madhouse! Oh, it's a rare place."[162]

Dalton continues:

"His reading really was different," Mrs. Nall said, relishing the opportunity to revisit the past, "and Jimmy was wonderful. He would be very crazy and the next minute perfectly sane just like an adjustable lunatic. But it was the subtlety of the change. He really loved it. And like I say, it was a monologue but it had about as many emotions as you could use in a reading. You never get more than five or six characters in a reading, and he had at least that many moods and voice changes."

161   Joe Hyams, *James Dean: Little Boy Lost,* p. 25.
162   David Dalton, *James Dean: The Mutant King*, p.51.

She sat watching from the back of the room in a school in Longmont as Jimmy took off his thick glasses so that cadaverous face and those malignant-looking eyes would loom out. She'd warned him that the piece, at twelve minutes, was too long.

"Perfect for Long-mont," he'd replied sarcastically.[163]

Dalton interviewed Jim McCarthy, who was another debater at the meet, and who recalled how he tried to convince Jimmy to change what he was wearing:

All day I kept trying to talk him into changing clothes. I'd brought my best suit and four white shirts and a couple of ties. So had everyone else, because we'd had it hammered into our heads that appearance counted for a lot and we had to be properly dressed. Jim was wearing an open shirt and jeans when I met him, and that's the way he went into the tryouts every time. At first he told me he just couldn't be bothered changing. But finally he admitted, "Look Jim, this bit I'm doing is a wild one. It's a Dickens thing called 'The Madman' and I've got to go crazy in it. How the heck can I go crazy in a shirt and tie? It wouldn't work."

"You won't win," I told him. "You've got to go along with what they want you to look like if you want to win."

"Then I won't, that's all," he said. "I don't need to win. Only I can't do the piece if I don't feel it, and I can't feel it all duded up."[164]

While Jimmy received good critiques during the preliminaries, he was told that it was too long during the second round. Adeline Nall made an attempt to cut it, but her attempt was unsuccessful. She later said, "…But you know, you can't tell 'em anything. You can never tell these kids; they know so much more than you do. So, I don't know if that's what was against Jim or not, but something was against us."[165] Interestingly, Val Holley notes:

163 David Dalton, *James Dean: The Mutant King,* p. 52
164 David Dalton, *James Dean: The Mutant King.* p. 52.
165 David Dalton, *James Dean: The Mutant King.* p. 52.

In Longmont, Dean placed sixth out of twenty-two contestants. He was eliminated after four rounds and just missed being one of five finalists. Brookshire says, "I can still remember seeing him huddled in his seat during the finals, heartsick that he was out of the running." She notes that he could have been penalized for exceeding the ten-minute time limit or for using a selection that was not the standard cutting from a play with two or more different characters. She also denies that he opened with a bloodcurdling scream or ripped his shirt, as later press accounts alleged. "I would never have a student begin so shockingly," she insists. "It was foreign to my training."[166]

I imagine that Adeline Nall revisited this experience many times through the rest of her life. She may have remembered it differently from time to time. And she may have ultimately decided that scream ended Jimmy's chances of winning.

There were five finalists in the contest. James Dean came in sixth place—something that remained a sore spot for him the rest of his life. [Possibly the fifth-place contestant was the brother-in-law of the volunteer Howard met at the Veteran's Hospital in Denver about ten years ago!] Jimmy blamed Adeline Nall for not insisting that he cut his performance and sometimes later referred to her as a "frustrated actress!" He also told some friends he did not go on to Colorado and invented another explanation for where he was. Yet,--

Even so, the day after the competition the Longmont Times Call printed a picture of Jim Dean on its front page as the sixth-place winner in the Dramatic Declamation Contest, and quoted Mrs. Nall with dramatic irony as saying, "Certainly great credit is given to Jim for interesting Fairmount students and citizens in speech... and I hope this is only the beginning of much more fine work in this field."[167]

Jimmy was gloomy all the way back to Indiana on the train. He and his teacher had a two-hour lay-over in Denver, and rather than endure his sulking, Adeline Nall took him to the Red Rocks Amphitheatre just

166   Val Holley, *James Dean: The Biography*, p. 25.
167   Qtd. In David Dalton, *James Dean: The Mutant King*, p. 53.

outside Golden, Colorado. Visitors to Denver and local residents know that Red Rocks is the place where touring bands have performed in concerts over the years. They were apparently the only two visitors at the amphitheatre that day. Even though in a dismal mood, Jimmy shouted his Madman's speech from the stage with Adeline as his only audience. We can say that James Dean once performed at Red Rocks, even though to an audience of one!

While he didn't win the competition, he learned something from it, and he never lost his focus again.

CHAPTER 11—"THREE LONG MOUNTAINS AND A WOOD..."

All I could see from where I stood
Was three long mountains and a wood;
I turned and looked another way,
And saw three islands in a bay.
So with my eyes I traced the line
Of the horizon, thin and fine,
Straight around till I was come
Back to where I'd started from;
And all I saw from where I stood
Was three long mountains and a wood.
Over these things I could not see;
These were the things that bounded me;
And I could touch them with my hand,
Almost, I thought, from where I stand.
And all at once things seemed so small
My breath came short, and scarce at all.
But, sure, the sky is big, I said;
Miles and miles above my head;
So here upon my back I'll lie
And look my fill into the sky.
And so I looked, and, after all,
The sky was not so very tall.
The sky, I said, must somewhere stop,
And -- sure enough! -- I see the top!
The sky, I thought, is not so grand;
I 'most could touch it with my hand!

And reaching up my hand to try,
I screamed to feel it touch the sky.
I screamed, and -- lo! -- Infinity
Came down and settled over me;
Forced back my scream into my chest,
Bent back my arm upon my breast,
And, pressing of the Undefined
The definition on my mind,
Held up before my eyes a glass
Through which my shrinking sight did pass
Until it seemed I must behold
Immensity made manifold;
Whispered to me a word whose sound
Deafened the air for worlds around,
And brought unmuffled to my ears
The gossiping of friendly spheres,
The creaking of the tented sky,
The ticking of Eternity.
I saw and heard, and knew at last
The How and Why of all things, past,
And present, and forevermore.
The Universe, cleft to the core,
Lay open to my probing sense
That, sick'ning, I would fain pluck thence
But could not, -- nay! But needs must suck
At the great wound, and could not pluck
My lips away till I had drawn
All venom out. -- Ah, fearful pawn!
For my omniscience paid I toll
In infinite remorse of soul.
All sin was of my sinning, all
Atoning mine, and mine the gall
Of all regret. Mine was the weight
Of every brooded wrong, the hate
That stood behind each envious thrust,
Mine every greed, mine every lust.
And all the while for every grief,

Each suffering, I craved relief
With individual desire, --
Craved all in vain! And felt fierce fire
About a thousand people crawl;
Perished with each, -- then mourned for all!
A man was starving in Capri;
He moved his eyes and looked at me;
I felt his gaze, I heard his moan,
And knew his hunger as my own.
I saw at sea a great fog bank
Between two ships that struck and sank;
A thousand screams the heavens smote;
And every scream tore through my throat.
No hurt I did not feel, no death
That was not mine; mine each last breath
That, crying, met an answering cry
From the compassion that was I.
All suffering mine, and mine its rod;
Mine, pity like the pity of God.
Ah, awful weight! Infinity
Pressed down upon the finite Me!
My anguished spirit, like a bird,
Beating against my lips I heard;
Yet lay the weight so close about
There was no room for it without.
And so beneath the weight lay I
And suffered death, but could not die.

Long had I lain thus, craving death,
When quietly the earth beneath
Gave way, and inch by inch, so great
At last had grown the crushing weight,
Into the earth I sank till I
Full six feet under ground did lie,
And sank no more, -- there is no weight
Can follow here, however great.
From off my breast I felt it roll,
And as it went my tortured soul

Burst forth and fled in such a gust
That all about me swirled the dust.

Deep in the earth I rested now;
Cool is its hand upon the brow
And soft its breast beneath the head
Of one who is so gladly dead.
And all at once, and over all
The pitying rain began to fall;
I lay and heard each pattering hoof
Upon my lowly, thatched roof,
And seemed to love the sound far more
Than ever I had done before.
For rain it hath a friendly sound
To one who's six feet underground;
And scarce the friendly voice or face:
A grave is such a quiet place.

The rain, I said, is kind to come
And speak to me in my new home.
I would I were alive again
To kiss the fingers of the rain,
To drink into my eyes the shine
Of every slanting silver line,
To catch the freshened, fragrant breeze
From drenched and dripping apple-trees.
For soon the shower will be done,
And then the broad face of the sun
Will laugh above the rain-soaked earth
Until the world with answering mirth
Shakes joyously, and each round drop
Rolls, twinkling, from its grass-blade top.
How can I bear it; buried here,
While overhead the sky grows clear
And blue again after the storm?
O, multi-colored, multiform,
Beloved beauty over me,
That I shall never, never see

Again! Spring-silver, autumn-gold,
That I shall never more behold!
Sleeping your myriad magics through,
Close-sepulchred away from you!
O God, I cried, give me new birth,
And put me back upon the earth!
Upset each cloud's gigantic gourd
And let the heavy rain, down-poured
In one big torrent, set me free,
Washing my grave away from me!

I ceased; and through the breathless hush
That answered me, the far-off rush
Of herald wings came whispering
Like music down the vibrant string
Of my ascending prayer, and -- crash!
Before the wild wind's whistling lash
The startled storm-clouds reared on high
And plunged in terror down the sky,
And the big rain in one black wave
Fell from the sky and struck my grave.
I know not how such things can be;
I only know there came to me
A fragrance such as never clings
To aught save happy living things;
A sound as of some joyous elf
Singing sweet songs to please himself,
And, through and over everything,
A sense of glad awakening.
The grass, a-tiptoe at my ear,
Whispering to me I could hear;
I felt the rain's cool finger-tips
Brushed tenderly across my lips,
Laid gently on my sealed sight,
And all at once the heavy night
Fell from my eyes and I could see, --
A drenched and dripping apple-tree,
A last long line of silver rain,

A sky grown clear and blue again.
And as I looked a quickening gust
Of wind blew up to me and thrust
Into my face a miracle
Of orchard-breath, and with the smell, --
I know not how such things can be! --
I breathed my soul back into me.
Ah! Up then from the ground sprang I
And hailed the earth with such a cry
As is not heard save from a man
Who has been dead, and lives again.
About the trees my arms I wound;
Like one gone mad I hugged the ground;
I raised my quivering arms on high;
I laughed and laughed into the sky,
Till at my throat a strangling sob
Caught fiercely, and a great heart-throb
Sent instant tears into my eyes;
O God, I cried, no dark disguise
Can e'er hereafter hide from me
Thy radiant identity!
Thou canst not move across the grass
But my quick eyes will see Thee pass,
Nor speak, however silently,
But my hushed voice will answer Thee.
I know the path that tells Thy way
Through the cool eve of every day;
God, I can push the grass apart
And lay my finger on Thy heart!

The world stands out on either side
No wider than the heart is wide;
Above the world is stretched the sky, --
No higher than the soul is high.
The heart can push the sea and land
Farther away on either hand;
The soul can split the sky in two,

And let the face of God shine through.
But East and West will pinch the heart
That can not keep them pushed apart;
And he whose soul is flat -- the sky
Will cave in on him by and by.

---Edna St. Vincent Millay
"Renascence" (1912)[168]

***

Something else happened to James Dean in Longmont, Colorado: he had tasted the experience of dramatic competition. Now at the end of his senior year in high school, he knew what he wanted to do.

"I want to become an actor," he told his aunt and uncle.

They had heard such statements before and thought those ideas would pass. His uncle had hoped he would enter his alma mater, Earlham—a nearby Quaker college--and study agriculture. But when graduation day arrived, his grandmother admitted:

> *"...It was becoming plain to all of us that acting was the thing Jimmy was best at. He'd won declamatory contests, even a state one; but the thing that convinced us that he was an actor was his appearance in a church play called, 'To Them That Sleep in Darkness.' Jimmy played the blind boy. Well, I'll tell you, I wished he wasn't quite so good at it. I cried all the way through."[169]*

While growing up in Fairmount, James Dean looked to his family members for nurturing and his drama teacher for dramatic advice.

---

168   Edna St. Vincent Millay, "Renascence". Archive of Classic Poems. The Poetry of Edna St. Vincent Millay. (Poem originally written in 1912) Everypoet.com Website. Accessed September 23, 2011. Available at: http://www.everypoet.com/Archive/poetry/Edna_St_Vincent_Millay/edna_st_vincent_millay_renascence.htm
169   qtd. In David Dalton, *James Dean: The Mutant King,* p. 54.

However, two adults in Fairmount had a significant impact on his life. David Dalton writes:

> *His mother had wished him into being, the Winslows nurtured him and Mrs. Nall, like some helper from folklore, led him along his destined path; but it was James DeWeerd, pastor of Fairmount's Wesleyan Church, who swung open the gates. He had a magnetic personality and an earthy quality. He was cultured, worldly and eccentric—if ever a name was meant to mean something, it was his—loved a good joke and dabbled in the mystic religions. He'd come home from the Second World War a hero of sorts: a Silver Star for gallantry, a Purple Heart with Oakleaf Cluster and a chestfull of scars from schrapnel. He was popular with the young boys in town and especially interesting to Jimmy.*[170]

Dalton goes on to say:

> *Fairmount remembers DeWeerd as a minor-league Billy Graham, a volatile combination of actor and minister. In his sermons he was outspoken, witty and openly critical of Fairmount and its way of life. "The more things you know how to do and the more things you experience, the better off you'll be," he told Jimmy. At the home that he shared with his mother, DeWeerd introduced him to art, classical records and yoga (which DeWeerd practiced because of his wounds), talked of poets and philosophers and showed him home movies of bullfights in Mexico. The world which lay beyond the Jonesboro Pike with all its wonders and terrors began to beckon to Jimmy.*[171]

Dalton concludes:

> *James DeWeerd appears in Jimmy's life like the wise old man in folk tales, the embodiment of the spirit world—"the weird"—a holy hobgoblin who arrived at that point in Jimmy's pubescence when he most needed a guide. DeWeerd had the insight, understanding and a certain sympathy for unformed ideas and*

---

170   David Dalton, *James Dean: The Mutant King*, p. 36.
171   David Dalton, *James Dean: The Mutant King*, p. 37

ambitions that Jimmy so sorely needed but could not muster from his own resources.[172]

Much has been written about James DeWeerd and the impact he had on young James Dean, and much of it has focused on the controversial aspect of the minister's life. Val Holley notes:

There are different schools of thought on DeWeerd. The traditional view was that he was a great guy whose influence on young James Dean was wholesome and constructive...Quoting Marcus Winslow, Nielsen (an apologist for the minister) said DeWeerd's "heroic war record" was what initially drew Dean's admiration. She [Nielsen] and a variety of sources report that Dean felt comfortable pouring out his heart to DeWeerd about the unrelenting reverberations of his mother's death. Eventually DeWeerd became Dean's "closest friend in Fairmount" and "the center of his life."

A different view of DeWeerd was held by Fairmount folk whose religious inclinations stopped short of fundamentalism. Sue Hill recalls DeWeerd coming into the Dairy Bar after speaking at a revival meeting in Fairmount. "DeWeerd was talking about how much money he had taken the previous night and how much of it was his take. I was disillusioned," she said. "My father knew DeWeerd right after the war and encouraged him to write about his experiences. However, when DeWeerd became an evangelist and embraced the sin-devil concepts, it was too far from our Quaker concepts, and my father spoke of him as more involved in the money than the help to others."

"As kids working in the Dairy Bar," Hill said, they would see people from the revivals come in, and "we were shocked at their pious conversations—'Are you saved by our Lord, Jesus Christ?'—but very sexually involved behavior in the shop. My folks would say, 'They're in heat.'"[173]

David Dalton concludes:

172   David Dalton, *James Dean: The Mutant King,* p. 37
173   Val Holley, *James Dean: The Biography,* pp. 25-27

DeWeerd delivered Jimmy from the conspiracy of littleness surrounding him. He encouraged his idea of separateness. "Everybody is the square root of zero," he used to tell him as they sat on wicker chairs on the pastor's porch. He introduced him to the Midwestern philosopher Elbert Hubbard. "Conformity is cowardice," this mad scribbler of moral precept had once said to his blotter. "It's better to die on the Horeb of isolation knowing you've been true to yourself than to rot away in the mephitic alleys of the commonplace." Jimmy took it to heart.

DeWeerd also taught Jimmy how to drive and in his senior year took him to the Indianapolis 500, where he introduced him to Cannonball Baker, a famous ace of the time. On the way home the pastor and Jimmy talked of cars, speed, danger and the possibility of sudden death. "I taught Jimmy to believe in personal immortality. He had no fear of death because he believed as I do," said Dr. DeWeerd, "that death is merely control of mind over matter." Personal immortality—it's a typical draft from DeWeerd's Morality Trust, Inc. and it made Jimmy then and there a shareholder in The Great Beyond.[174]

Concerning Jimmy's infatuation with James DeWeerd, Al Terhune, who was then editor of the *Fairmount News* noted in an interview with David Dalton:

"Jimmy was a parasitic type of person…He hung around DeWeerd a lot, picked up his mannerisms and absorbed whatever he could." [175]

Dalton continues:

Unlike most people Jimmy knew in Fairmount, DeWeerd had tested himself in the outside world; he was cosmopolitan and had been a friend of Winston Churchill, later attending his funeral on invitation from the Queen herself. Jimmy started to rely on him and, according to DeWeerd, confided his deepest secrets to him. "Jimmy poured out to me his belief that he must be evil, or his

---

174   David Dalton, *James Dean: The Mutant King*, pp. 37-38
175   David Dalton, *James Dean: The Mutant King*, p. 36

mother would not have died and his father wouldn't have sent him away."[176]

On June 16, 1965, James DeWeerd made application to join the Indiana Chapter of the National Society of the Sons of the American Revolution. He was accepted for membership June 23, 1965, and his application is now available on Ancestry.com. According to the application, James Arthur DeWeerd was born May 23, 1916 in Olivet, Elwood Twp., Vermillion, Illinois to Fred DeWeerd (1881-1923) and Lelia Zay Benedict (1881-1955). His Revolutionary War ancestor was Jonathan Benedict on his mother's line.[177] A summary of DeWeerd's ancestry follows:

1. Fred DeWeerd, b. 6 Dec 1881, Holland, Michigan; d. 8 Jan 1923, Fairmount, Indiana; m. Lelia Zay Benedict 14 Sep 1908, Holland, Michigan. Lelia was born 11 May 1881, Muskegon, Michigan; d. 11 Jun 1955, Fairmount, Indiana.

2. James E. Benedict, b. 4 Jan 1848, Ohio; d. 28 Aug 1923, Belding, Michigan; m. Barbara Ann McCrea 29 Jun 1873 (place unknown.) Barbara was born 11 Dec 1850, Michigan; d. 7 Nov 1911, Holland, Michigan.

3. Alfred Robinson Benedict, b. 23 Apr 1810 (unknown location; death date and location unknown ; m. 23 Jul 1837 (location unknown) Cynthia Aldrich. Cynthia was born 1 Mar 1820 (location unknown) and died 9 Aug 1864 (location unknown.)

4. Cyrus Benedict, b. 23 Nov 1785 (location unknown); d. 9 Aug 1864 (location unknown); m. Martha Robinson 3 Apr 1744, Danbury, Connecticut. Martha was born in 1785 and died in 1869.

5. Jonathan Benedict, b. 12 Apr 1744, Danbury, Connecticut; d. 20 Jul 1834, Pompey, New York; m. Huldah Seelya 11 Jun 1782, Bethel Parish, Danbury, Connecticut.

176 David Dalton, *James Dean: The Mutant King*, pp. 36-37
177 James Arthur DeWeerd Sons of the American Revolution Application for Membership National Number 93009, State Number 1860. Dated June 16, 1965; Accepted June 23, 1965. Ancestry. com. Accessed September 25, 2011. Available at http://www.ancestry.com

6. Nathaniel Benedict, b. 1716 - whose wife was Hannah.[178]

Concerning Jonathan Benedict's Revolutionary War Service, the application states:

Battles engaged in: Danbury, Fairfield, Norwalk

From bound volumes of documents in Connecticut State Library 1832—Revolutionary War Pay Tables, Vol XVII, Document 73, Soldiers and Accounts 1780-1781 (for Jonathan Benedict). His pension record is available on request as he was a pensioner when he died. His father, Nathaniel, also served, and his son, E. Lemuel, fifteen years of age, took his father's place when he became disabled.[179]

It is interesting to note that Fred DeWeerd died when his son James was only seven years old, thereby creating another bond between James Dean and his mentor . They both lost parents at early ages. DeWeerd lived with his mother, who never remarried.

James DeWeerd died in March 1972. He is buried in the Brookside Cemetery in Montpelier, Indiana.[180] The controversy surrounding him did not appear in print until after his death.

***

There was another adult James Dean turned to in Fairmount. Her name was Bette McPherson, whose homeroom at Fairmount High during the 1948-1949 school year consisted of seniors. James Dean

---

178   James Arthur DeWeerd Sons of the American Revolution Application for Membership National Number 93009, State Number 1860. Dated June 16, 1965; Accepted June 23, 1965. Ancestry. com. Accessed September 25, 2011. Available at http://www.ancestry.com

179   James Arthur DeWeerd Sons of the American Revolution Application for Membership National Number 93009, State Number 1860. Dated June 16, 1965; Accepted June 23, 1965. Ancestry. com. Accessed September 25, 2011. Available at http://www.ancestry.com

180   James Arthur DeWeerd, Social Security Death Record. Ancestry.com. Accessed September 25, 2011. Available at http://www.ancestry.com.

was a member of the class. She taught art and physical education at the school. As told to Val Holley, McPherson states:

> "...He was very good as an artist. Since I drove from Marion to school every day, Jim asked to ride with me. My route went by where he lived anyway, so I would pick him up. He was always joking, so it made the days. When I moved to Fairmount, my landlady would get annoyed when he roared up on his motorcycle."[181]

Holley continues:

> McPherson, who died after a 1990 automobile accident, maintained she was eight years older than Dean, but her family genealogy shows that she was actually eleven years his senior. She and her husband, who had infantile paralysis and used crutches, lived in an apartment over a bar in Marion; they separated sometime during the 1948-49 school year. In the evenings McPherson worked for Joe Payne, an interior decorator of churches and public buildings, in Payne's warehouse near the center of Fairmount. "After basketball practices, Jim would come by and spend time with me there," she said. "We had a lot of good times together. He didn't seem that different to me then, although he was very dramatic about things." She was aware, she said, that Marcus Winslow did not approve of her, but he never tried to dissuade Dean from seeing her.

> During Dean's brief suspension from school for punching David Fox, he turned to McPherson for consolation. "He was unhappy about people talking about him," she said. "One night he came in with three watercolors he had painted. The first painting depicted people running him down. The second one was eyeballs that are crushing him, and the third represents his wanting to get back at everybody and show them, but he can't because his foot is tied down."

> One day at school a student was taking pictures on the front lawn. "Jim came up to me and put his arm around my neck for the pictures," McPherson said. "That's the first time I knew he liked

---

181   Val Holley, *James Dean: The Biography*, p. 29.

me. Later on he fell in love with me. For a long time after his death I didn't talk about him or see his movies. I had phone calls asking for information, but I did not want my personal experiences in print. I wouldn't mind now—some of them."[182]

A week before graduation, the senior class went on a trip to Washington DC and stayed in the Roosevelt Hotel. That hotel was the hotel for housing classes of touring students in those days; my American Heritage class stayed there in April 1960! Howard and I were in Washington D.C. in 1992, and I recall finding the building. I believe that today it is a senior citizens' residence.

James Dean's trip to Washington DC was not without controversy— something that tended to follow him around. According to Val Holley:

As a senior class sponsor, McPherson chaperoned the class trip to Washington, D.C., at the end of the school year. Denying a persistent Fairmount legend of her involvement in a boys' beer bust in Washington's Roosevelt Hotel, she said, "I did not get beer for any of the kids, nor did I drink beer on the D.C. trip! I was accused of a lot of things in Fairmount; it was a real Peyton Place." Partying aside, Dean made a special pilgrimage to Ford's Theater during some free time, which Adeline Brookshire had urged him to do. On the bus back to Indiana, some of the young women snipped locks of hair off Dean and another male student while they were snoozing.[183]

Later in Santa Monica, he had a short relationship with Bette McPherson, which will be covered more completely in the next chapter. He would later send McPherson "...an empty beer bottle wrapped in a napkin on which he had written a few nostalgic and cryptic words about past shared beer-drinking sessions as well as wishes for a superb New Year."[184]

James Dean's constant search for substitute parents placed him in a number of situations such as those described here. His mother's

---

182   Val Holley, *James Dean: The Biography*, pp. 29-30.
183   Val Holley, *James Dean: The Biography*, p 30.
184   Val Holley, *James Dean: The Biography*, pp. 40-41

death and father's absence left a huge void in his life that no one could understand unless experiencing the same dilemma.

Jimmy graduated from Fairmount High School May 16, 1949. The Winslows did not stand in the way of his dream to become an actor, which is typical of the Quaker manner. Quakers believe that people need to find themselves. As David Dalton notes, "If the boy wanted to act, let him learn to do it well." [185] He was asked to give a prayer at the baccalaureate service, and turned to James DeWeerd for advice. Val Holley notes: "The preacher loaned him some prayer books, from which Dean chose a supplication by John Henry Newman invoking 'safe lodging and a holy rest and peace at last.'"[186]

In June 1949, James Dean left Fairmount for Santa Monica, California, where he would rejoin his father and embark upon the next stage of his life. The *Fairmount News* noted his departure:

JAMES DEAN WAS HONORED AT FAREWELL PARTY MONDAY NIGHT. A farewell party was held Monday night in honor of James Dean who left Tuesday for Santa Monica, Calif., where he will enter the University of California at Los Angeles, planning to take a course in dramatics and fine arts.

Joyce Wigner and Barbara Middleton acted as hostesses at the party. Games were played and Donald Martin played the piano while the guests sand "California Here I come," and "Back Home Again in Indiana."

Refreshments were served by Mr. and Mrs. Charles Dean, Mr. and Mrs. Marcus Winslow and son, Jerry Brown, Kenneth Bowers, Donald Martin, Virginia Payne, Joan Roth, Wilma Smith, Ethel and Edith Thomas, Norma Banister, James Dean, Joyce Wigner, Barbara Middleton, Phyllis Wigner, Mr. and Mrs. Denzil Thompson and Mrs. Cecil Middleton.

The party was brought to an end with the guests offering their best wishes and singing "Now is the Hour."[187]

185   David Dalton, *James Dean: The Mutant King*, p. 54.
186   Val Holley, *James Dean: The Biography*, p. 30.
187   Qtd. In David Dalton, *James Dean: The Mutant King*, pp. 54-55.

CHAPTER 12—"THE ROAD NOT TAKEN"

Two roads diverged in a yellow wood,
And sorry I could not travel both
And be one traveler, long I stood
And looked down one as far as I could
To where it bent in the undergrowth;   5

Then took the other, as just as fair,
And having perhaps the better claim,
Because it was grassy and wanted wear;
Though as for that the passing there
Had worn them really about the same,   10

And both that morning equally lay
In leaves no step had trodden black.
Oh, I kept the first for another day!
Yet knowing how way leads on to way,
I doubted if I should ever come back.   15

I shall be telling this with a sigh
Somewhere ages and ages hence:
Two roads diverged in a wood, and I—
I took the one less traveled by,
And that has made all the difference.

--Robert Frost
"The Road Not Taken" (1920)

***

Jimmy must have anticipated his trip to California with some appre-hension. He would be living with his father Winton, a man he had little contact with over the last ten years. They wrote to one another, but the letters were brief and formal. And he would also be living with his stepmother, Ethel Case Dean, whom Winton had married four years after Mildred's death. According to David Dalton:

> Jimmy was polite enough to his stepmother, but she was a wom-an he never became close to; and, in the new family situation, they occupied mutually distrustful corners. Ethel never became one of Jimmy's "Moms" and is as absent from his story as his own mother is spectrally ever present.[188]

Unlike Jimmy's Quaker family back in Fairmount, who believed that he needed to find his own way in life, Winton Dean had definite plans for his son:

> Winton had selected Santa Monica City College as the school in which Jimmy should enroll for the fall. It was nearby and offered a good practical curriculum—business, teaching, physical educa-tion—courses you could use to earn a better living. Winton didn't realize that one of the reasons Jimmy had come to Los Angeles was because Indiana's Earlham College did not have a theater arts major. When Jimmy announced his desire to act, Winton didn't want to hear about it. The nine-year separation created a huge communication gap—Jimmy didn't want to fight with his father now that he was finally living with him again, and Winton had no idea how talented Jimmy was on a stage. Jimmy gave in to his father, but hoped to change his mind by the time fall registra-tion came.[189]

In an interview with Dalton, Bill Bast noted:

> Jimmy's father is very mid-mannered. Very quiet. I knew him in California because he was working at Sawtelle Hospital. But if

---

188   David Dalton, *James Dean: The Mutant King*, p.58.
189   David Dalton, *James Dean: The Mutant King*, p. 58.

you're looking for the source of Jimmy's dynamism you can forget his father.

"Jimmy related 'nicely' to his family. Very nicely. I can't imagine there ever being a family feud unless it was over something he couldn't have. He was always respectful and very kind. Overly kind, overly considerate. And generally gentle with his father. I don't think there was ever an unpleasant scene. Maybe once I think there was a little friction over the car. But not the kind of dynamic friction we would imagine.

"I couldn't see any family problems, though I know they were there. His father was very hard to approach and I know Jimmy wanted to extract more from him. And if you've met Marcus and Ortense, you can't imagine that they were very demonstrative or physically affectionate either. He looked for more, especially as a budding young actor. Jimmy was learning to respect the ability to value and demonstrate love and emotion...

"I don't think there were any specific difficulties between Jimmy and his father...but I always wondered why they didn't talk to one another. We'd go over to the house to get something and no one would say anything. We'd be there an hour and five words would be exchanged. And later Jimmy would interpret for me. 'Oh, he'll give it to me.' And I'd think, 'Really?' I never heard him say anything about it. They had their own language."[190]

Jimmy joined a summer stock company in Santa Monica that summer, where he acted under the stage name Byron James in a musical production called *the Romance of Scarlet Gulch.* He had just received a car from his father—a 1939 Chevy—in an attempt to bridge the gap between them. And the following item appeared in the *Fairmount News:*

JAMES DEAN JOINS THEATRE GROUP AT SANTA MONICA, CAL. Mr. and Mrs. Charles Dean received a letter last week from their grandson, Jimmy Dean, who recently went to Santa Monica, Calif., to make his home with his father, Winton Dean. He stated

---

190   David Dalton, *James Dean: The Mutant King,* p.59.

in his letter that he was enjoying his vacation bowling and playing golf with his father, and also wrote, "I have registered for summer and fall sessions at UCLA. I take a subject A English examination Monday. I am now a full-fledged member of the Miller Playhouse Theatre Guild troop. I wasn't in time to be cast in any production, but my knowledge of the stage and the ability to design and paint sets won me the place of head stage manager for the next production of four one-act plays, starting Thursday."[191]

He was careful not to mention that Bette McPherson from Fairmount had joined him in California. Not surprisingly, Bette McPherson's teaching contract had not been renewed for the following year at Fairmount High School. She decided to spend the summer with several female friends in Los Angeles who were from her hometown and who were also schoolteachers. Her cousin, Marjorie Armstrong, noted in an interview with Val Holley:

"Bette loved to go to bars...She just wanted to have a beer and talk. She wasn't promiscuous. I can assure you she wasn't an alcoholic."[192]

McPherson described her firing from Fairmount in an interview with Holley:

"I had been told that an apartment over a cocktail lounge was not a good place for a teacher to live...Then on weekends I would go with my boss, Joe Payne—who also happened to be president of the school board—to paint churches. Rumors started about him and me, and the superintendent called me in about it. I said, "Do you think I'm that hard up?' and that sounded worse than it was. This was my undoing. I was fired by the end of the 1949 school year."[193]

Holley continues:

McPherson said when she notified Dean she was coming, he was happy "because he would know someone with a car. [This was

191   David Dalton, *James Dean: The Mutant King*, p. 60.
192   Val Holley, *James Dean: The Biography*, p. 32.
193   Val Holley, *James Dean: The Biography*, p.32.

prior to his father's giving the Chevy to him.] When I arrived, my cousin was away for the weekend. So I called Jim and he found a place for us to stay that Sunday night. He took Julia and me to the place, drove my car on home, and came back for us the next morning.

"Jim didn't have anything to do that summer, so he went around with us. He showed us a lot—Alvarado Drive, Forest Lawn Cemetery, with lots of famous people buried there. I remember admiring the stained glass. I don't how on earth he knew so many places. He hadn't been in L.A. too much longer than I, and Winton certainly hadn't shown him..."[194]

Then came *The Romance of Scarlet Gulch,* described as "a melodrama with a California gold rush motif" in which James Dean billed himself as Byron James; he played Charlie Smooch, a habitual drunk.[195] Jimmy recruited McPherson to help him with the scenery. She later told Val Holley, "He wanted me to be in the play...I took him to rehearsals a lot. He didn't have a car, so we used mine. By this time, we were arguing a lot—all day."[196] Holley continues:

Dean's feelings for McPherson had grown intense. In spite of their eleven-year age difference, he asked her to marry him. "I said no," she recalled. "So he said we could just live together. He was hurt." In 1989, McPherson said she had lingering mixed emotions about discussing Dean. "It still makes me sad," she confessed. "Maybe if I would have stayed in L.A., he would still be alive, but not famous. Who knows?"[197]

Holley adds:

Despite his wounded feelings at her rejection of his marriage proposal, the two of them parted as friends when she returned to Indiana. "We kept in touch. He wrote—I didn't keep the letters," she later said. "I was supposed to meet him when he was back

---

194   Val Holley, *James Dean: The Biography,* p. 32
195   Val Holley, *James Dean: The Biography,* p. 33
196   Val Holley, *James Dean: The Biography,* p. 34
197   Val Holley, *James Dean: The Biography,* p. 34

*in Indiana the following summer, but couldn't make it. Actually, I
never saw him again. But we stayed in contact, because I called
him in Texas, during the filming of Giant, because I happened to
be in Albuquerque. Unfortunately, it was a weekend and the cast
was on a break. We were planning to get together at my cousin's
place in the summer of 1956."[198]*

Winton won out and Jimmy did not enroll in UCLA as planned, but
in Santa Monica College instead as a physical education major. He
compensated for his disappointment by enrolling in as many drama
classes as possible, where he met a sympathetic instructor named
Jean Owen. She took him under her wing and gave him the encouragement he needed. She later said in an interview which appeared
in an article "An Unforgettable Day with Jimmy Dean" in *Movieland*
Magazine:

*I never knew him to be a complex and difficult personality...Jimmy
was not moody, temperamental, unpredictable or rude. These
terms did not describe the Jimmy Dean I knew. When I read some
of the stories about Jimmy, it is almost as though I were reading
about another person entirely. I do not understand why so many
write about him as though he were a sort of juvenile delinquent.
He was never that. I never knew him to be untidy or rebellious. He
was always polite and thoughtful; his enthusiasm for everything
that pertained to the theatre was boundless.*

*Jimmy was in my radio class...When I first met him, I wasn't par-
ticularly impressed by his looks. He just seemed to be another college boy—quiet, shy, not prepossessing in size—and, of course, he
always wore glasses. I never realized what arresting eyes he had
until I saw him on a TV show in 1951. He was never aware of his
good looks. It was one of his more charming qualities.*

*One day in class, Jimmy read some scenes from Edgar Allen Poe's
"Telltale Heart." He was magnificent—but then he always had a
spectacular emotion for any scene he played. Later, during that
same class, I asked Jimmy to read some scenes from Hamlet. That
night when I returned home I informed my husband that I finally*

---

198   Val Holley, *James Dean: The Biography,* p. 35.

found the right student to play Hamlet as I felt it should be played. That student was, of course, Jimmy Dean."[199]

Val Holley sums up James Dean's freshman year of college as follows:

In some ways, Dean's freshman year was simply an extension of high school; once again he would have a nurturing drama teacher and go out for basketball and field events. He was still thoroughly Indianan that fall but would continue the process of social and intellectual climbing that had started with his emulation of James DeWeerd. He would pursue and date the homecoming queen [a young woman by the name of Dianne Hixon—that relationship also ended], campaign for and win membership in the Opheleos (an elite male service organization), and fraternize with students whose sophistication he hoped would rub off. "The Jim Dean we knew at Santa Monica," said Larry Swindell, "was entirely different from the Dean of legend", suggesting a personal evolution that has never really been tracked.[200]

Concerning his relationship with Dianne Hixon, Joe Hyams wrote that while she was "a slim, well-proportioned blonde," Jimmy broke up with her because—in the words of Bill Bast—"she was put off by the prospect of becoming a mother substitute."[201] A search of Ancestry.com yielded a picture of a young woman who may have been Diane Hixon in the 1954 UCLA Bruin Yearbook. The name is spelled "Hasin"—but school yearbooks are notorious for their misspelling of names. She appears to have been born in 1933.

David Dalton views it this way:

Jimmy was beginning to experiment with himself, expanding his repertoire of gesture and impersonation. He watched the way the California kids behaved, mimicking a beach boy's bop or a freshman's moon-faced stare. He wanted a reaction, an environment in which he could grow, but Winton and Ethel suffocated him with their lack of response. Bill Bast: "Like anybody when they first

---

199   David Dalton, James Dean: The Mutant King, p. 61.
200   Val Holley, James Dean: The Biography, p.35.
201   Joe Hyams, James Dean: Little Boy Lost, p. 35.

*learn something, Jimmy went home and tried it out on the folks,
and the folks recoiled. They didn't want to deal with anything like
that. They didn't want to feel. They didn't want to express something they're not used to expressing."*

*Jimmy's need for feedback and the ensuing ferocities of rejection
were never expressed against Winton but waited for release in
East of Eden and Rebel Without a Cause.*[202]

Having outgrown the boundaries of Santa Monica College and the
confines of his home, in the fall of 1950, Jimmy finally entered UCLA
as a drama student and the Sigma Nu Fraternity.

***

*"I have more important things to do than sit around and listen to
some old moss-walled academician!"*

James Dean's comments about his experience at UCLA may not have
been too far afield. In a 2005 Commencement Address at Stanford
University, Steve Jobs, founder and CEO of Apple Computer noted
that this commencement was the closest he came to a college graduation. Jobs said that he dropped out of college and then dropped in
on the only courses appealing to him. Had he not dropped in on a
calligraphy class, Apple Computer would never have been![203] (After
thirty years of teaching, I have reached the conclusion that the "hal-
lowed halls of ivy" are indeed "moss-walled" and often stifle those
who find lecture notes cumbersome and bars to real learning.)

According to the Picture Show 1890-1960 Website, Winton threw
Jimmy out of his house when he refused to give up the idea of becoming an actor, although I'm not sure whose decision made the major
part for the move. I believe that his move was by mutual agreement:

---

202   David Dalton, *James Dean: The Mutant King*, p. 62.
203   "You've Got to Find the Job You Love: Text of Steve Jobs Commencement
Address, Stanford University, June 12, 2005. Stanford University News
Website. Accessed October 7, 2011. Available at: http://news.stanford.edu/
news/2005/june15/jobs-061505.html

After graduation James returned to California to live with his father, and at the beginning of the following year (1950) enrolled at Santa Monica City College where he majored in pre–law. The following semester, however, he switched to UCLA (*The University of California*, Los Angeles) and immediately changed his major to Theater Arts. This change of major enraged his father who suddenly refused to support James any longer. His father believed strongly that "acting" would get James nowhere in life, and after a number of impassioned arguments he finally kicked James out of his home. They would never again be fully reconciled.[204]

In the fall of 1950, Jimmy was living on his own and was a theater arts major at UCLA. He landed the part of Malcolm in *Macbeth,* which was UCLA's first major theatrical production that year. He was ecstatic over the part and wrote home about it:

> *"The biggest thrill of my life came three weeks ago...after a week of grueling auditions for UCLA's four major theatrical productions, the major one being Shakespeare's Macbeth which will be presented in Royce Hall (seats 1600). After the auditioning of 367 actors and actresses, I came up with a wonderful lead in Macbeth the character being Malcolm (huge part)..."[205]*

Bill Bast wasn't so impressed, as he noted in his book, *James Dean: A Biography:*

> In the darkness of Royce Hall Auditorium I slipped deeper into my seat and braced myself for more garbled Shakespeare. The unimpressive figure wearing a kilt stepped forward on the badly lighted rehearsal stage. I froze in anticipation. He spoke.
>
> "We shall not spind a large expinse of time berfer we reckon with yer several loves, and make us evin with you...

---

204   James Dean: Hollywood's Rebel, The Picture Show Man 1890-1960 Website: Articles—Personalities: The History of Motion Pictures. Accessed January 5, 2012. Copyright 2004-2012, Key Light Enterprises, L.L.C. Available online at http://www.pictureshowman.com/articles_personalities_dean.cfm

205   Qtd in David Dalton, *James Dean: The Mutant King*, p. 63.

"We will perform in misure, time, and place, So thanks to all at once and to each one, whom we invite to see us crown'd at Scone."

Like an agonizing dental extraction, it was over, but the pain lingered. I turned to an anonymous Theater Arts student seated next to me and asked, "Who is that?"

I would have preferred to know how whoever-it-was got cast in this production of Macbeth, but around campus a question like that smacked too much of envy.

"Dunno," came the answer.

The slouched young man with the bad diction on stage was obviously going to remain an enigma. Then, out of the blackness from a distant corner of the empty auditorium, a name was dropped.

"James Dean" came the harsh whisper out of the void, followed by an appreciative snicker from another direction.

"James Dean," I remarked to myself. "A name to forget."[206]

Jimmy's stint at UCLA was short-lived. According to Dr. Walden Boyle, a professor at UCLA, "I didn't think he was happy in school. I guess the university life was much too slow for him. I got the feeling he wanted to act and nothing more than that, so he didn't take to the rest of the academic requirements."[207] Dalton adds:

A friend at Santa Monica, Richard Shannon, actually spoke of Jimmy using images of light: "He was like a rainbow. You don't ever see one color; you see a maze of them. Nothing stands out in my memory of Jimmy but a bright light."[208]

A number of breaks happened for Jimmy, taking him in the direction where he was headed. The Coke commercial came first, followed by the Pepsi commercial (which I recall seeing in the 1950s.) Then came "Hill Number One", an Easter special in which James Dean played

---

206   William Bast, *James Dean: The Biography,* p. 1
207   David Dalton, *James Dean: The Mutant King,* p. 63.
208   David Dalton, *James Dean: The Mutant King,* p. 63.

John the Apostle.[209] He had a cold during the production, giving him a raspy voice. David Dalton describes the experience:

> Hill Number One brought Jimmy his first fan club and his first reli-gious following: The Immaculate Heart James Dean Appreciation Society. The girls at the Immaculate Heart High School had been required to watch the television show, and they thought Jimmy's St. John was divine. They contacted him through his agent (though his Malcolm was a critical failure, agent Isabelle Draesmer had taken him on as a client) and requested he attend a party in his honor.
>
> Bill Bast went along with him to the party, which was lucky for Jimmy because they ended up pushing his car the last block and a half. "A lot of giggling went on as far as I recall. They made a cake for him," said Bill. "The girls were between fourteen and eighteen. It was one of those embarrassing affairs where everyone just ands around a lot. Jimmy got to play the star to the hilt and he loved it, and don't think he didn't take full advantage of the situation."[210]

James Dean's situation at the Sigma Nu Fraternity house deteriorated over the semester. He was more interested in acting than in the re-quirements of the "brothers" and spent his time in Hollywood and Burbank, looking for parts and an eventual studio contract. While on an expedition one day, he ran into Bill Bast, who was also searching for parts, and suggested that they would make a great team. Jimmy had been evicted from Sigma Nu and was in search of a new resi-dence—something he could not handle on his own. He definitely did not want to return to Winton and Ethel's house. As David Dalton notes:

> Jimmy had a capacity for binding apparent strangers dramati-cally into his toils and making them almost his closest friends on the spot—even those who did not care to become involved in his life—as casually as fate. "In the flat glare of the bus lights I could

---

209   NOTE: James Dean's part in "Hill No. 1" was that of John the Apostle, also called John the Beloved. Some writer's have erroneously identified him as John the Baptist (who was not one of the Apostles.)
210   David Dalton, *James Dean: The Mutant King*, p.67

see his intense blue eyes peering out at me from behind his thick lenses, magnifying the sincerity of his expression" Bill recalled. *Jimmy outlined his irresistible scheme to Bill and, like D'Artagnan and Porthos, they found themselves in their steel carriage hurtling toward some unknown destiny.*[211]

They found their "dream place"; however, Jimmy's behavior was highly unpredictable:

Bill found living with Jimmy a stimulating, but rather unnerving, experience. For one thing, he could turn off his magnetic charm as abruptly as it appeared. He employed its surging power defensively and aggressively, and often almost ruthlessly, rarely staying long enough in any one place or with any particular friend to form a lasting bond. This way he became a tantalizing blur, irritating those upon whom he intruded and infuriating those who would have liked to know him better.

Far from being the promised "team," Bill found Jimmy secretive about almost everything he did—and the more tense Jimmy became about his role as an actor, the more furtive he would be, reluctant to discuss his sullen art. "I sometimes had the feeling that he thought that by talking about the job, or admitting that it even existed, he would lose it," Bill said. "Once or twice it seemed to me that he was hoarding his pleasure and excitement for fear that I, or someone else, might steal it from him if he left it unguarded.[212]

Then came Beverly Wills and the fight that would end their friendship for a while. Dalton describes their meeting:

The girl in the picture is Beverly Wills, one of Jimmy's dates, who was articulate and sensitive enough to give us a picture of Jimmy during what must have been one of the most insecure periods of his life. She is the daughter of the late comedienne Joan Davis. Bill had met Beverly at CBS, where she played "Fluffy Adams" on a weekly radio show. She first met Jimmy on a double date—

---

211   David Dalton, *James Dean: The Mutant King,* p. 69
212   David Dalton, *"James Dean: The Mutant King,"* pp. 69-70.

Beverly with Bill and Jimmy with Jeanetta Lewis, a classmate from the Theater Arts Department at UCLA:

"I thought he was pretty much of a creep until we got to the picnic and then all of a sudden he came to life. We began to talk about acting and Jimmy lit up. He told me how interested he was in the Stanislavsky method, where you not only act out people, but things too.

"Look," said Jimmy, "I'm a palm tree in a storm." He held his arms out and waved wildly. To feel more free, he impatiently tossed off his cheap, tight blue jacket. He looked bigger as soon as he did, because you could see his broad shoulders and powerful build. Then he got wilder and pretended he was a monkey. He climbed a big tree and swung from a high branch. Dropping from the branch, he landed on his hands like a little kid who was suddenly turned loose. He even laughed like a little boy, chuckling uproariously at ever little thing. Once in the spotlight, he ate it up and had us all in stitches all afternoon. The "creep" turned into the hit of the party."[213]

They double-dated for a while, and then Beverly made the announcement to Bill concerning her relationship with Jimmy:

"Bill, there's something we have to tell you," she said without looking at him. "It's Jimmy and me. I mean, we're in love."

There was a long pause, during which I [Bill] imagined I was supposed to react. I could think of nothing to say. I wasn't shocked by the announcement, since I had not become emotionally involved with Beverly. I seriously doubted 'love' would have been the word Jimmy would have chosen...I knew him better than that. But he made no effort to correct her.

"We tried not to let it happen," she explained with all the sincerity at her command. "But there was nothing we could do. These things just happen."

---

213   David Dalton, *"James Dean: The Mutant King,"* pp. 70-71.

Beverly was only eighteen at the time and she had seen a lot of movies.[214]

The blow up happened when Jeanetta Lewis heard the news. She and Jimmy were still dating, and she didn't appreciate being two-timed, as is evidenced by her exclamation: "Why, the two-timing little weasel!"[215]So she convinced Bill Bast to move out of the apartment and leave Jimmy to fend for himself. That news did not sit well with James Dean. Bill Bast describes the encounter:

As the car slid up to the curb across the street from the Penthouse, we could see Jimmy, prepared to greet us, blocking the walkway. He was standing there, arms folded, glowering at us with a look that far exceeded anger. Obviously the landlady had rushed to him with the news, after my phone call. He had had plenty of time to let his anger grow to the stage of violence.

"You'd better stay in the car," I advised Jeanetta, remembering the torn photograph.

As I went to face my adversary, he removed his glasses and drew threw them onto the lawn.

"You dirty little snake!" he hissed, and grabbed me by the throat. He was so furious the words stuck on his tongue, rendering him inarticulate. He pulled me within focus and ripped my insides apart with the hatred in his tear-filled eyes.

"If you're going to do it, do it!" I cried out at him.

Jeanetta, who had come running when he grabbed me, was tugging at his sleeve.

"Cut it out," he warned her.

"If you're going to hit somebody, why don't you hit somebody who won't hit back? That's your speed, isn't it?"

"Get off my back! This doesn't concern you," he spat at her.

---

214   David, Dalton, *James Dean: The Mutant King,* p. 71
215   William Bast, *James Dean: A Biography,* p. 43.

"Oh, yes it does! I talked him into it," she insisted.

Jimmy loosened his grip on my throat.

"C'mon, Jimmy, hit me!" she needled. "I can't defend myself."

"Just shut up, or I will!"

She tugged harder at his arm. "Oh, you're brave! Big brave man! C'mon, get some real satisfaction. Why don't you—"

He released his hold on me and smashed her across the face with all the violence he had accumulated. She staggered backward.

"Oh, you can do better than that," she insisted, tears flooding her eyes. "C'mon, Jimmy, hit me again, why don't you?"

Before I could grab his arms, he had smashed her twice more across the mouth, this time drawing blood. I steadied him, and the sight of the blood drained him of resistance.

Somehow I managed to get them both upstairs into the Penthouse. Jeanetta became sick and went into the bathroom, where she made terrible retching sounds. Jimmy fell apart, apologizing profusely for his animal behavior. I was shaken and ignored him, packing my clothes quickly. He turned his attention to Jeanetta, whose performance had completely unstrung him, and attentively offered her handkerchiefs, aspirin, anything that would help stop the bleeding and the sickness. He ran downstairs to the landlady to borrow a tea bag so that he could make her some hot tea.

"I'm not really sick. Let him squirm a little," she confided when he was gone.

"I think we've had enough. Maybe you'd better lay off."

"No," she laughed. "I'm enjoying this."

Jimmy returned with the tea and put some water on to boil, all the time apologizing to Jeanetta, comforting her, and explaining himself to me. The more he apologized, the more I hated myself. I couldn't even talk. All I could think of was getting out of that place as fast as possible. Jeanetta continued the performance, obviously pleased with the effect of her acting.

I gathered my things and moved them down to the car. On the last trip I picked up the remaining suitcase and told Jeanetta I was ready to go. Jimmy began to cry. Whoever said revenge was sweet had evidently never tasted it.

"So long, Bill," he said, offering his hand for me to shake.

For a long moment I looked at his hand. Then, with a helpless shrug, I shook my head and left."[216]

[A search of Ancestry.com yielded two photographs of Jeanetta Lewis, an attractive brunette: one photo in the 1950 UCLA Bruin Yearbook and the second in the 1951 UCLA Bruin. She appears to have been born in 1930 or 1931 , and she was in the theater department at UCLA. I could find nothing further about her. However, I located three marriage records for a Jeanetta Lewis and one divorce record. I don't know whether any of these records pertain to the Jeanetta Lewis in this narrative. Since I was unable to decide upon her most recent married name, the Social Security Death Index could not be used. There was one thing I noticed from the pictures, however. Jeannetta Lewis bore some resemblance to James Dean's mother!]

Jimmy was on the move again since he couldn't afford the penthouse by himself. He first moved in with Ted Avery, another usher at CBS, and then moved in with Rogers Brackett, who quickly became a significant individual in the life of James Dean. Jimmy was working as a parking lot attendant when he first met Brackett. Val Holley writes:

Why would Dean accept the amenities and charms Rogers Brackett could offer?" "Jimmy was an opportunist," says Isabel Draesemer. "He would latch onto anyone who could do something for him." But Brackett, beyond his usefulness, was an immensely appealing and entertaining fellow. "Dean must have been impressed with Rogers's great flair and style and, above all, by Rogers's abundant store of movie history, lore and gossip from D. W. Griffith to

*Thelma Todd to Paul Bern to whoever might be the centerpiece
of this morning's scandale," says a close friend of Brackett. "The
Rogers that Dean first encountered must have been charming
and full of droll fun: the sophisticated sprite who could make you
laugh at and embrace Hollywood's dream factory at the same
moment. And he may have been quite as ardent in his private life
as he was witty publicly."[217]*

No doubt, Jimmy drew comparisons between Rogers Brackett and
James DeWeerd. According to Ron Martinetti in *The James Dean
Story:*

*A tall, curly-haired bachelor with good looks and an elegant man-
ner, Brackett was some fifteen years Dean's senior. He was the
son of Robert Brackett, an early Hollywood film producer who
was once in partnership with Lewis J. Selznick. Born in Culver City,
Brackett had literally been raised in Hollywood, and his connections in the film industry were numerous. He had served an ap-
prenticeship with David O. Selznick, Lewis's son, and had worked
at the Walt Disney Studio. He had left the film business to accept
a high-paying position with the advertising firm of Foote, Cone,
and Belding as account supervisor. One of his accounts sponsored
Alias Jane Doe, and Brackett doubled as the show's director, an
arrangement that was not uncommon.[218]*

James Dean parked his car one night and made it known that he
was an actor as soon as he learned about Brackett's connections.
Martinetti continues:

*A brilliant stage director, Brackett had had the first Equity com-
pany in California, and he began to coach Dean in plays and readings. They rehearsed Hamlet on the grand staircase of the Sunset
Plaza, overlooking the pool. "Elsinor with room service," Rogers
quipped. Then, for contrast, Dean would recite some poems by
James Whitcomb Riley he had learned as a boy. "'Little Orphant*

217   Val Holley, *James Dean: The Biography,* p. 3.
218   Ron Martinetti, *The James Dean Story*, p. 36.

Annie' was quite one of his favorites," Brackett remembers. "It was very funny and very touching..."[219]

Although Jimmy first learned about bullfighting through James DeWeerd, he would actually see it in action through Rogers Brackett:

> *Along with David Wayne, the actor, and his wife, Dean and Rogers went to Tijuana for a weekend to see a bullfight, first staying overnight in Laguna. Another time, Dean traveled with Brackett to Mexicali where they saw the matador Arruza in the ring. In Mexicali Jimmy met Budd Boetticher, a movie director and bullfight aficionado who had served as technical adviser for the film Blood and Sand. Boetticher gave Dean a blood-stained cape that had once belonged to Sidney Franklin, the Brooklyn-bred matador who had achieved fame in the rings of Spain and about whom Hemingway had written.*

> *The cape became Dean's prized possession and, thereafter, wherever he traveled, the cape traveled with him.*[220]

Concerning their relationship, Brackett told Ron Martinetti:

> *"Jimmy was like a child," Brackett said. "He behaved badly just to get attention." But he added, "He was a kid I loved—sometimes parentally, sometimes not parentally."*[221]

Martinetti continues:

> *Like a child, too, Dean seemed to be forever testing the affection of those closest to him. "The only way he could be sure you really loved him," another friend, Stewart Stern, later said, "was if you loved him when he was truly at his worst."*[222]

Brackett secured numerous radio parts, television parts and some small parts in three motion pictures for James Dean: *Sailor Beware, Fixed Bayonets,* and *Has Anybody Seen My Gal?*

---

219   Ron Martinetti, *The James Dean Story*, p.38
220   Ron Martinetti, *The James Dean Story*, p. 39.
221   Ron Martinetti, *The James Dean Story*, p.40
222   Ron Martinetti, *The James Dean Story*, p. 40

There was also in a Toni commercial on the radio—a commercial for Toni home permanents--which I remember from childhood! Against a background of violin music the "husband" crooned lovely words to his "wife" about her beautiful hair. My mother kept her kitchen radio turned on throughout the day, so I heard this commercial frequently in the early afternoon. The minute the violins struck the air waves, I waltzed around our dining room table, mimicking the playing of a violin and then crooning beautiful words to my dolls, and I did this each time I heard that commercial. Years later I would read that the "husband crooner" was James Dean. And years later, I would also read about the difficult time he had recording that commercial. The "wife" was a comedienne who kept making faces at him from the other side of the microphone, causing him to "crack up." He finally had to not look at her in order to get through it!

Brackett also introduced Jimmy to a world of books he had never encountered:

> *Rogers gave him books to read by writers like Saint-Exupery and Camus, and introduced him to a movie house on Fairfax that showed silent films. Dean absorbed all this excitedly, asking for more. "He sapped the minds of his friends," Bast once noted, "like a bloodsucker saps the strength of an unsuspecting man."*

> *But Dean's intelligence was largely intuitive, Brackett felt. He amazed Rogers with his ability to do mime, though he had never seen a performance. Once Dean surprised him by making a mobile, using wire and some chicken bones that had been left over from dinner the night before. When Rogers told him how much he liked the mobile, Jimmy answered, "What's a mobile?"*[223]

It was through Rogers Brackett that James Dean first encountered *The Little Prince*—his favorite book, although he stated to someone that he did a dramatic reading of the book in his drama class in high school. The friendship ended eventually. Later, Alec Wilder made Jimmy sit down and write Brackett a letter, thanking him for all the things he had done for him. Brackett, who was born September 30, 1916, died of throat cancer August 20, 1979.

---

223   Ron Martinetti, *The James Dean Story*, p. 37.

James Dean had long departed from UCLA. Patience was not one of his virtues, and he grew steadily impatient. According to David Dalton:

> ...Jimmy was one of a group of students who weren't satisfied with bit parts or "moss-walled academicians" as Jimmy later referred to the university atmosphere. They wanted the kind of experimental classes that Strasberg and Kazan were conducting at the Actors Studio in New York...

> Never one to give credit to anyone but himself for his ascendancy ("No one helps you," he said to Hedda Hopper in a reverse switch on long-established Hollywood pieties. "You do it yourself."), he nevertheless considered [James] Whitmore—at that time an up and coming actor from the New York school—a great catalyst in his career.

> "I owe a lot to Whitmore. I guess you can say he saved me when I got all mixed up. One thing he said helped more than anything. He told me I didn't know the difference between acting as a soft job and acting as a difficult art.

> People ask me these ridiculous questions like, "When did you first decide to become an actor?"...I don't know that there was ever any such time. I realized I was an actor because of James Whitmore.

> There's always someone in your life who opens up your eyes. For me, that's Whitmore. He made me see myself. He opened me up, gave me the key."[224]

Jimmy's elated mood evaporated when the summer of 1951 came to an end and jobs in Hollywood became scarce again. He was dating Beverly Wills as his steady. She later recalled:

> I soon learned that it was nothing for Jimmy to run through a whole alphabet of emotions in one evening. His moods of happiness were now far outweighed by his moods of deep despair.

---

224   David Dalton, *James Dean: The Mutant King,* p.72

He was almost constantly in a blue funk. He still couldn't get an acting job and he was growing increasingly bitter. I hated to see Jimmy become so blue. When he was happy, there was no one more lovable. When he was depressed, he wanted to die.

These low moods became so violent that he began to tell me that he was having strange nightmares in which he dreamed he was dying. The nightmares began to give him a certain phobia about death.[225]

Their love affair lasted until the summer of 1951. David Dalton states that it ended "in a sudden outburst of petty jealousy, the result of gradually aggravating pressures."[226] It happened when Jimmy saw her dancing with someone else. According to Beverly, "Jimmy saw red. He grabbed the fellow by the collar and threatened to blacken both of his eyes...I ran out to the beach and Jimmy walked after me, scuffing angrily at the sand, complete misery on his face. We had an argument and I pulled his gold football off the chain."[227] Then he called her to say goodbye and tell her he was leaving for New York: "I was glad he called," she said. "I had been thinking of Jimmy ever since we broke off, and I realized more and more that this was a hurt and misunderstood boy. I wanted to remain his friend. I wished him luck."[228],[229]

In summing up James Dean's experiences in California during that two-year period, David Dalton writes:

His two years in California had been a series of steadily deteriorating relationships—first with his father and stepmother, then the grotesque parody of brotherhood at Sigma Nu, then the alienation of his only intimate friend, Bill Bast—and by the end of the

---

225   Qtd. In David Dalton, *James Dean: The Mutant King,* p.73.
226   Qtd. In David Dalton, *James Dean: The Mutant King,* p. 73
227   Qtd. In David Dalton, *James Dean: The Mutant King,* p. 74
228   Qtd. In David Dalton, *James Dean: The Mutant King,* p. 74
229   Beverly Wills died in a house fire October 24, 1963 with her grandmother, Nina Davis, and her two children by her first husband, Alan Grossman. Her second husband was Martin Colbert. Beverly Wills Biography, IMDb Website. Accessed September 30, 2011. Available at http://www.imdb.com

summer he had managed to sever himself from Beverly too. He had shrunk to a pulsing nuclear knot, a critical mass waiting to explode.

"Jimmy was very sensitive and it hurt him very much to be looked down on," Beverly said about the way her friends at Paradise Cove treated Jimmy. "He sensed their patronizing attitude and withdrew deeper and deeper into a shell. I think he wanted to hurt them back too. I've often wondered if he recalled this period in his life when he portrayed the sensitive feelings of the rejected youth in Rebel Without a Cause."

These tiny slights—the wrong clothes, hair that just won't do, a shyness that keeps poking through—are the huge animals of the teenage nightmare, the agony of exposure, grafts that will not take. It is a misery in which monsters crawl. Jimmy later relished his role as loner, but it was something else to be helplessly impelled toward it. In his films he played this mirror image of his own life against solid backgrounds, but here was stripped of all Method handles in an unnerving, slippery free fall. He depicted this sensation of a person being absorbed into an element he cannot recognize in a painting described by Bill Bast: "It was an oil and portrayed the skeleton of a man, stretched over with nothing but horrid green skin, who was standing waist deep in the mire which flowed through a long sewerlike tunnel that diminished in perspective. His head and one arm raised upward, as if pleading to be saved, he was slowly melting into and becoming part of the very mire that flowed beneath him. Jimmy titled the picture 'Man in Woman's Womb.'"[230]

James Dean left California for New York City in the fall of 1951. David Dalton notes: "Beverly's recollection of her goodbye to Jimmy reads like a transparent poem as he ambles forlornly toward an eastern vanishing point:

I kissed him

On the cheek, wished

---

230   David Dalton, *James Dean: The Mutant King.* pp. 74-75.

Him well, and watched

Him walk down the street.

He

Kicked at some stones

Like a little boy scuffling

Down the street, and he

Stopped under a lamppost

To light a cigarette.

Then

He squared his shoulders,

Turned the corner,

And was gone...[231]

---

231   David Dalton, *James Dean: The Mutant King.* p. 75.

SECTION THREE
THE CREATION OF "JAMES DEAN"

James Dean in Indianapolis
*February 1955. Photo taken during his last
trip to Indiana by Bob Middleton.*

CHAPTER 13—"NEW YORK! NEW YORK!"

*A*t first I couldn't see anyone. Then, as my eyes adjusted to the darkness, I noticed a young man slumped in a couch against the far wall. He hadn't bothered to remove his rain coat. He was rumpled from head to foot. Soggy and wet. So soggy, you could practically see the steam rising from him. His feet were on the coffee table. God forbid Miss Carleton should walk in and see such wanton disregard for her precious furniture! The light played across his sandy hair and boyish face. His glasses had slipped far down his nose, and he appeared to be reading a magazine. Now, here is someone different, I thought to myself. The flash was instant.

I plopped myself down on the small couch across from him and picked up a magazine from the coffee table. We were the only two people in the huge room...total strangers. But the patter of rain on the windows, and the soft lamplight falling on our shoulders, made everything seem very intimate. He looked up, nodded at me, and smiled. I nodded back, and we both returned to reading our magazines.

I didn't want him to see me staring, so I would sneak a peek every time I turned a page. He was smoking and I liked the way he put his cigarette to his lips, gracefully cocking his head as he inhaled, his hand covering his chin. He had a manner that made him seem manly and self-assured far beyond his years. He started to mumble something. But he wasn't talking to me, and it took a minute before I realized that he was reading out loud:

"Although the birds returned tethered to oranges," he said...and then there was a long pause, as though he was waiting. I decided to take a chance. Glancing down at my own magazine, I read *some gibberish. Words taken from here and there that made no sense together:*

"Egg salad sandwiches were raining everywhere."

Without looking up, he added another line. "The pancakes of the Universe fell through the cracks..."

"Who reinvented the future if not Mother Goose?...That's what I want to know," I read back.

Back and forth, on and on, we kept up this surreal exchange until we were both howling with laughter.

"Who are you?" he finally asked me. "I'm Jimmy."

I sat up, suddenly struggling to catch my breath. My stomach did a little flip-flop.

"I'm Dizzy."[232]

When James Dean arrived in New York, it is as though his whole life pulled together into a single focus. David Dalton notes that while he had been frustrated in California, "It is here in New York that Jimmy gathers visibility. He would no longer be anonymous."[233] Dalton continues:

> *Within two years he would "press the Broadway theater to its feet," within three years he would "conquer Hollywood" and within four years he would be dead.[234]*

The sights and sounds of New York must have terrified Jimmy at first. He had a small hotel room off Times Square and did not stray too far from the building. He wrote:

---

232   Liz Sheridan, *Dizzy & Jimmy: My Life with James Dean—a Love Story*, pp. 10-12.

233   David Dalton, *James Dean: The Mutant King*, p. 78.

234   David Dalton, *James Dean: The Mutant King*, p. 78.

"For the first few weeks I was so confused that I strayed only a couple of blocks from my hotel off Times Square. I would see three movies a day in an attempt to escape from my loneliness and depression. I spent most of my limited funds just on seeing movies..."[235]

Marcus and Ortense Winslow and James DeWeerd gave him the money when he stopped to see them while on his way to New York, enabling him to get a room at a midtown YMCA. He later wrote to another lover, Barbara Glenn:

"...across from Leon and Eddies, and above the so called Brown Derby and the Flamingo, and the Famous Door, and the Harem, and...It's so lovely! In the pensiveness of night the cheap, monotonous shrill, symbolic, sensual beat of suggestive drums tattoos orgyistic images on my brain. The smell of gin and 90 cent beer, entwine with the sometimes suspenceful slow, sometimes labored static, sometimes motionless, sometimes painfully rigid, till finally the long awaited for jerks and convulsions that fill the now thick chewing gum haze with a mist of sweat, fling the patrons into a fit of suppressed joy. The fated 7 days a week bestial virgin bows with the poise of a drunken pavlova. Rivilets of stale perspiration glide from and between her once well formed anatomy to the anxious, welcoming front-row celebrities who lap it up with infamous glee. The Aura of Horror. I live above it and below it. It is now 6:30 Monday morning and if I wish; the drawer to my left, 2nd from the bottom is filled with a collection of not so subtle representation of the more imaginative. Photographs and drawings. I did not ask for this; I did not seek it; it is. It is my Divine Comedy. The Dante of 52nd Street. There is no peace in our world. I love you.

"I would like to write about nicer things or fiction but we shouldn't avoid reality should we? The things I have just written are the truth. They are very hard to write about. I am lonely. Forgive me. I am lonely."[236]

235 David Dalton, *James Dean: The Mutant King*, p. 78.
236 David Dalton, *James Dean: The Mutant King*, pp. 78-79

He carried a letter from Rogers Brackett, but that opened no doors for him in the beginning. Finally, he was hired to be a stunt tester for a television show called "Beat the Clock". His job was to test the stunts prior to their being performed in front of the camera. (Note: "Beat the Clock" is another show I remember watching regularly, and it was one of the most popular shows of the time.) David Dalton notes:

> ...Audiences love nothing more than to watch normal people making fools of themselves for money by attempting "impossible" stunts.

> But they were possible, and week after week for one year, one person singlehandedly solved all of them, thereby justifying the impossible logic of nursey rhymes, of dishes and spoons, cows and moons, candles and cats. The conjurer who mastered all of these feats was, of course, Jimmy Dean, that athlete of transcendence.[237]

Jimmy quickly and carefully selected those elements from the New York environment that he wanted to acquire. According to David Dalton, in describing "the man who invented himself":

> He was both mechanic and machine, and his creation was to have monstrous proportions, for as Victor Frankenstein had said, "with the scarcity of parts these days, why make a midget?"

> Even before he tried out for the Actors Studio, Jimmy was a student of the Stanislavsky method. Combing the city streets with a derelict's fever, Jimmy would pick up a soft, round moment from a fat lady at a lunch counter or steal a wink from an orphaned eye. Stanislavsky, the founder of "Method" acting, recommended collecting these awful treasures to his students—a repertoire of gestures and mannerisms—the material of life from which an actor can build a character:

> Both a cat and an elephant can walk, wiggle its ears, wag its tail. But each has its own distinct way of doing it. Master these differences. Ask yourself—is it hard for a fat man to turn his neck? How

---

237   David Dalton, *James Dean: The Mutant King*, p. 79

does he sit down, stand up? Does he eat and drink in a certain way? Do not pretend; do not overact as if you were fat. Observe fat men in life and try as correctly as possible to reproduce them.[238]

He finally outgrew the confines of the room at the YMCA and went searching for a new situation. That's when he met Dizzy Sheridan, the daughter of pianist Frank Sheridan, in the lobby of the Rehearsal Club. The two became inseparable. And it was Dizzy Sheridan who noticed how his features could change:

...his habit of taking whatever he needed to complete the image he kept of himself in his mind's eyes. She said of his larcenies: "He would take from people—he took their voices, their expressions, their gestures, and it would become part of him without his having to work on it. I don't think he did it so much as it overtook him because he was so impressionable."[239]

According to Dizzy:

"Sometimes he would come home and be a completely different person. Like later when he was in See the Jaguar [his first Broadway role] and was working with Arthur Kennedy, who's kind of big, blustery, drinks and is loud—which Jimmy isn't. Well, that wasn't so good. But fortunately these stages would never last too long."[240]

Dizzy and Jimmy shared an apartment together, which they couldn't afford. Dizzy continues:

"...so Jimmy left to live with Jim Sheldon, a friend of Rogers Brackett, which he didn't want to do—but that's another story. I got a room on Eighth Avenue that was about as big as this coffee table.

"Jimmy came and spent a couple of nights there, and we would have a ball pretending we knew Elsa Maxwell and we planned a big party and made lists of all the people we were going to invite.

---

238   David Dalton, *James Dean: The Mutant King,* p.82.
239   David Dalton, *James Dean: The Mutant King*, p. 83.
240   Qtd. In David Dalton, *James Dean: The Mutant King*, p. 83.

You couldn't even open the door all the way in this place because the bed got in the way.

"I guess it was time for us to break up, because when we were together we were both hiding out. We stayed in a lot and clung to each other. But you can't live that way for very long. Our lives were full of fantasy and we were so young, with long futures ahead of us, and of course we would be together forever to share it. There's a point in your life when everything seems to be forever. And you should never lose that. But it's good to pull yourself together once in a while and I realize that it's not forever."[241]

Noting that true to his Quaker stoicism, James Dean never "elaborated on the lean days in New York," David Dalton found other people who would tell those stories:

"Once I found out he'd gone for two days without eating," said television writer Frank Wayne. "You know how I found out? Well, we had a sponsor that made tapioca pudding. And we always had gallons of it around because the commercials were live in those days. And after the show we'd throw it away. So one day Jimmy came up to me and said, 'Hey, Frank, if you're gonna throw that pudding away, can I have it?' And I said, "You sure you want to eat a lot of tapioca?' And he said, 'Man, anything would taste good right now. I haven't had anything to eat in two days.' So I gave him the pudding and took him out to dinner as well."[242]

It was through James Sheldon that James Dean met his future agent, Jane Deacy. Val Holley writes:

"When I first met Jane," said Sheldon, "I was not married. She was a switchboard operator at the Shurr Agency. I wanted tickets for a show that Shurr handled, and the agent said there were none left. 'But,' I was told, her switchboard operator's husband doesn't like the theater and she has tickets; why not go with her?' So Jane Deacy was a 'blind date.' We got along very well..."[243]

241   Qtd. In David Dalton, *James Dean: The Mutant King,* p. 83.
242   David Dalton, *James Dean: The Mutant King,* p. 84.
243   Val Holley, *James Dean: The Biography,* p. 99.

Sheldon continues:

> *"Jimmy had become a responsibility, and I had a wife, and a social life, and a career... He started to be a pest—in a nice way—and I didn't have much time for him. I sent him to Doris Quinland on Mama, Bob Stevens on Suspense, and to other people. But I realized he needed someone to take care of him, and thought Jane Deacy would be good for him. He needed someone to talk to, and she would be good, instead of him talking to me. It wasn't that I was annoyed by him; we were always friendly. It was just a matter of who could help him more."*[244]

Jane Deacy never wavered in her refusal to discuss Jimmy with the media or with writers. Val Holley estimates their first meeting about May 1952: "As such, she had no role in Dean's early television jobs, which he got principally through Sheldon and Brackett. When they met, she was still with the Shurr Agency; she became a solo agent in August 1952."[245] Reportedly, she kept a photograph of James Dean on her desk for years, until George C. Scott raised an objection about it. She immediately put the photo away and ended up exclusively representing Scott.

Then Bill Bast relocated to New York. Val Holley writes: "He phoned Dean and then found his way to the Brackett-Dean residence on West Twenty-third street, only to discover that his old friend had fallen back into a heavy sleep."[246] [A known insomniac, Jimmy would suddenly crash any time, any place, anywhere!] Shortly after his arrival, Jimmy introduced Bill to Dizzy Sheridan, whom he liked immediately. Bill describes an afternoon in Central Park:

> *The hour or so in the park eased my worried mind. Arriving unprepared in a new place, I had many plans to make, and concern for my future pressed heavy on my mind. But laughter soothes all strain, and my friends had made me laugh.*

---

244 Val Holley, *James Dean: The Biography,* p. 99.
245 Val Holley, *James Dean: The Biography,* p. 99.
246 Val Holley, *James Dean: The Biography,* p. 100

"Well, I've got to take off," I announced, refreshed. "Got to find a place to live."

Gracefully, Dizzy sprang to a sign pole and swung lightly around it through the air, landing at my feet. "Why don't you two get a place together?" she asked casually.

I turned a quick look on Jimmy, who was staring at me with the expression of a man who has just been offered a water moccasin for a pet.

"What's the matter?" Dizzy inquired after a long moment of silence. "I say something wrong, or do you both usually look like a scene from a wax museum around this time each day?"

Jimmy broke first. He began to laugh, first giggling, then roaring, until the tears rolled down his face. The Penthouse incident became vivid in my mind, and the clearer it became, the funnier it seemed. I began to laugh with him. Dizzy was at a total loss, but since she liked to laugh in general, she joined us.

For Jimmy and me, all the tensions and guilts of the year before were poured into that laughter. Dizzy, ignorant of the situation, was a sort of buffer between us, and we could explain away our individual motivations in the Penthouse incident and excuse our behavior toward one another. We jabbered incoherently, as if to let Dizzy in on the big joke. When we finished, Dizzy understood less than she had at the start, but Jimmy and I knew one very important thing: our friendship had weathered a very serious storm. And, once again, without a word, our ties were strongly re-established.[247]

They finally settled on a room at the Iroquois Hotel. According to Bill Bast:

A single room with twin beds and bath for ninety dollars a month was, I was assured by Jimmy and Dizzy, a real bargain in midtown. As I scanned the room with an appraising eye, I could only remember how much larger and more atmospheric the Penthouse

247   William Bast, *James Dean: A Biography*, pp. 56-57.

had been, and how much cheaper. But the day was short, and the uncomplicated procedure of simply taking what was at hand appealed to me.

"Okay," I agreed. "Let's try it for a month, anyway."[248]

***

First, there were two: Jimmy and Bill. When that living situation ended, they formed a group of three. And then there were four. According to Bill Bast:

> *I had run into a girl who had been with us in the Theater Arts Department at U.C.L.A. She had been sharing a one-room apartment on Forty-sixth Street with another girl since her arrival in New York. The apartment was a summer sublet, rented from June until the middle of September, and it was the largest apartment I had seen up to that time in New York.*

> *Just before Jimmy left on the boat trip, the girl's roommate decided to accept another offer of an even nicer apartment on the East Side. So our friend from U.C.L.A., being of a generous nature and somewhat afraid to stay in so large a place alone, offered Jimmy and me living quarters in the back bedroom...*

> *When Jimmy returned, he joined us, and for several weeks all went well. Gradually, however, our funds dwindled to a panic level. It was only through the combined resources of Dizzy's salary, our friend's salary, my salary, and Jimmy's infrequent television checks that we were able to buy enough food for our four enormously hungry mouths*[249]

When the owners returned to New York and demanded their apartment back, the original three: Jimmy, Bill and the girl from UCLA were forced to surrender the premises. By this time, Dizzy Sheridan was looking for another place, so they asked her to join them in their new adventure. Bill continues:

---

248   William Bast, *James Dean: A Biography,* p. 58.
249   William Bast, *James Dean: A Biography,* pp. 71-72

The night before we moved we were particularly broke, because we had had to make an advance payment of the rent on the new place. We had between us less than a dollar on which to eat. So, like scavengers, we took all the left-overs from the refrigerator and made with them a soupy stew into which Jimmy dumped a half package of month-old vermicelli. It was late by the time we sat down to dinner, and our stomachs were singing out in a discordant chorus of hunger cries. As we sat eating the mess, not one of us would acknowledge the presence of the tiny bugs floating atop the broth. Each of us surreptitiously dipped out the little intruders and continued to eat in silence. Necessity is the mother of many things, one of which is not choosiness.[250]

Their adventure was not without humor, as is described by Bill Bast:

One night, returning from a dinner at the home of one of his theatrically securer friends whose mother had been visiting town, Jimmy entered the apartment carrying a large box and looking as though he had never seen us before. Completely ignoring our presence, he carefully set himself to taking from the box two very clean and very blue bed sheets, one equally clean and blue pillow slip, a downy pillow, and a very warm-looking blue wool blanket. In a performance that did justice to his art, he began to make his bed, making certain that every shake of the sheet, every tuck, every smoothing, was done with casual, careless ease. He never said a word as we sat watching him with longing, envious eyes. When he had finished, he slipped into the neatly made dream bed, cooing and gurgling like a freshly fed baby. Without a conference, without a decision, without a word, the three of us rose in unison, walked calmly to his bed, and tore the sheets out from under him. Satisfied that his bed was a total mess, we all retired, leaving Jimmy to laugh uncontrollably in a tangle of sheets on the floor.[251]

While the friends spent their evenings amusing themselves with "bullfights"—Jimmy always with the cape and Dizzy wearing the horns—the novelty of the apartment soon wore off. Bast continues:

250   William Bast, *James Dean: A Biography,* p. 72.
251   William Bast, *James Dean: A Biography,* p. 73.

...In such an arrangement, much consideration of the other fellow is required. Jimmy was not used to making such compromises, nor, for that matter, was I. We had learned to tolerate one another in a living situation, but neither of us had learned to tolerate the habits of the girls. The girls, too, had their complaints. If we weren't battling over the maze of bras, panties, and stockings that were making access to the bathroom impossible, we were haggling over the unwashed dishes, the open windows, the closed windows. The selection of food, the selection of radio programs, etc. etc. etc. For a time this can be fun and often amusing, but when you are suffering the pressures of being jobless and when you have just been through a torturous summer in New York, it isn't the kind of game you care to play for very long.[252]

One afternoon, Jimmy walked into his agent's office, where he noticed a pretty blonde busy at a typewriter. He had never seen her before and decided to see what she was doing. The following dialogue of their meeting is provided by David Dalton:

"What is that?"

"It's a scene."

"What's your phone number?"

"I don't know." (still typing)

He doesn't look like an actor, she thought to herself, not with that slouch and those thick glasses. But Jane Deacy (who, it turned out, was her agent as well) told her who Jimmy was.

Later that afternoon, over a cup of coffee at Cromwell's Drugstore, Christine (White) told Jimmy that she was an actress working on a scene to use in her audition for the Actors Studio. Since James Whitmore had told him about the Studio, Jimmy had been trying to figure out a way to approach it. By the end of the afternoon it occurred to Chris that she needed a partner, and, with apparent casualness, Jimmy wrote himself into her little existential drama.[253]

---

252   William Bast, *James Dean: A Biography,* p. 74.
253   David Dalton, *James Dean: The Mutant King,* pp. 89-90

They spent about five weeks rehearsing the script, and then decided they were ready after they felt it could be mistaken for a lovers' quarrel. Dalton describes their performance:

> *Jimmy was so nervous the day of the audition Chris was almost sure he would run out on her. But a few beers (conveniently written in as props) cured pre-audition shakes. Jimmy, with a can of beer in hand, ran on stage. "Without his glasses on he couldn't find center stage," recalled Christine, "and was almost in the opposite wing. He was out of both overhead amber lights, but the scene was supposed to be nighttime anyway. I waited twenty seconds out of the five minutes we were allowed, ran out and plunked down center stage and refused to look at him. I knew he was startled, but he immediately made the adjustment. He rolled over twice on the floor, laughed and said, 'Hi!' which wasn't in the script.*[254]

Jimmy and Christine White were two of the twelve chosen as finalists and were ultimately the only two accepted. However, Elia Kazan recalled him vaguely. "To begin with, Dean was scarcely at the Studio at all. He came in only a few times. I remember him sitting in the front row, a surly mess. He never participated in anything."[255] David Dalton notes the reason:

> *Jimmy stomped out of a session after doing one scene and then having his performance analyzed by students and [Lee] Strasberg. For an actor whose method was so totally personal, it was a scraping and slicing he couldn't sit still for.*
>
> *"If I let them dissect me, like a rabbit in a clinical research laboratory or something, I might not be able to produce again," he told Bill Bast. "For chrissake, they might sterilize me!"*
>
> *Though the reputation of the Actors studio as an institution rests on its stars, Strasberg readily admits that neither Brando, Clift nor Dean ever trained themselves rigorously there: "Perhaps they didn't need it; perhaps their talent was enough. But Jimmy would*

254   David Dalton, *James Dean: The Mutant King*, p. 90.
255   Qtd. in David Dalton, *James Dean: The Mutant King*, p. 92.

sit and watch. He didn't work much; I think he was a little bit afraid of the work. But you'd see him sitting there, watching."[256]

One evening in October, Jimmy, Bill and Dizzy went to a local hamburger joint for a three-way bowl of chili and beans, when Jimmy made a suggestion: "Let's go to Indiana, to the farm!"

James Dean's suggestions were often impulsive and not uncommon. According to David Dalton:

Jimmy practiced the "Method" on himself almost daily, continually taking himself apart, tearing away the superfluous tissue of his body image and examining that crystal skeleton at the center in its bone-white light: ripping away layers to find roots, as he wrote for himself in his audition.

Close friends saw that such hair-raising experiments must lead to a final dissolution. It was just a sum of all the little destructions that he worked so relentlessly on himself.

Barbara Glenn, who was one of the few people in whom he would confide, said, "Jimmy was a terribly destructive person. Our relationship was destructive. I knew he would destroy himself in the end and that's why when it came, it wasn't a surprise; it was as though my reaction to it had happened long before. From the first time I met Jimmy I felt it. Whenever I waited for him I always wondered, 'Is he going to make it?'"

"He bought a new bike and said, 'I'm going to go home.'" It was winter. 'How?' I said. "please, if you're going to die, why don't you do it around here?' 'No, I've got to try it. It's great. Don't worry.'

"So Jimmy went to Indiana and I didn't hear from him for a couple of weeks. He went through the snowstorms and through the ice and practically froze to death, but drove all the way out and back. I was doing rehearsals one day and I looked in the back of the theater and saw him and just said, 'Whew! Okay.'"

---

256   David Dalton, *James Dean: The Mutant King*, p. 92

...Most actors shrink from the specter of the white bear. Jimmy embraced it as he worked at building the character of James Dean, not realizing that in self-creation are the roots of self-destruction.[257]

In the present situation, the mode of transportation became the prime concern. Three people could not ride a motorcycle at the same time; however, Jimmy had plans already in his mind:

"It won't cost us a thing...We'll hitchhike out there, and it won't cost a cent on the farm."

"Hitchhike!" both Dizzy and I shouted.

"Sure," Jimmy said. "It's only eight hundred miles."

"Three of us hitch eight hundred miles to Indiana and eight hundred miles back. That's a laugh. Nobody would pick us up. All we've got is about ten dollars between us. What if we got stranded someplace? I should also take the chance of losing my job? No thanks, It all sounds very nice, but not for me," I concluded.

"Maybe he's right," mumbled Dizzy dejectedly.

"Well, it was just an idea," Jimmy grumbled.

The next morning, after taking a bus from New York to the New Jersey Turnpike, the three of us stood with our thumbs flapping in the whoosh of passing cars. We had packed a single suitcase, gathered our pennies, and slipped out on our sleeping friend, leaving her a note with instructions to call C.B.S. every day and report that I was sick. After two rides, we found ourselves at the western end of the Pennsylvania Turnpike.[258]

I seriously doubt that James Dean knew about his Western Pennsylvanian ancestors, but fortune smiled upon the trio as they stood there. They were picked up by Clyde McCullough, catcher for the Pittsburgh Pirates, who was heading west for an exhibition game

---

257   David Dalton, *James Dean: The Mutant King,* pp. 94-95.
258   William Bast, *James Dean: A Biography,* pp. 76-77.

in Des Moines, Iowa. He drove them through the night and dropped them off at a highway intersection north of Fairmount, Indiana. According to Bast:

Jimmy took us to his old high school, where, with a bit of his ego showing and the flourish of his own special brand of bravado, he took over for a few days. His drama teacher, Adeline Nall, was more than pleased to see him and turned her class over to the three of us. Jimmy spoke elaborately on the art of acting; Dizzy spoke on modern dance techniques, demonstrating some of the movements, to the enchantment of her audience; and I lectured on television directing and writing.

None of us was anywhere near enough of a master of his craft to warrant the display of unabashed authoritative lecturing, and we were aware of it. But it was greatly rewarding to our starving egos to have those youngsters pay such close attention and regard us with such inappropriate awe. After a year or so of trying to convince the professional world in New York of our capabilities, it was a wonderful boost to have so many accept us as masters of what we were trying to attain.[259]

After several days of fun and food on the farm, a call came from Jimmy's agent, necessitating the long eight hundred mile trip back to New York.

---

259   William Bast, *James Dean: A Biography,* p. 80.

CHAPTER 14—FILMOGRAPHY

Over the years, some people have wondered why James Dean is so remembered since they believe that he only made three films. This chapter focuses on the artistic development of James Dean's film image and lists his radio, stage, television and film performances. The filmography included here is taken from my 2005 book *The Legacy—A Fifty Year Tribute (1955-2005)*[260] The remaining chapters in this section focus on the creation of the character *JAMES DEAN*.

Miscellaneous Radio Dramas

Alias Jane Doe

Stars Over Hollywood

[Note: July 1951] There were others, but they are unknown. Neither recordings nor transcripts of these programs survive. According to Donald Spoto in his biography *Rebel*, there was a radio commercial for Toni Home Permanent, "in which he—JD—told his 'wife' how lustrous and silky her hair looked while violins swooned romantically in the background."]

"Prologue to Glory," *U.S. Steel Radio Hour:* 21 May 1952. James Dean cast as Abraham Lincoln's friend. Also in the cast: John Lund and Wanda Hendrix. [Note: There has been some debate about whether this was a radio show or a television show.]

---

260   Barbara Inman Beall, Ph.D. *The Legacy—A Fifty Year Tribute (1955-2005)*, pp. 77-81

Stage (Broadway)

See the Jaguar by N. Richard Nash; opened 3 Dec 1952, Cort Theater: Cast: James Dean as Wally Wilkins. Also Arthur Kennedy, Constance Ford, Phillip Pine, Arthur Batanides, Dane Knell, Margaret Barker, Roy Fant, Florence Sundstrom. Director: Michael Gordon. Producers: Lemuel Ayers and Florence Jacobson. Incidental music: Alec Wilder.

The Immoralist, adapted from the novel by Andre Guide by Ruth and Augustus Goetz; opened 8 Feb 1954, Royale Theater. Cast: James Dean as Bachir. Also, Geraldine Page, Louis Jourdan, David J. Stewart, Charles Dingle, Adelaide Klin, Bill Gunn, Vivian Matalong (Philadelphia only). Director: Daniel Mann. Producer: Billy Rose.

Stage (Off-Broadway)

End as a Man by Calder Willingham; workshop performances 10 and 17 May and 11 June 1953. Actors Studio. Cast: James Dean in a nonspeaking role as a scribe; also Ben Gazzara, Arthur Storch, William Smithers, Albert Salmi, Anthony Franciosa, Peter Mark Richman. Director: Jack Garfein.

The Scarecrow by Percy Mackaye; opened 16 June 1953, Theatre de Lys. Cast: James Dean as the scarecrow's mirror image; also Patricia Neal, Douglas Watson, Eli Wallach, Anne Jackson, Bradford Dillman. Director: Frank Corsaro. Producer: Terese Hayden.

The Fell Swoop by Jonathan Bates; rehearsed reading 23 June 1953, Palm Garden. Cast: James Dean. Remainder unknown. Director: Sherwood Arthur. Producer: New Dramatists Workshop.

Trachiniae (Trachis) by Sophocles and translated by Ezra Pound; rehearsed reading 14 Feb 1954, New School of Social Research. Cast: James Dean as Heracles' son; also Ann Jackson, Eli Wallach, Adelaide Klein, Earle Montgomery, Joseph Sullivan. Director: Unknown.

Television

"Hill Number One," *Family Theatre* (Easter special, broadcast on all stations nationwide), 25 Mar 1951. Cast: James Dean as John the Beloved; also Regis Toomey, Gene Lockhart, Joan Leslie, Ruth Hussey. Director: Arthur Pierson. Producer: Father Patrick Payton. Writer: James D. Roche.

"Jackie Knows All," *The Trouble with Father*, 1951. Cast: James Dean as Randy, Martin Milner

"T.K.O", *The Bigelow Theatre* (Dumont), 29 Oct 1951. Cast: James Dean, Martin Milner, Jack Bernardi, Carey Loftin. Director and Producer: Frank Woodruff. Writer: Ted Thomas. [Note: Dean's exact character in this show is unknown.]

"Into the Valley," *CBS Television Workshop* (CBS), 27 Jan 1952. Cast: James Dean as a G. I. Also George Tyne, Robert Baines, Michael Higgins, John Compton. Director: Curt Conway. Producer: Norris Houghton. Story: John Hersey. Adaptation: Mel Goldberg.

"Sleeping Dogs," *The Web* (CBS), 20 Feb 1952. Cast: James Dean as a boy trying to solve his brother's murder. Also, Anne Jackson, E. G. Marshall, Robert Simon, Nancy Cushman. Director: Lela Swift. Producer: Franklin Heller. Writer: Marie Baumer.

"Ten Thousand Horses Singing," *Studio One* (CBS), 3 Mar 1952. Cast: James Dean as a bellhop. Also John Forsythe, Catherine McLeod, Vaughn Taylor, Joe Morass. Director: Paul Nickell. Producer: Worthington Minor, Writer: Karl Tunberg.

"The Foggy, Foggy Dew," *Lux Video Theatre* (CBS), 17 Mar 1952. Cast: James Dean as Kyle McCallum; also James Barton, Muriel Kirkland, Richard Bishop. Director and Producer: Richard Goode. Writer: J. Albert Hirsch.

"Abraham Lincoln," *Studio One* (CBS), 26 May 1952. Cast: James Dean as a court-martialed soldier named William Scott; also Robert Pastene. Director: Paul Nickell. Producer: Donald Davis. Story: John Drinkwater. Adaptation: David Shaw.

"The Forgotten Children," *Hallmark Hall of Fame* (NBC), 22 June 1952. Cast: James Dean as Bradford, an 1887 Georgian aristocrat. Also Cloris Leachman, Nancy Malone, Don McHenry, Lee Lindsey. Director and Producer: William Corrigan. Writer: Agens Eckhardt.

"The Hound of Heaven," *The Kate Smith Hour* (NBC), 15 Jan 1953. Cast: James Dean as an angelic messenger dressed as a hillbilly. Also John Carradine, Edgar Stehli, Director: Alan Neuman, Producer unknown. Writer, Earl Hamner, Jr.

"The Case of the Watchful Dog," *Treasury Men in Action* (NBC), 29 Jan 1953. Cast: James Dean as Randy Meeker (son of a mountain moonshiner). Also Crahan Denton, Dorothy Elder, Thom Carney, John Fecher, Bill Elliot. Director: Daniel Petrie. Producer: Robert Sloane. Writer: Albert Aley.

"The Killing of Jesse James" (sometimes listed as "The Capture of Jesse James"), *You Are There* (CBS), 8 Feb 1953. Cast: James Dean as Bob Ford. Also Walter Cronkite, John Kerr, Helen Warnow, Addison Powell, James Westerfield, Carl Frank. Director: Sidney Lumet. Producer: Charles W. Russell. Writer: Leslie Slate.

"No Room," *Danger* (CBS), 14 April 1953. Cast: James Dean as a safecracker. Also Martin Kingsley, Irene Vernon, Kate Smith. Director and Producer unknown. Writer: Mary Stern.

"The Case of the Sawed-Off Shotgun," *Treasury Men in Action* (NBC), 16 April 1953. Cast: James Dean as Arbie Ferris, a would-be gas station robber. Also Joseph Downing, Anita Anton, Coe Norton, Humphrey Davis, Ben Gazzara. Director: David Pressman. Producer: Everett Rosenthal. Writer: Albert Aley.

"The Evil Within," *Tales of Tomorrow* (ABC), 1 May 1953. Cast: James Dean as Ralph, the lab assistant. Also Rod Steiger, Margaret Phillips. Director: Don Medford. Producer: Mort Abrahams. Writer: Manya Starr.

"Something for an Empty Briefcase," *Campbell Soundstage* (NBC). 17 July 1953. Cast: James Dean as an ex-convict Joe Adams. Also Susan Douglas, Frank Maxwell, Robert Middleton, Don Hamner,

Director: Don Medford. Producer: Martin Horrell. Writer: S. Lee Pogostin.

"Sentence of Death," *Summer Studio One* (CBS), 17 Aug 1953. Cast: James Dean as death row prisoner Joe Palica. Also Betsy Palmer, Gene Lyons, Ralph Dunn, Virginia Vincent, Barnet Biro. Director: Matthew Harlib. Producer: John Haggott. Story: Thomas Walsh. Adaptation: Adrian Spies.

"Death is my Neighbor," *Danger*, (CBS), 25 Aug 1953. Cast: James Dean as JB—psychotic janitor. Also Walter Hampden, Betsy Palmer, Frank Marth, Andrew Duggan. Director: John Peyser. Producer: Franklin Heller. Writer: Frank Gregory.

"Rex Newman," *The Big Story* (NBC), 11 Sept. 1953. Cast: James Dean as Todd Ingalls. Also John Kerr, Carl Frank, Wendy Drew, Donald McKee, Ken Walken. Director: Stuart Rosenberg. Producer: Robert Lewis Shayon. Writer: Alvin Boretz.

"Glory in the Flower," *Omnibus* (CBS), 4 Oct 1953. Cast: James Dean as Bronco Evans. Also Hume Cronyn, Jessica Tandy, Mark Rydell, Ed Binns, Frank McHugh. Director: Andrew McCullough. Producer: Fred Rickey. Writer: William Inge.

"Keep Our Honor Bright," *Kraft Television Theatre* (NBC), 14 Oct 1953. Cast: James Dean as Jim. Also, Joan Porter, Michael Higgins, Larry Fletcher, Addison Richards, Bradford Dillman. Director and Producer: Maury Holland. Writer: George Roy Hill.

"Life Sentence," *Campbell Soundstage* (NBC), 16 Oct 1953. Cast: James Dean as Hank Bradon, an imprisoned felon. Also Georgann Johnson, Nicholas Saunders, Matt Crowley, Charles Mendick. Director: Gary Simpson. Producer Martin Horrell. Story: Margaret Kleckner. Adaptation: S. Lee.

"A Long Time Till Dawn," *Kraft Television Theatre* (NBC), 11 Nov 1953. Cast: James Dean as Joe Harris. Also, Naomi Riordan, Ted Osborn, Robert Simon, Rudolph Weiss. Director and Producer: Richard Dunlap. Writer: Rod Serling.

"The Bells of Cockaigne," *Armstrong Circle Theatre* (NBC), 17 Nov 1953. Cast: James Dean as stevedore Joey Frasier. Also Gene Lockhart, Donalee Marans, Vaughn Taylor, Karl Lucas. Director: James Sheldon. Producer: Hudson Faussett. Writer: George Lowther.

"Harvest," *Robert Montgomery Presents* (NBC), 23 Nov 1953. Cast: James Dean as Paul Zalenka. Also Dorothy Gish, Ed Begley, Reba Tassell, Vaughn Taylor, John Dennis, John Connell. Director: James Sheldon. Producer: Robert Montgomery. Writer: Sandra Michael.

"The Little Woman," *Danger* (CBS), 30 Mar 1954. Cast: James Dean as Augie, a counterfeiter on the lam. Also Lydia Reed, Rank Maxwell, Albert Salmi, Lee Bergere. Director and Producer: Andrew McCullough. Writer: Joe Scully.

"Run Like a Thief," *Philco Television Playhouse* (NBC), 5 Sept 1954. Cast: James Dean as Rob, the busboy. Also Kurt Kaszner, Gusti Huber, Ward Costello, Barbara O'Neill. Director: Jeffrey Hayden. Producer: Gordon Duff. Writer: Sam Hall.

"Padlock," *Danger* (CBS), 9 Nov 1954. Cast: James Dean as an escaped felon. Also Mildred Dunnock, David Hardison, Ken Konopha. Director and Producer unknown. Writer: Louis Peterson.

"I'm a Fool," *General Electric Theatre* (CBS), 14 Nov 1954. Cast: James Dean as a racetrack stable boy. Also Eddie Albert, Natalie Wood, Roy Glenn. Director: Don Medford. Producer: Mort Abrahams. Story: Sherwood Anderson. Adaptation: Arnold Shulman.

"The Dark, Dark Hours," *General Electric Theatre* (CBS), 12 Dec 1954. Cast: James Dean as a "hepcat" killer. Also Ronald Reagan, Constance Ford, Jack Simmons. Director: Don Medford. Producer: Mort Abrahams. Writer: Arthur steuer.

"The Thief," *U. S. Steel Hour* (ABC), 4 Jan 1955. Cast: James Dean as Fernand Legarde. Also Mary Astor, Paul Lukas, Diana Lynn, Patrick Knowles, Nehemiah Persoff. Director: Vincent J. Donehue.

Producer: the Theatre Guild Story: Henri Bernstein. Adaptation: Arthur Arent.

"The Unlighted Road," *Schlitz Playhouse of Stars* (CBS), 6 May 1955. Cast: James Dean as Jeff Latham, a Korean War veteran. Also Pat Hardy, Mervyn Vye, Edgar Stehli. Director: Justus Addis. Producer: William Self. Writer: Walter C. Brown.

Note: There are others: various episodes of *Mama* (CBS), an unknown episode of *Suspense* (CBS), 1952. And an interview to promote *East of Eden* preceding "Life of Emile Zola," *Lux Video Theatre* (NBC), 10 March 1955. Plus there are various commercials for Pepsi-Cola, for Coca Cola, and the Highway Safety Spot with Gig Young filmed 29 July 1955.

Films

East of Eden, Warner Brothers, released March 1955. Cast: James Dean as Cal Trask. Also Julie Harris, Richard Davalos, Raymond Massey, Jo Van Fleet, Burl Ives, Lois Smith, Albert Dekker, Lonny Chapman, Timothy Carey, Betty Treadville, Harold Gordon. Director and Producer: Elia Kazan. Screenplay: Paul Osborn, based on a novel by John Steinbeck. Music: Leonard Rosenman. Photography: Ted McCord.

Rebel Without a Cause, Warner Brothers, released October 1955. Cast: James Dean as Jim Stark. Also Natalie Wood, Sal Mineo, Jim Backus, Ann Doran, Edward Platt, Marietta Canty, Jack Simmons, Corey Allen, Dennis Hopper, Jack Grinnage, Frank Mazzola, Nick Adams, Beverly Long, Steffi Sidney, Virginia Brissac, William Hopper, Rochelle Hudson. Director: Nicholas Ray. Producer: David Wisehart. Screenplay: Stewart Stern. Adaptation: Irvin Shulman from a story by Nicholas Ray. Music: Leonard Rosenman, Photography: Ernest Haller.

Giant, Warner Brothers, released October 1956. Cast: James Dean as Jett Rink. Also Rock Hudson, Elizabeth Taylor, Mercedes McCambridge, Jane Withers, Chill Wills, Carroll Baker, Dennis Hopper, Sal Mineo, Victor Millan. Director: George Stevens. Producers: George Stevens and Henry Ginsberg. Screenplay: Fred

Guiol and Ivan Moffatt, based on the novel by Edna Ferber. Music: Dmitri Tiomkin. Photography: William C. Mellor.

Cameo Roles in Films

Fixed Bayonets, 20th Century Fox, released November 1951. James Dean uncredited as a G. I. Cast: Richard Basehart, Gene Evans, Michael O'Shea, Bill Hickman, Tony Kent. Director: Samuel Fuller, Producer: Jules Buck. Screenplay: Samuel Fuller, suggested by a novel by John Brophy. Music: Roy Webb. Photography: Lucien Ballard.

Sailor Beware, Paramount, released January 1952. James Dean uncredited as a boxer's second. Cast: Jerry Lewis, Dean Martin, Corinne Calvert, Marion Marshall, Leif Erickson. Director: Hall Walker, Producer: Hal Wallis. Screenplay: Martin Rackin and James Allardice, from a play by Kenyon Nicholson and Charles Robinson. Music: Joseph Lilley. Photography: Daniel L. Fapp.

Has Anybody Seen My Gal? Universal, released July 1952. James Dean uncredited as a malt-drinking college student. Cast: Piper Laurie, Rock Hudson, Charles Coburn, Gigi Perreau, Rod Barkely (uncredited). Director: Douglas Sirk. Producer: Ted Richmond. Screenplay: Joseph Hoffman, based on a story by Eleanor H. Porter. Music: Joseph Gershenson. Photography: Clifford Stine.

There has been some discussion over whether James Dean appeared in an uncredited role in the John Wayne movie *Trouble Along the Way* (1953).[261] The general consensus is that he did not.

---

261   *Trouble Along the Way* (1953). Actors: John Wayne, Donna Reed, Charles Coburn. Director: Michael Curtiz. Released April 4, 1953. Warner Bros.

CHAPTER 15—LOOKING THROUGH A GLASS DARKLY[262]

His name was Charles. A veteran of Vaudeville, he had moved to Denver, Colorado, where my student encountered him again. She had known him from Hollywood years ago while she was working in wardrobe and make-up. And in Fall 2002, she was on her way to a restaurant where she would interview him for a paper she was writing.

Charles remembered James Dean. He met him on a Hollywood set, and they developed a friendship. Charles described one evening at either a restaurant or a bar. Everyone was talking. All of a sudden, James Dean began miming playing a violin. Charles soon followed by miming playing a piano. Someone else joined in by miming another instrument. They soon had a full orchestra of soundless instruments playing a symphony. All conversation ceased and all eyes were on the players. It was a moment to remember. At the end of the interview, Charles added, "James Dean was so beautiful, he would light up a room the minute he entered it."

***

James Dean lit up Broadway in two performances. The first, *See the Jaguar*, will be covered in this chapter. The second, *The Immoralist*, will be covered in Chapter 16.

Auditions for *See the Jaguar* had been underway for some time, but in his *James Dean: A Biography*, John Howlett notes that no final casting decisions had been made, although "Dean knew there were

---

several young actors on the short list for the part of the 'Jaguar", Wally Wilkins."[263] In describing the play, Howlett states:

> The play told the story of a teenager who had been shut away all his life by a protective and frightened mother. After the mother's death the boy comes out of his prison, a sixteen-year-old freak, illiterate, and wholly unprepared for the cruelties of the small town world in which he finds himself. The part was well suited to Dean, and the puzzled bewilderment he could project so convincingly.[264]

This was Jimmy's first real part, and he fully immersed himself into that character. According to Howlett:

> Dean would return home to the brownstone apartment in the evenings full of the excitement of the day's rehearsals, acting out for his room-mates each of the main parts in the play and explaining to them the subtleties of Gordon's staging. He had mastered his lines within a few days, but experienced more trouble with the song he had to sing in the play: a little folk tune written by his friend Alec Wilder especially for the production, "Green Briar, Blue Fire'. Being practically tone-deaf Dean had a terrible time trying to learn the tune. He was intensely self-conscious of his singing and would only practice in a dark room at dead of night, to the amusement but eventual despair of his flatmates.

> Rehearsals went smoothly until they moved out of town into Connecticut for trial previews. Then, during one of the final runthroughs in the theatre at Hartford, Dean had a fight with one of the stage-hands and ending up pulling a switchblade on him. It was apparently Arthur Kennedy who broke up the fight, not without some harsh words for his young co-star. The incident could have been a simple quarrel, a stage-hand's ill-timed remark; it could have been an accumulation of nervous tension; it could even have been a calculated moment of self-triggering by Dean, trying perhaps to spark off some detail of insight or invention within his role as Wally Wilkins. In an impasse Dean needed adrenalin as badly as some actors need liquor. Two years later, when they

263   John Howlett, *James Dean: A Biography*, p. 47.
264   John Howlett, *James Dean: A Biography*, p. 47.

were working together on Rebel Without a Cause, he would tell Dennis Hopper a propos of the mechanics of invention: 'When you know there's something more to go in the character and you're not sure what it is, you just got to go out after it. Walk out on the tightrope. If the rope's hard it's got to be leading somewhere.'[265]

The knife-pulling incident is described by Val Holley:

Broadway legend holds that Dean pulled a knife on someone in Hartford. According to Nash, it was Gordon. "During a rehearsal or maybe a scenery setup, Jimmy stood on the apron of the stage and flashed a knife at Michael and said, 'You come up here, you son of a bitch, and you'll get this!' I'm not sure what provoked it, but I was there, and those were his exact words. I hadn't been paying attention, but I did see that incident. A stagehand broke it up. Jimmy got on well with the stagehands but not with Michael, who was a formalist and believed in doing the professional thing. There was never any artistic quarrel between them; Jimmy just didn't go by the rules. He would come late to rehearsal, or he would pretend to forget the lines. But Michael wouldn't have fired him; you can't fire someone that good."[266]

Holley further describes opening night:

Opening night in Hartford had its share of glitches. Due to problems backstage, the curtain rose nearly a half hour late. Then, at the end of Act Two, where Gramfa is clubbed to death and Wally is captured, Dean threw in some unexpected business. It was crucial for Pine to drag Wally offstage as the lights came up on a dying Gramfa. But in this performance, Dean surprised Pine by struggling with him, even though he had previously been submissive. "Did I miss a rehearsal?" Pine wondered to himself. With no time for argument, Pine stomped on Dean's foot. Offstage, an aggravated Dean protested, "I was only doing what my character would have done." "Well," Pine countered, "that's what my character would have done in response."[267]

265   John Howlett, *James Dean: A Biography*, pp. 47-48.
266   Val Holley, *James Dean: The Biography*, p. 136.
267   Val Holley, *James Dean: The Biography*, p. 136.

The play received dismal reviews in the press, where critics described it as "over-symbolic" and "naïve." However, James Dean received favorable notice from Walter Kerr, in the *New York Herald Tribune*:

> *James Dean adds an extraordinary performance in an almost impossible role: that of a bewildered lad who has been completely shut off from a vicious world by an over-zealous mother, and who is coming upon both the beauty and brutality of the mountain for the first time.*[268]

See the Jaguar marked the real beginning of James Dean's acting career. Jane Deacy could now reject the superficial roles and concentrate on roles leading to a substantial future. John Howlett describes Jimmy's transformation:

> *There were an increasing number of these roles available. The 'hep teenager' was creeping into contemporary drama, the young television writers of the day influenced on one level by the emergence of the Kerouac-style wanderers, the first of the hippie-beats; and on another level by the cynical alienation of Salinger's Holden Caulfield from The Catcher in the Rye, the problem teenager from East Coast city affluence.*[269]

There were three male actors who were primarily competing for these parts at that time: James Dean, Paul Newman and Steve McQueen. According to John Howlett:

> *If they had been competing on a league basis Dean would have been out in front during that year, and his success at picking up the better parts was due more than anything else to the audience reaction he inspired. The Schurr office would have made programme sponsors aware of the fan mail: rave letters from young girls, brotherly letters from young boys, pornographic letters from old ladies and gentlemen. The scale of response was nothing to compare with the deluge that followed his first feature film, but it*

---

268   John Howlett, *James Dean: A Biography*, p. 48.
269   John Howlett, *James Dean: A Biography*, p. 49.

was already an indication of the magnetic strength of his screen personality.[270]

His behavior became more unconventional, as John Howlett notes:

[He was] drifting in and out of people's lives apparently at will and random. He would call unannounced, and sometimes sit for hours in a friend's house without speaking. At other times he could be the clowning life and soul of any gathering; extempore champion of the absurd, like the day he carried an armchair down four flights of stairs to sit himself in the middle of a busy New York street.

Night or day he would walk the city, watching, listening and learning. He would talk for hours with cabbies and waitresses, the news-stand operators, his old friend 'Moondog', the blind musician who wandered the New York streets...For Dean wanted to absorb everything and everybody, good and bad, the whole Technicolor pageant, his collection of characters and emotions sometimes strung out behind him, the Pied Piper—at other times instead, crowded uncomfortably and uneasily inside his head.[271]

He was devoid of any serious commitments. As Howlett notes, "That was almost the precondition, his rule."[272] Howlett goes on to say:

Love and dependence were emotions Dean could not easily cope with, either in himself or in other people—an almost inevitable consequence of the loss of his mother and the close relationship they had shared: love is everything but love can be taken away, therefore it is dangerous.[273]

Bill Bast recalled:

He would run into a new face in the Schurr office, or at Walgreen's, or at Cromwell's, and attach himself to her for a few hours, or, at the most, a day. The girls would accompany him wherever he

270 John Howlett, *James Dean: A Biography,* p. 49
271 John Howlett, *James Dean: A Biography,* p. 53.
272 John Howlett, *James Dean: A Biography,* p. 54.
273 John Howlett, *James Dean: A Biography,* p. 54

went to his agent's office, or interviews, to rehearsals, to dinner, on walks, or to his room.[274]

Besides Dizzy Sheridan, who was supportive and who learned how to deal with his mood swings, there were two other women who sustained a relationship with him: Christine White, who was a close friend and with whom he auditioned for the Actor's Studio, and Barbara Glenn, a relationship that was intermittent and stormy.

Dance and rhythm music became a part of James Dean's life during his second year in New York. He studied dancing with Katherine Dunham, and he learned to play the bongo drums in the Greenwich Village cellars.[275] According to Howlett:

The dancing was an exercise on his part to achieve greater physical flexibility in his acting and lose the inhibited stiffness that apparently marked some of his television performances. On a cramped TV set movement could not be expressed with too much exuberance, and the only alternative, in Dean's opinion, was to learn the more controlled expressions of modern dance or ballet.[276]

Although he had already appeared in numerous television shows, television would remain a staple in his acting career.

***

Sunday night television programming at our house included a program hosted by Ronald Reagan called *The General Electric Theater.* And on one such Sunday night, we settled in to watch a program called "The Dark, Dark Hours." I was eleven years old at the time and afraid of my own shadow. What I found so terrifying that evening was the character with the gun, who kept dancing around the room, waving the gun in the doctor's face (Ronald Reagan)—and who talked in the "hep cat" dialect—something we were not allowed to use in my

---

274   qtd. In John Howlett, *James Dean: A Biography,* p. 54.
275   John Howlett, *James Dean: A Biography*, p. 56.
276   John Howlett, *James Dean: A Biography,* p. 56.

house! People who talked that way were dangerous, and I certainly thought this guy was dangerous. That hep-cat killer was James Dean!

Our house was old and squeaky, and the boards played their own music at night. They creaked loudly that evening after I went to bed, and I imagined the "hep-cat killer" from that show sneaking up the stairway, gun in hand. I remember hiding under the covers, trying to go to sleep, emerging only to hear the wind outside and the creaking boards! As I recall, I had some vivid dreams once I actually fell asleep.

My suspicions were all confirmed the next day by Ronald Reagan, in the form of a press conference. What follows is the rest of the story:

> "The original script, as was our habit, was sent to the sponsor [General Electric] for approval," Medford recounts. "They rejected it because they didn't want to show sympathy with juvenile delinquents. Mort Abrahams, the producer, and I were disappointed, because it was a labor of love for us. So I had an idea: 'Let's get Jimmy Dean to play it—let's have the writer take out the controversial dialogue and let Jimmy fill it in.' So the script was resubmitted after the names and title had been changed, and it was accepted!
>
> "As part of his deal with G.E. as its weekly host, Ronald Reagan could choose to play in up to six shows per season. To our horror, he chose this one. He was delighted to be in it. Jimmy was a smashing success. We got telegrams and raves from other directors, which never happens.
>
> "Well, the next day, Mort Abrahams and I were fired. G. E. realized the script had been a ruse. And Reagan called a press conference. He stated that he hated the role and had been coerced into playing it, and all juvenile delinquents were bastards who deserved what they got.
>
> "But Jimmy was fabulous. He did things on the air that rocked us in the control room. Peewee was lying on the doctor's table, terribly scared. The doctor left the room, and in an effort to calm Peewee, Jimmy turned the radio up and took his hand and pre-

tended to jitterbug with him. That was original! Another thing he did was to tap on the lens of Peewee's glasses and ask, 'Are you home, Peewee?"

"Jack Simmons was just a person at Googie's, really. Jimmy would sit at Googie's and study people by the hour. That was his key to people, I felt. He was delighted that we cast Jack. But I'm afraid we did Jack a terrible disservice by casting him, because after that he thought he was an actor!"[277]

Ronald Reagan would later say:

"I think in a way he was experimenting with his part...because in an all-day rehearsal he would vary the performance, [but] by showtime he had arrived at the performance he wanted...he was...not easy to know."[278]

For many years, copies of James Dean's early television shows were practically non-existent. After his death in 1955—an event that occurred just when the public was becoming acquainted with him—public demand for those old television shows was nonstop. The shows were initially live productions; however, backup tapes existed. They were played and replayed through the late 1950s, especially during the summer months when the regular shows were "on vacation." That is the reason why I saw so many of them. I saw some of the original productions in the early 1950s when we were visiting friends. But we didn't get our first television set until August or September 1954. By 1960, the tapes were shelved, forgotten, or even destroyed. Then many of the tapes were rediscovered and were made available on cassette tapes and are today available on DVD.

A few of the shows have yet to be found, including the *You Are There* production of the killing of Jesse James. I remember reading that when James Dean was trying out for the part of Jett Rink, he had a tape of that show sent over to Warner Bros. for consideration. It is

277   Val Holley, *James Dean: The Biography*, pp. 246-247
278   Qtd. In Donald Spoto, *Rebel: The Life and Legend of James Dean*, p. 197.

possible the tape is in some vault at Warner Bros., and I continue to hope that it will eventually be found.

It was during another *General Electric Theater* production of "I'm a Fool" where Jimmy initially met Natalie Wood. Her description, as told to John Howlett, follows:

> *It was a half-hour drama for General Electric Playhouse. Eddie Albert was also in it. It was based on a rather well-known short story—I can't remember the name of the author. All I remember is that it was the story of a man looking back on his youth, so that Jimmy was playing Eddie Albert as a young man and remembering his first love. For me it was the first time I had done a love scene on screen. As for Jimmy, he was unusual for that time in that he arrived at work on a motorcycle looking rumpled—though he was nice and clean. Just rumpled. He didn't comb his hair a lot, He arrived through a garage side entrance and had to jump down into the rehearsal hall, which was really an old building. He had a safety-pin holding his pants together. He was introspective and very shy. The producer, Mort Abrahams, told him to sit with me since we were the young lovers in the piece. But he just grunted, and we'd got half-way through the reading before he did come and sit by me. He was introspective during the read-through and very indirect in his manner towards people. I remember when I went to lunch I noticed him soundlessly following me. We had lunch together every day while we were working. He always had a radio with him and played classical music. At that time he was very much in love with Pier Angeli. But her mother was breaking off their romance because she didn't believe he had the necessary social graces.*[279]

Natalie Wood described their first lunch together in several documentaries. He looked at her suddenly and said, "I know who you are. You're a child actor!" And then he referenced something about a child acting like an adult. She responded by saying, "Well, I'd rather be a child acting like an adult than an adult acting like a child." He didn't

279   qtd. In John Howlett, *James Dean: A Biography,* p. 82.

get it at first. Then it soaked in, and he started laughing. After that, they were good friends!

The important thing about James Dean's television roles—as corny as some of the plot lines may seem—viewers can see many of his moods and gestures that he employed later in his major films. His depiction of anguish in "A Long Time 'Til Dawn" is regenerated as Jim Stark in *Rebel Without a Cause*. In the television episode, an anguished Joe Harris sprawls backward on the bed with a gun in one hand and a football on the other. In the motion picture, an anguished Jim Stark sprawls backward on the couch after rubbing a milk bottle across his face. The prone positions in both cases are almost identical. The dancing actor appears in several of those shows. James Dean was never one to stand still. He was always moving—whether as Joe Adams in "Something for an Empty Briefcase," ["I'm going to buy myself a briefcase"], Cal Trask in *East of Eden* jumping on a base beneath a tree, hands in pockets, legs spread, moving back and forth. ["You wanna go someplace with me, Aron?"], Jim Stark in *Rebel Without a Cause* using the same movement while talking with Judy, ["You wanna go there with me?"], the "hep-cat killer" dancing with Peewee. In *Giant*, Jett Rink could never stand still either, even in background scenes where he appears as a shadow. Viewers' eyes are continually drawn to him to see what he is doing!

Another play on Broadway—*The Immoralist*—would launch his film career.

CHAPTER 16—THE IMMORALIST

"If certain distinguished minds have chosen to regard this drama as no more than the account of a strange case, and its hero as a sick man; if they have failed to see that some very urgent ideas of very general interest may nonetheless be found in it—that is not the fault of these ideas nor of this drama, but of the author, and I mean: of his clumsiness—though he has put into this book all his passion, all his tears, and all his care. But the real interest of a work and the interest taken in it by the public of the moment are two very different things. One may without too much conceit, I think, prefer the risk of failing to interest the moment by what is genuinely interesting—to beguiling momentarily a public fond of trash.

Be that as it may, I have tried to prove nothing, but to paint my picture well and light it properly."

Andre Giide

Preface

"The Immoralist"

***

Andre Gide's *The Immoralist* was first published in 1902 and was immediately assailed for its "themes of omnisexual abandon and perverse aestheticism."[280] According to the description on the jacket of the novel:

---

280   Andre Gide, *The Immoralist*, Back Jacket.

Gide's protagonist is the frail, scholarly Michel, who shortly after his wedding nearly dies of tuberculosis. He recovers only through the ministrations of his wife, Marceline, and his sudden, ruthless determination to live a life unencumbered by God or values. What ensues is a wild flight into the realm of the senses that culminates in a remote outpost in the Sahara—where Michel's hunger for new experiences at any cost bears lethal consequences. The Immoralist is a book with the power of an erotic fever dream— lush, prophetic, and eerily seductive.[281]

Sometime in November or December 1953, James Dean auditioned for a part in Billy Rose's production *The Immoralist.* The play was an adaptation by Ruth and Augustus Goetz of Andre Gide's novel by the same name. Howlett describes the play as "the story of a French archaeologist (Louis Jourdan in the play) on a honeymoon with his young wife (Geraldine Page), and how the marriage breaks up under the strain of his homosexuality.[282] James Dean auditioned for the part of the corrupt young Arab houseboy who tempts Jourdan. According to Howlett, "In one scene of the play the house-boy dances for Jourdan and this was the scene Dean insisted on playing at the audition, with apparent success."[283] This was the famous "scissors" dance, which Dalton describes:

In this scene, which is the only physically suggestive scene in the play, Jimmy plots to steal a pair of scissors from the house while the mistress of the house is out. Playing on the weakness of Michel and the sexual desires he is trying weakly to suppress, Bachir tempts him with a tour of all the night places. "I know them all. With money you can buy anything that pleases you..." Bachir says.

Michel refuses and Bachir says, "Then maybe I amuse you sir. I dance for you." Then he takes scissors from the taborer where he had put them down and snips them in a rhythm, then slips the

281   Andre Gide, *The Immoralist,* Back Jacket.
282   John Howlett, *James Dean: A Biography,* p. 56.
283   John Howlett, *James Dean: A Biography,* p. 56.

scissors in his burnoose and continues the rhythm by snapping his
fingers and dancing sensuously, his arms extended into the air.[284]

During the time when he was preparing for the role, Jimmy turned down television roles. Rehearsals were postponed for a couple of weeks, and this time offered him the opportunity to return to Indiana. Howlett notes:

It was more than a year since he had been home, and he had
missed any chance of a summer vacation due to his television
work…To the great consternation of his future producer and di-
rector he decided to make the journey to Indiana by motorbike.
The original motorbike sent out to him from the farm had been
chanced several times during the year. Each time Dean's television
fees had been raised he had bought a bigger and faster machine.
That December he was riding an English Triumph 500, and there
were friends and interested parties in New York who believed they
would never see him again when he set out on it into the snow-
bound midwinter interior of the continent.[285]

Friction developed after the play was well into rehearsal, involving the replacement of the director Herman Schulman with Daniel Mann, restaging of the show, and some rewriting of the script. Howlett says that although the Philadelphia reviews had been very good, "Dean was confused and upset by the sudden changes."[286] Howlett contin-ues:

His own part as the Arab boy had been singled out for special
praise and now he found the part shrinking with each day's re-
hearsing. Nor was there any time for tact or sympathy. The show
had to transfer onto Broadway within a week…

Wherever the blame and whatever the faults, tension and friction
finally climaxed in a showdown between Dean and Mann only a
day or so before the New York opening. Dean asked a question,
and Daniel Mann rounded on him: "What makes you think you're

---

284   David Dalton, *The Mutant King,* pp. 144-145.
285   John Howlett, *James Dean: A Biography,* p. 56.
286   John Howlett, *James Dean: A Biography,* p. 57

so important here? The row had been brewing all week, and in the heat of the moment Dean walked out of the theatre. When he had cooled down enough to come back he found the rehearsal progressing with his understudy playing for him (the black actor Billy Gunn). A diplomatic intervention by an Equity official, and apparently some strong pressure from Geraldine Page, restored Dean to the cast and the play opened as planned.

But Dean's commitment to the play was now lost. He believed the changes had cheapened the drama and bitterly resented the way he had been steamrollered by Daniel Mann. The Immoralist opened at the Royale Theatre on 1 February 1954, and on that first night, a night of triumph both for Dean and for the play, he handed in his two weeks' notice to quit.[287]

Concerning the friction in the play, David Dalton writes:

Jimmy still pulled ironic and testy little "numbers" as he developed the character during final rehearsals. For a traditionalist like Daniel Mann, who was brought in the replace the original director of The Immoralist during out-of-town tryouts, it was an annoying repetition of destructive games that infuriated him to such a point that once during a rehearsal in Philadelphia he jumped on the stage and chased Jimmy out of the theater down the street!

"I had this strange young man who was defying the whole company. Well, there's only so much you can take. I would ask him to do what he had to do, try to communicate with him, but it was extremely difficult. But I wouldn't sugar-tit Jimmy because I had a play to do in a certain amount of time. He was a rebel, and that has a negative connotation if rebelling is against progress, and the play meant progress. You have to play the play, not your own whims. If you're playing music...if someone stands up and plays the wrong notes or holds his note too long, he's gonna stick out, right? That's what Jimmy did to get attention. Jimmy would decide to play a scene differently—but it wasn't interpretation, it was defiance! Jimmy played what came to his mind and nothing was ever the same twice. He had an attitude toward me that I

---

287   John Howlett, "James Dean: A Biography", p. 57.

was a policeman, worse than a policeman, a pig. But it was a big loss for him because I would have helped him the way I helped Louis Jourdan if only he would let me. But I couldn't make him understand that my approach was a positive one, that the director's job is to help an actor help himself.

"He had all these adolescent notions about being a man—he carried a knife, he rode a motorcycle around—but it couldn't have nourished him very much or else he would have been much calmer and enjoyed it. I thought he was a very, very disturbed, very compulsive young man."[288]

The night *The Immoralist* opened, James Dean gave a performance that won two Broadway awards—the Antoinette Perry Award, better known as the "Tony," and the Daniel Blum Award—"both for most promising young actor of the year."[289]

It was also on opening night when Jimmy had a huge fight with his then girlfriend, Barbara Glenn, which she recalled for David Dalton:

"I remember the opening night of The Immoralist...I was all dressed up for opening night—and I met his aunt and uncle there from Indiana. After the show I went backstage and asked Jimmy what he wanted to do. He said, 'They're all going to Sardi's, do you want to go?' as he was putting on his torn dungarees and his tee shirt. I said, 'Jimmy, you can't go to Sardi's that way; they won't let you in.' 'C'mon, they'll let me in,' he said. And of course they didn't.

"So he said, 'What do you want to do?' I wanted to go in, so he told me to wait there for him, that he'd go home and change. So he got on his bike and went home, and came back in a suit—one of the rare occasions—and he even had on a tie! And it was so funny because I had been sitting at this table—and it was like a bad Hollywood novel, everybody gossiping and bitching—and I'd gotten so uptight that when he walked in the door in his little choir boy's suit I just stood up and said, 'I'm leaving.'"

288   David Dalton, *The Mutant King*, pp. 145-146.
289   David Dalton, *The Mutant King*, p. 148.

"We had a violent, violent fight. I can't tell you what a sacrifice this was, for Jimmy to go home and put on a suit. We didn't talk to each other for two days after that. The reason I bring it up is that Jimmy never dressed up for any occasion or for anybody. I think that was the only time I ever saw him in a suit. But I had no choice. I didn't know it would be the nightmare it was. It sounded like so much fun—a party full of stars. Ugh."[290]

While he may have been discouraged with the manner in which his part as Bachir was rewritten, he used that part to the best of his ability on stage, as is noted by John Howlett:

Both audience and critics had given the play a good reception and Dean won the last laugh over the director, a mild thumbing of his nose at the way his part had been camped up in the alterations: at his curtain-call he stepped forward, lifted up his robe, and curtsied. While his performance that night, cursty and all would earn him a mention as one of the most promising newcomers in the Theatre World yearbook, the audience reception was particularly gratifying for Dean since his uncle and aunt had come out from Indiana to be present at the opening night. Dean had told them nothing about the quarrels that had led up to his decision to quit, and the two of them returned to Fairmount having seen Jimmy at one of his rare peaks, prince of Broadway and Manhattan for one brief evening.

Most of his friends were now telling him to retract his decision to quit. The play was sure to have a long run, and a quarrel with the management could only damage his reputation. They warned him he would end up one day with no one prepared to employ him.

Dean ignored the advice and shut himself away for the remainder of his two weeks' work on the show; intransigent, moody, unapproachable. Though he didn't yet know it himself, his obstinacy was about to reap an unexpected reward.[291]

---

290   David Dalton, *The Mutant King*, p. 149.
291   John Howlett, *James Dean: A Biography*, p. 57.

CHAPTER 17—*EAST OF EDEN:* THE ESSENCE OF CAL TRASK

"**N**o need," said Samuel. "Liza let me take her mother's. It's here in my pocket." He took out the package and unwrapped the battered book. "This one has been scraped and gnawed at," he said. "I wonder what agonies have settled here. Give me a used Bible and I will, I think, be able to tell you about a man by the places that are edged with the dirt of seeking fingers. Liza wears a Bible down evenly. Here we are—this oldest story. If it troubles us it must be that we find the trouble in ourselves."

"I haven't heard it since I was a child," said Adam.

"You think it's long then, and it's very short," said Samuel. "I'll read it through and then we'll go back. Give me a little wine, my throat's dried out with wine. Here it is—such a little story to have made so deep a wound." He looked down at the ground. "See!" he said. "The boys have gone to their sleep, there in the dust."

Lee got up. "I'll cover them," he said.

"The dust is warm," said Samuel. "Now it goes this way. 'And Adam knew Eve his wife; and she conceived, and bare Cain, and said, "I have gotten a man from the Lord."'"

Adam started to speak and Samuel looked up at him and he was silent and covered his eyes with his hand. Samuel read, "'And she again bare his brother Abel. And Abel was a keeper of sheep, but Cain was a tiller of the ground. And in the process of time it came to pass that Cain brought of the fruit of the ground an offering unto the Lord. And Abel, he also brought of the firstlings of his *flock and of the flat thereof. And the Lord had respect unto Abel and to his offering. But unto Cain and to his offering he had not respect.'"*

Lee said, "Now there—no, go on, go on. We'll come back."

Samuel read, "'And Cain was very wroth, and his countenance fell. And the Lord said unto Cain, "Why art though wroth? And why is thy countenance fallen? If thou doest well, shalt thou not be accepted. And if thou doest not well, sin lieth at the door. And unto thee shall be his desire, and thou shalt rule over him."

"'And Cain talked with Abel his brother: And it came to pass, when they were in the field, that Cain rose up against Abel his brother and slew him. And the Lord said unto Cain, "Where is Abel thy brother?" And he said, "I know not. Am I my brother's keeper?" And he said, "What hast thou done? The voice of thy brother's blood crieth unto me from the ground. And now art thou cursed from the earth, which hath opened her mouth to receive thy brother's blood from thy hand. When thou tillest the ground it shall not henceforth yield unto thee her strength; a fugitive and a vagabond shalt thou be in the earth." And Cain said unto the Lord, "My punishment is greater than I can bear. Behold, thou hast driven me out this day from the face of the earth, and from thy face shall I be hid. And I shall be a fugitive and a vagabond in the earth; and it shall come to pass that everyone that findeth me shall slay me." And the Lord said unto him, "Therefore, whosoever slayeth Cain, vengeance shall be taken on him sevenfold." And the Lord set a mark upon Cain lest any finding him should kill him. And Cain went out from the presence of the Lord and dwelt in the land of Nod on the east of Eden."[292]

When once asked about the source for his novel, *East of Eden*, Steinbeck responded he had two sons who fought like that. His novel created a sensation in 1951 and by 1954, Hollywood embarked upon a film by that name. But while the book encompasses a huge period of time filled with a host of characters, the movie focuses only on the last half of the novel and the lives of two grown sons: Aron (played by

---

292   John Steinbeck, *East of Eden*, Penguin Classics, pp. 267-268.

REBEL FROM BACK CREEK   221

Richard Davalos) and Caleb (Cal) Trask (played by James Dean). In the Introduction to the Penguin Classic, David Wyatt notes:

> Steinbeck defines his major characters as children. He makes the point that, after Adam and Eve, everyone is the son or daughter of some human parent. From the standpoint of family romance, the dilemma faced by our first parents is profoundly unique. Yet everyone who has been a human child has felt, Steinbeck argues, a common terror: "The greatest terror a child can have is that he is not loved and rejection is the hell he fears. I think everyone in the world to a large or small extent has felt rejection. And with rejection comes anger, and with anger some kind of crime in revenge for the rejection and with the crime guilt—and there is the story of mankind." In the model of human development the key figure is not a parent or a child but a sibling, or the idea of one. The threat to the self is having to share love, and the root of all evil, if there is one, is the impulse that leads a parent to say, as Cyrus Trask does to Adam, "I love you better."[293]

Explaining Adam and Cathy (Kate in the film) as "figures for two character functions that throw the notion of character into question: depression and difference,"[294] Wyatt states:

> A thoroughly passive hero, Adam moves through his life as though absent from it. If it seems to Samuel that he "might be pleasuring himself with sadness," this is often how depression looks to an outsider...After Cathy leaves, he finds himself "clothed in a viscosity that slowed his movements and held his thoughts down. He saw the world through gray water."...From the beginning, Adam will not fight. The best he can do is "Act out being alive," as Samuel urges him, willfully disguise a mental illness for which the culture of his day was only beginning to find a name...Steinbeck's treatment of Adam is not clinical, it is moral, and it deserves to be so by acknowledging that Adam will not change and cannot be judged.[295]

---

293   David Wyatt, Introduction to *East of Eden*, Penguin Classics, p. xxii.
294   David Wyatt, Introduction to *East of Eden,* Penguin Classics, p. xxiv
295   David Wyatt, Introduction to *East of Eden,* Penguin Classics, pp. xxiv-xxv

Cathy (Kate) on the other hand, represents difference. Wyatt incorporates Steinbeck's words in describing her:

> *"Her life is one of revenge on other people because of a vague
> feeling of her own lack." Here is a woman who rapes herself, in-
> cinerates her parents, beds down with her brother-in-law, shoots
> her husband and abandons her children. Eve and Tamar and
> Delilah and Jezebel are rolled into one. She is realized through her
> actions rather than her motivations. Steinbeck tries once or twice
> to refer her back to the order of nature, as in the sentence "As
> though nature concealed a trap, Cathy had from the first a face of
> innocence." He throws out the notion of a "twisted gene or a mal-
> formed egg." But the tone of his opening sentence about her gets
> it right: "I believe there are monsters born in the world to human
> parents." This is right because it presents and does not explain.
> What Steinbeck creates in Cathy is an affront to the interpretative
> schemes that police the category we call "human."[296]*

The decision to focus on the last half of the book in the motion picture eliminated Charles Trask, Adam's brother, and Cal's real father.
Cathy slept with her husband Adam and brother-in-law Charles on
her wedding night. While the two boys had the same mother, they
had different fathers: Aron was Adam's son while Cal was actually
the son of Charles! Given the period of time when the film was made
(1954), it is doubtful the Motion Pictures Censorship group would
have approved of such an inclusion, although Charles is included in
a later *East of Eden* miniseries appearing on television in the 1980s.
What remains in the motion picture film is Cal's search for love and
identity: the unloved child striving for recognition. Concerning the
original novel, Wyatt notes:

> *The writer faces an earlier story the way people in the story face
> their ancestors. "This is our father," Adam says of the Cain and
> Abel story. We are children of the story: "This is our father. Some
> of our guilt is absorbed in our ancestry. What chance did we have?
> We are the children of our father. It means we aren't the first.
> It is an excuse, and there aren't enough excuses in the world."*

296   David Wyatt, Introduction to *East of Eden*, Penguin Classics, p. xxv.

Adam gets it half right. The first motion East of Eden asks us to perform is one of reverse projection—to take on the story, to take it in. Adam does this and stops. Cal does this and proceeds. When he says to Kate "I don't have to be you," he begins the second and crucial motion; he begins to rewrite the story. In doing so, he must call down God himself, the Father who wrote the father of all stories. He must call down God in the figure of Adam, his father, in order to get him to see his part in the story. In doing so, he rewrites "the story of original sin" and relocates it not in Eve's disobedience but in God's rejection of Cain's gift. The point being made about human life is that parents and Gods make a world in which children can spend a lifetime trying to decipher the expressions of their love.

So Lee takes Cal into the dying Adam's bedroom. Whether one is really loved, this cannot be known. The only love one feels is the love one feels for someone else. This is the love declared in the last scene of East of Eden: Adam raises his hand, but it is really Cal who has gotten him to raise it, and who gives the blessing. This is the third and final motion Cal must make, beyond taking on the story or revising it. It is a motion of brave indifference, the leap of an intention that can have confidence in nothing beyond itself. Cal blesses his father and forgives him, but he does not know, as he never has or will, whether that father loves him. Like the mind, love is lonely, an emotion necessarily self-confirmed. It is time for Cal to stop caring whether his father's love exists or is true, and time to admit that the pain he feels in being human is not because he is not loved, but because he loves.[297]

Cal's brother Aron, is not able to do this. As Wyatt notes:

Aron cannot renounce his family romance and dies of it. "He couldn't stand to know about his mother because that's not how he wanted the story to go—and he wouldn't have any other story. So he tore up the world." Aron repeats the stubborn credulity displayed by Adam when faced by the lies of his father: "I believe in my father." He inhabits a world where stories are either lies

297   David Wyatt, Introduction to *East of Eden*, Penguin Classics. p. xxviii.

or truth; he cannot make the difficult transit to a world in which all stories are seen as things that people make, fictive things. A fiction can never have the killing force of a lie because it is never presented as a truth. Steinbeck's novel studies "the difference between a lie and a story."[298]

***

Elia Kazan saw James Dean's performance in *The Immoralist* and knew he had found his Cal Trask. James Dean *was* Cal Trask! Years later, Emma Woollen Dean (Jimmy's grandmother) said that *East of Eden* was her favorite of the three films. Jimmy was like the character he portrayed on the screen. Her favorite scene was Cal running about the bean patch, trying to make the beans grow faster. He would do that at home on the farm. According to David Dalton:

> *Before long, the publicity mill was grinding out stories about Kazan's "new genius," the temperamental star who would be coached by Kazan, live in isolation at the studio and be protected by a closed set. It was true that Kazan and Jimmy didn't want anyone hanging around while Eden was shot, but the reaction was to make sensational comparisons to Greta Garbo.[299]*

Dalton further notes:

> *Kazan has been a prime creator of the anti-hero in American movies. He democratized and linked this rebellious figure to root American values by using such fundamentally recognizable types as Brando and Dean—i.e., Brando as a dock worker, Dean as a farmboy. For Kazan, East of Eden was not only a symbolic vision, it was also a vehicle for change. He has always believed that movies "change human life," and through movies like On the Waterfront and East of Eden, he tried to show how the discordant, disruptive elements of American society could effect wide-ranging changes in attitude, behavior and awareness. By making Jimmy the pivotal*

298   David Wyatt, Introduction to *East of Eden*, Penguin Classics.p. xxiv.
299   David Dalton, *The Mutant King*, p. 159.

character in the central American story of Eden, he identified him with the original spirit of revolution in America.[300]

Central to the success of *East of Eden* was the reaction/interaction between the characters on and off the screen. The conflict between James Dean and Raymond Massey (who played Adam Trask) is obvious. Massey had a keen dislike for the young actor playing the part of his son, something that is evident in his facial expression when Adam states, "But I'm not interested in making money, Cal." According to David Dalton:

> *Raymond Massey, who played Jimmy's father, Adam, was dignified, poised and temperate enough in real life to embody all the rigidity Jimmy railed against. Massey had not been cast by Kazan, but had made it a condition for accepting a role in Battle Cry, agreeing to play in the war movie only if he could also appear in the more prestigious Kazan film. Massey is not a Method actor and found Jimmy's long preparations for the scenes—exercising, shaking his wrists, bouncing up and down, long meditations in the dressing room—both excessive and unprofessional. He found Jimmy, who would sometimes not talk nor acknowledge someone's presence if he were "in character," rude and offensive.*[301]

I remember watching an interview with Julie Harris, who played Abra in the film, in which she stated that he was always pushing Raymond Massey's buttons, as though delighting in antagonizing him. David Dalton notes:

> *Kazan is notorious for drawing out emotional tensions and resources for dramatic use. If Jimmy began to spoil after Eden, Kazan, who drew on the lush bottom land of Jimmy's childhood for four intense months of shooting, had something to do with it.*
>
> *He took from this ripe moment of Jimmy's life the plasma for his film. Kazan himself recognized the loss of vitality suffered by his victim.*

---

300   David Dalton, *The Mutant King*, p.161.
301   David Dalton, *The Mutant King*, p. 165.

*"The more success an actor has," said Kazan, "the more he ac-
quires the look of wax fruit; he is no longer devoured by life . . . I
try to catch my actors at the moment when they are still, or again,
human. And if you have a human actor, at that moment, you can
slip your hand inside, touch him and wake him . . . Jimmy Dean . .
. was just a young fellow who prowled about the front offices. But
he had violence in him, he had a hunger within him, and he was
himself the boy that he played in the film."[302]*

And it was during the filming of *East of Eden* when James Dean met
the love of his life.

***

When James Dean met Anna Maria Pierangeli (Pier Angeli), she
was appearing in a Paul Newman film called *The Silver Chalice*. Jimmy
wandered over to the set on a break to see his friend Newman, and
that's when he met her. Although some writers have said the relationship was a studio-orchestrated romance and that it wasn't real,
evidence to the contrary certainly exists. Fourteen years later, Pier
Angeli told the *National Enquirer:*

*We used to go together to the California coast and stay there se-
cretly in a cottage on a beach far away from all prying eyes.*

*We'd spend much of our time on the beach, sitting there or fool-
ing around, just like college kids. We would talk about ourselves
and our problems, about the movies and acting, about life and
life after death.*

*Sometimes we would just go for a walk along the beach, not actu-
ally speaking, but communicating our love silently to each other.*

We had complete understanding of each other.

*[She put a handkerchief to her eyes to wipe away the tears as she
told the story of her young love.]*

---

302   David Dalton, *The Mutant King*, p. 172.

We were like Romeo and Juliet, together and inseparable. Sometimes on the beach we loved each other so much we just wanted to walk together into the sea holding hands because we knew then that we would always be together.

It wasn't that we wanted to commit suicide.

We loved our life and it was just that we wanted to be that close to each other always.

We didn't have to be seen together at film premieres or night-clubs.

We didn't need to be in the gossip columns or be seen at the big Hollywood parties.

We were like kids together and that's the way we both liked it.

We saw a great deal of each other when we weren't making films. We were young and wanted to enjoy life together and we did.

Sometimes we would just drive along and stop at a hamburger stand for a meal or go to a drive-in movie. It was all so innocent and so emphatic.[303]

But their relationship soon ended. Pier's mother, a staunch Catholic, disapproved of the relationship. In the words of David Dalton:

Pier's mother disapproved of Jimmy's tee-shirted appearance, the late dates, the fast car and, worst of all, he was not a Catholic. His manners left even more to be desired. On a particularly late outing, Mrs. Pierangeli remarked that such behavior was not per-mitted in Rome. Jimmy mumbled sarcastically, "When in Rome do as the Romans do; when in Hollywood ..." But it wasn't only Pier's mother who disapproved. MGM, where Pier was working, felt the relationship was not a good idea, and Jimmy's business "mom" Jane Deacy, advised him against marriage. "If you marry

---

303   Pier Angeli—qtd. In David Dalton, *The Mutant King*, p. 196.

her, you'll be Mr. Pier Angeli," she warned him. Shades of the Montagues and Capulets![304]

James Dean went on a trip to New York and while he was gone, Pier announced her engagement to singer Vic Damone and their subsequent wedding put together in less than two months shocked not only James Dean, but the press as well. The Hollywood legend for years centered around the story about the heart broken actor, sitting on his motorcycle across the street from the church, gunning it as the wedding party emerged from the church. This story has been both validated and denied. In *Pier Angeli: A Fragile Life*, Jane Allen describes the scene:

> *Exiting from the candlelit church into the sudden brightness of the midday sun, Pier was aware of a crowd of people on the steps, and photographers up close and shouting, "Hey Pier!" "Look this way Vic," then "Kiss him, go on Pier." Vic had his arm around her, and as Pier turned toward him for their first married kiss for the cameras, she was aware of the noise of a motorbike revving up across the street, and glimpsed a familiar figure taking off at high speed. Her heart lurched; she knew who it was. So did Esme Chandlee who was right behind her and witnessed the moment. By now the whole wedding party had arrived on the steps beside them, being grouped for a formal portrait. In the crush it took some time for guests to make their way out of the church, and by then Jimmy Dean was long gone. The pictures taken that day say it all. Pier smiled and smiled, and laughed like an overexcited child, but not a single photograph records a loving glance between her and Vic—he seldom looked at the camera and not once did he look at her.*[305]

I remember another account of the marriage ceremony that supposedly happened the night before the wedding. Unfortunately, I can no longer remember where I read this. On the night before his wedding, Vic Damone was celebrating at a restaurant with some friends. James Dean walked in. Vic Damone walked up to him and extended his

304   David Dalton, *The Mutant King*, pp. 196-197
305   Jane Allen, *Pier Angeli: A Fragile Life*, p. 111.

hand. James Dean's response? He yelled, "YOU MAY HAVE HER NOW, BUT YOU WON'T HAVE HER FOR LONG." And that's when they started swinging at one another. It took a number of men on both sides to separate them. It is quite possible this incident did happen. There was no love loss between the two men. According to Jane Allen:

> *He told Kendis Rochlen that Pier had stunned him with the news that she was getting married before the engagement was officially announced, "but she wouldn't tell me who the guy was," he said. "I was floored when I learned it was Vic Damone. I figure that when I went back to New York after finishing East of Eden her family and friends got in her ear and changed her mind about me. I won't try to pretend I'm not sorry—Pier's still okay with me. Oh well," he added flippantly, "maybe she likes his singing. I hope they'll be happy."*
>
> *Only some of that was true. The flippancy was a cover for something approaching rage. What he said off the record to Rochlen paints a different picture. "....I know how we can cure her of Damone. We lock her in a five-by-five room plastered with pictures of him before his nose job." He expressed the same sentiments to Christine White in New York, early in November. "He called Damone a jerk, among other four letter words," White recalled. "He couldn't believe that out of all the competition, Damone was the one to beat him: The attitude Dean adopted seemed to depend largely on who he was talking to.[306]*

Jane Allen writes:

> *Apart from Dean momentarily spoiling the atmosphere with bad-tempered exhaust fumes, there were remarkably few mishaps on the day, given that the wedding was assembled in less than two months. Connolly records that Vic suffered a mild attack of nerves in the car on the way to church and, asking his driver to turn on the radio because he thought music might help, found himself listening to another groom-to-be, Eddie Fisher. Vic also left the marriage certificate behind at the Church, and Pier, who'd*

---

306   Jane Allen, *Pier Angeli: A Fragile Life*, p. 98.

*forgotten for two months to give the official photographer Earl
Leaf his gift of cufflinks, remembered only just in time to bring
them to the church.*[307]

Concerning whether James Dean was actually on a motorcycle across
the street from the church, Jane Allen states:

*Dean returned to Hollywood in time for the wedding, to which
he was not invited. He told several friends he was going to be
there anyway, wearing the black leather jacket Enrica hated and
sitting on his motorcycle outside the church. He was there, said
Esme Chandlee, who saw him gunning his bike and speeding off
in a cloud of acrid blue smoke when the newly-weds appeared on
the steps of St. Timothy's church. He had to talk about it to someone. According to his friend Maila Nurmi, known as Vampira, "He
came into Googies when I was having coffee and said 'I've just
come from a wedding.'"*

*"Well, I knew which wedding—Pier Angeli and Vic Damone. Then
he said, 'I revved my motorcycle and I took off outa there.'"*

*"His heart broke," said Vampira theatrically, "He was deeply,
deeply in a state of love with her."...*

*...Several people who knew Dean in the last months of his life
attest that he never got over Pier. Joe Hyams claims he went to
visit Dean shortly after the wedding and found him on the floor,
rocking back and forth in misery with a picture of Pier in his arms.
He withdrew without speaking and Dean had no recollection of
the visit.*[308]

[Hyams supplies two versions of this encounter: the one described
here and another where he took the distraught Jimmy in his arms and
rocked him.]

James Dean's love for Pier Angeli has been substantiated by a number
of people:

---

307   Jane Allen, *Pier Angeli: A Fragile Life,* p. 112.
308   Jane Allen, *Pier Angeli: A Fragile Life,* pp. 98-99.

Natalie Wood: ...remembered that during the filming of Rebel Without a Cause, Dean would buy all the fan magazines and read about his romance with Pier, and that could have been because he loved the publicity about himself. But her close friend Mary Ann Marinkovich claims that by the end of filming Rebel, Natalie and Dean were close friends, and she comforted him in his distress when the news broke that Pier was pregnant. "Pier was Jimmy's whole life, I mean eat, live, sleep, breathe—it was so sad that whole thing"...

Jane Withers: "After that it was Pier Angeli,...We had talked of many things, but it always came back to Pier. He talked of her constantly. He just worshipped the ground she walked on."

Elizabeth Taylor: "Sometimes he would come over to my house and we'd talk until three in the morning. Then we had to be on set together at 7 A.M. He would tell me things you'd only tell to a very good friend... Wouldn't you love to know!"[309]

In addition, Julie Harris recalled during an interview for a documentary that James Dean wore an Ankh on a chain around his neck. According to Harris, he once opened it and showed her a lock of Pier's hair that he carried inside. He grew really emotional about it, and she firmly believed that he really loved Pier.

After his death, a pamphlet outlining *The Order of Matrimony* was found among his effects with "blanks for the names of the bride and groom. In every space indicated for the bride, the name Pier was penciled in".[310] But there is another story about the James Dean-Pier Angeli romance that takes an interesting twist, as noted by Jane Allen:

In 1955, Harrison Carroll in the L.A. Herald-Examiner reported on the case of a grief-crazed fan who, having written many letters to Dean during his lifetime, following his death turned her attention to writing to Natalie Wood and Rebel Without a Cause director, Nick Ray. According to Carroll, these letters were unsigned, and all postmarked Erie, Pennsylvania. Ray was sufficiently concerned

309   Jane Allen, *Pier Angeli: A Fragile Life*, pp. 99-100.
310   Jane Allen, *Pier Angeli: A Fragile Life*, p. 100.

by their morbid tone to telephone the manager of the Erie cinema to find out if anyone was known to have been attending showings of Dean's films an unusual number of times.

Many years later, a bundle of unsigned letters dated 1955, post-marked Erie Pennsylvania, and purporting to have been written by Pier to Dean, was sold to a member of Dean's family in Fairmount. These most likely are the same letters. They are on display in the museum.[311]

Pier had two unhappy marriages that both ended in divorce. Her first was to Vic Damone, and her second was to Armando Trovajoli. It is true in her later years that she romanticized her young love with James Dean, as noted in *The Fragile Life,* by Jane Allen, when discussing the *National Enquirer* interview:

The story was accompanied by old file photos of Dean and Anna (Pier), pictures of both her weddings, and of Dean's Porsche before and after the crash. It was wildly inaccurate. It did nothing to revive her image in any positive way in the public eye, and certainly didn't lead to any offers from Hollywood. The Dean merchants meanwhile set about catering to the burgeoning market they'd helped to create, making documentaries about his life that always included one of the few MGM publicity shots of Dean and Anna together, and sometimes brief newsreel footage of her wedding to Vic. Whether portrayed as the pure Madonna—the only love of Dean's life—or as just another girl in a string of starlets he dated, or even as the wicked heartless woman who abandoned him for another, she was part of the legend.

Another part of the fiction, according to Marisa [Pier's sister], was the creation of their "great but contentious love." Anna had never experienced the passionate feelings for Dean that the press wrote about. There was tenderness, flirtation, but no more. "In that climate of fantasy," Marisa continued, "even if Anna had wanted to forget Dean, it was in no way possible. For years, in fact, journalists and others continued to speak to her about him

311   Jane Allen, *Pier Angeli: A Fragile Life,* pp. 100-101.

until he became like a restless ghost which greatly disturbed my sister's peace of mind."

Why then did Anna always carry a photo of him? Patrizia remembers that Anna always had two photos beside her bed, one of her father and one of James Dean, the two men she claimed to have loved the most, who died young, and whom she idealized in death.[312]

Anna Maria Pierangeli died September 14, 1971 of what her family believes was anaphylactic shock resulting from Dr. Ramon Spritzler's administration of Compazine.[313] Her sister, Marisa, found out later that she should have been carefully monitored after receiving the injection, and she wasn't. For the sake of Pier's two sons, no charges against the doctor were ever pursued. Her funeral service was held at The Church of the Good Shepherd in Beverly Hills and she is buried in France.

Like Cal Trask and Abra of *East of Eden*, James Dean and Pier Angeli fell in love and were caught in a tangled situation. Cal and Abra were eventually drawn together. On the other hand, James Dean and Pier were separated by overwhelming odds. Unfortunately, this seems to be the story of James Dean's life. He was never "lucky in love."

After her second marriage ended, Pier had this to say about James Dean:

"He is the only man I ever loved deeply as a woman should love a man. I never loved either of my husbands the way I loved Jimmy.

I tried to love my husbands but it never lasted. I would wake up in the night and find I had been dreaming of Jimmy. I would lie awake in the same bed with my husband, think of my love for Jimmy and wish it was Jimmy and not my husband who was next to me.

---

312   Jane Allen, *Pier Angeli: A Fragile Life*, pp. 182-183.
313   Jane Allen, *Pier Angeli: A Fragile Life*, p. 199.

> *I had to separate from my husbands because I don't think one can be in love with one man—even if he is dead—and live with another."*[314]

In answering why Pier would hastily marry someone else if she and Jimmy were so much in love, David Dalton writes:

> *Leonard Rosenman suggested a sinister reason for their break-up: "Jimmy would get drunk on a couple of glasses of wine, and when he got drunk he could become very nasty. His personality completely changed; he was completely uncontrollable and could get vicious. It was very Jekyll and Hyde. He also became violent, and he had a reputation for beating up his girlfriends. He did this to Pier once too often and I think she had just had enough."*[315]

Possibly, since his temper had gotten the best of him on prior occasions. Regarding his temper, James Dean was once quoted as saying: "I'm trying to get ahold of the violence in my life, for only the gentle are ever really strong."

314   David Dalton, *The Mutant King*, p. 198.
315   David Dalton, *The Mutant King*, p. 198.

CHAPTER 18—*REBEL WITHOUT A CAUSE*: IN SEARCH OF JIM STARK

*T*he wide and continuing interest in this book confirms what The New York Times predicted in its review: "It may develop to be epochal in its field. The indomitable pioneering implicit in Dr. Lindner's quest of the real secret of criminalism will surely one day prevail."

The entire course of a scientific experiment is presented in this remarkable book.

By means of a novel telescoped technique utilizing the methods of psychoanalysis and hypnosis, the author uncovers the crucial episodes and the basic characterologic factors in the life of a youthful criminal and reconstructs the mental history of a baffling abnormal personality from earliest infancy, through a perverted, lawbreaking boyhood, to the young manhood phase in a pentintiary environment.

The subject unfolds his own story, and in his deepest revelations relives the experiences that dynamically shaped his aberrant being.

Eminent criminologists have hailed this unique full-length psychologic life record as a courageous and ingenious innovation, foreshadowing a new instrument of scientific insight and possibly a means of rehabilitation of the psychopathic individual that will help to allay the problem he presents to society with ever increasing threat.

In a significant passage the author says:

> "This is the menace of psychopathy: The phychopath [sic] is not only a criminal; he is the embryonic storm trooper; he is the disinherited...whose aggressions can be mobilized on the instant by that leader under whose tinseled aegis license becomes law, secret and primitive desires become virtuous ambitions..." [316]

> From the jacket of Rebel Without a Cause:
> Robert M. Lindner (1944)

***

The original material for *Rebel Without a Cause* appeared in a study of a psychopath by Dr. Robert M. Lindner in 1944. Titled *Rebel Without a Cause: The Hypnoanalysis of a Criminal Psychopath*, the book focused on the motivation of one young man from childhood to young adult. In his preface, Lindner writes:

> In preparing the material for publication, the writer was torn between two desires which apparently exerted almost equal weight. He was anxious to offer for discussion and experiment a psychotherapeutic technique of promise especially at a time when it could be used to such advantage in the armed services and on the home front where the strains of living in a period of chaos are reflected in mental casualties. At the same time, he earnestly desired to present the findings of research with a type of personality disorder that is responsible for much of crime and has broad social and even political implications. If this book does both, it will have realized such intentions. [317]

Between 1944 and 1954, Hollywood toyed with the idea of making a film based on Lindner's material, but the project did not take hold until a maverick director by the name of Nicholas Ray seized the moment. The period of the late 1940s/early 1950s was a challenging

---

316   Robert M. Lindner, *Rebel Without a Cause: The Hypnoanalysis of a Criminal Psychopath,* Book Jacket.
317   Robert . Lindner, Preface, *Rebel Without a Cause: The Hypnoanalysis of a Criminal Psychopath,* xiii

time for film makers, as is described by Douglas L. Rathgeb in his *The Making of Rebel Without a Cause:*

> *Despite the threats of communism and nuclear annihilation, America was comfortably complacent; weekend barbeques, the Sunday paper, shopping trips, long-meandering drives in the country. For the nation's middle-class adults, who still remembered the Great Depression, life had never been better. For ever-increasing numbers of their teenage children, however, the Good Life was flawed by powerful feelings of alienation and anger.*

> *More and more, teens seemed to express those feelings through violence and crime. According to an article in the September 17, 1954, issue of U.S. News and World Report, juvenile delinquency had increased more than 40 percent between 1948 and 1953, right along with the post-war prosperity. More than a million teenagers a year now came to the attention of the police.*

> *A rising divorce rate, television, teenage drinking, even comic books took part of the blame for teenage violence, but too much of it had no explanation. Especially difficult to understand was criminal activity among the most affluent and privileged of America's youth. The spread of delinquency from the urban lower class to the suburban middle and upper classes was an ominous trend. Yet, these "concealed delinquents," as U.S. News called them, seemed mainly the problem of parents and child psychiatrists, not police or social workers. Like Leopold and Loeb, the rich, spoiled thrill killers of the 1920s, such teenagers were exceptions, anomalies, oddities. Despite the threat they posed to post-war society, they were not a concern of America's growing social consciousness movement.*[318]

Thus the classic film, *Rebel Without a Cause*, was born with James Dean in the starring role of Jim Stark!

Dean was well suited for the lead role in this film. Nicholas Ray had read about some of his antics. According to Rothgeb:

---

318   Douglas L. Rathgeb, *The Making of Rebel Without a Cause*, 6.

...James Dean...had been a controversial figure at Warner Bros. since his arrival the previous April. Ray had undoubtedly heard some of the stories about Dean: that he was moody, insolent and uncooperative; that he had once kept a loaded revolver in his trailer on studio property; that he drove his motorcycle at dangerous speeds down studio streets and through sound stages; that he had bizarre and unsavory friends.

He had heard also that Dean was emotionally unstable, and that Kazan had been forced to baby-sit the young actor in side-by-side studio trailers to keep him from running away during the production [East of Eden]. Dean's co-star, Julie Harris, whom Kazan called "an angel on the set," had worked overtime quelling Dean's frequent attacks of panic.[319]

Their first meeting left Ray somewhat perplexed. According to Rothgeb:

...Leonard Rosenman, the film's composer, was improvising at the piano while Kazan screened the film. James Dean stood inconspicuously in a corner. Wearing eyeglasses, unshaven and hunched over, he did not remotely resemble a movie star. Ray's first reaction was undoubtedly puzzlement. How could this shy, awkward young man possibly be the subject of so much media attention? How could he possibly be Hollywood's newest phenomenon? The discrepancy between the man and the image seemed to intensify as Ray watched Dean portray Cal Trask so powerfully on the screen. It did not seem possible that these were both James Dean. Dean himself did not seem to believe it. He watched himself with an odd, almost adolescent fascination, as if he were admiring someone else.[320]

Thereafter, they met periodically, James Dean picking with Ray about the details of the film. He would ask, then vanish, only to return later with another question or two. But he seemed to develop a keen interest in the role of Jim Stark and "seemed genuinely intrigued by the

319   Douglas L. Rathgeb, *The Making of Rebel without a Cause,* 20.
320   Douglas L. Rathgeb, *The Making of Rebel Without a Cause, 20-21.*

concept of middle-class delinquency."[321] Somewhere along the line, Ray decided he had found his Jim Stark. And the rest is history.

The only resemblance between the film *Rebel Without a Cause* and Lindner's initial study is the title. The script engaged several writers before it was finally finished, beginning first with Leon Uris (whose vision of the film was completely opposite that of Nicholas Ray's). Robert Lindner began objecting to the title of the film, an objection leading to a great deal of legal maneuvering. Irving Shulman next tackled the script, and when his vision diverted from Ray's, Stewart Stern was then employed to finish the task. And then came his first meeting with James Dean. According to Rathgeb:

> *Stern had never met James Dean. When Stern arrived at the home of Arthur Loew, Jr., that December afternoon, Dean was sitting in a swivel chair in the living room. As usual, he was keeping to himself. He gave Stern a terse greeting and then ignored him. When Stern sat in the swivel chair across from him, Dean swiveled the other way in his, turning his back. Stern did the same. After about ten minutes of silence, Stern heard a loud mooing sound from across the room. Stern mooed back convincingly. After a few variations on cows, they moved on to imitations of sheep, chickens, horses, and pigs. This odd encounter created an instant friendship between the two men.[322]*

A number of actresses were considered to play the part of Judy in the film. Warner Bros. wanted Debbie Reynolds. Nicholas Ray's first choice was Carroll Baker and then switched his allegiance to Natalie Wood. Margaret O'Brien hoped to get the part. Jayne Mansfield tested for the part. James Dean recommended his friend, Christine White (she never tested for the part)--but Natalie Wood would eventually win the role. Sal Mineo was eventually cast in the role of Plato, Jim and Judy's lonely friend. Billy Gray from the television show *Father Knows Best* was also a contender for that part, as was Jack Simmons, who had acted with Jimmy as one of the delinquents in "The Dark, Dark Hours." Both Natalie Wood and Sal Mineo later received Oscar nominations for their portrayals of Judy and Plato.

---

321   Douglas L. Rathgeb, *The Making of Rebel Without a Cause,* 21.
322   Douglas L. Rathgeb, *The Making of Rebel Without a Cause,* 40.

Completion of the film was by no means easy. Originally shot in black and white, the film was switched to a color format, requiring all the earlier scenes to be reshot. Encounters between Ray and the studio heads were constant with script reworkings and other changes. And the use of real switchblades in the fight scene at the Planetarium caused concern. Rathgeb describes the situation:

...James Dean and Corey Allen [Buzz, the gang leader] used real knives. It was illegal in California to manufacture or own switch-blades, so the Property Department had borrowed thirty of them from Juvenile Hall. The police had confiscated the knives from young hoodlums picked up on various charges. After Frank Mazzola coached Dean and Allen in handling the weapons, they began a carefully choreographed ballet of thrust and parry. The prop man had dulled the blades, and both actors wore chest pro-tectors under their shirts, but there was still some danger. The work was physically exhausting for the two actors, who had to make a convincing display without actually hurting each other. Ray appeared relaxed enough as the cameras rolled, but Dean and Allen quickly showed signs of stress. After several attempts, they still hadn't found the nerve to fight at close range.

When they finally did engage, the safety precautions failed. One of Allen's thrusts caught Dean on the neck just below the right ear. As soon as Ray saw the blood, he stopped filming. The First Aid Man, wearing a bright red windbreaker, rushed to give Dean assistance. Fortunately, the wound was superficial...

...During one of the breaks in the action, Corey Allen found a quiet spot on the front lawn of the observatory. As he tried to focus his thoughts and calm his jittery nerves, he also kept a wary eye on Dean. Allen had made a point of keeping track of Dean on the set, watching him as if he were a real adversary. Suddenly, Dean walked over to him and, without saying a word, handed him a cup of water. The gesture startled Allen, who asked, "How did you know I wanted a drink of water? Dean answered, "I'm a lot older than you!."[323]

---

323   Douglas L. Rathgeb, *The Making of Rebel Without a Cause*, 107-108.

In addition to the mechanics of making the film and ensuing prob-
lems, the theme of the film was beginning to cause it some trouble.
In a large part, this was due to another film released in March titled
Blackboard Jungle. A review of that film by Bosley Crowther of *The
New York Times* was consistent with the view of others:

> *It is a full-throated, all-out testimonial to the lurid headlines
> that appear from time to time, reporting acts of terrorism and
> violence by uncontrolled urban youths. It gives a blood-curdling,
> nightmarish picture of monstrous disorder in a public school. And
> it leaves one wondering wildly whether such out-of-hand horrors
> can be.*
>
> *...From scenes that show the painful inability of the teacher to
> control his class, let alone interest his pupils and get something
> into their heads, to incidents of straight assault and battery, cul-
> minating with an attack upon the teacher with a knife, the em-
> phasis is wholly upon impudence, rebellion and violence...*
>
> *...More than a question of entertainment is involved, however, in
> this film, since it treats of a contemporary subject that is social
> dynamite. And it is on the question of its faithfulness to over-all
> conditions that we suspect it may be challenged not only as re-
> sponsible reporting, but also as a desire stimulant it to spread
> before the young.*[324]

Another review of *Blackboard Jungle* in *Variety* decided:

> *Exhibition of "The [sic] Blackboard Jungle" at Proctor's Theater
> was blamed for prompting several teenagers last week to form
> a gang, which proposed to wage a battle with an Albany group.
> Other juvenile outbreaks were attributed to the motion picture,
> which deals with delinquency in a public school. Local papers
> played up the film as an alleged contributing factor.*[325]

---

324 Bosley Crowther, *The New York Times*. Qtd. In Douglas L. Rathgeb, *The
Making of Rebel Without a Cause,* 92.
325 Douglas L. Rathgeb, *The Making of Rebel Without a Cause,* 146.

Because the turmoil over *Blackboard Jungle* began spilling over to *Rebel Without a Cause,* James Dean provided a spirited defense of his film in the *Los Angeles Mirror-News:*

> *There's a new burst of celluloid juvenile delinquency coming up on the screen in "Rebel Without a Cause" that may again bring out the "excessive violence" blue pencils.*

> *This time it's James ("East of Eden") Dean packing a switch-blade knife and, in one scene, hurling his father down a flight of stairs following an argument.*

> *But if the censors black out the violence Dean thinks "they'll be doing the country an injustice."*

> *It's Dean's private theory after playing the role:*

> *"Since juvenile delinquency is based on violence, it is justified violence. We picture a very real situation that exists in this country—something that should be stamped out. Movies like "The Blackboard Jungle" and "Rebel" can help."*

> *Any arguments?*[326]

That was in 1955. Today in 2012, the film is considered a classic. Teachers use it in the classroom. Fans cluster about it. Of the three main films that James Dean made, *Rebel Without a Cause* is best remembered. The rest of this chapter will focus on an answer to the question: why?

***

Films like *Rebel Without a Cause, Blackboard Jungle,* and *The Wild One* came under fire by one U.S. Senator, Estes Kefauver, who started his one-man war against violence in motion pictures. And Jack Warner was summoned to appear before Kefauver's sub-committee. Rathgeb describes that encounter:

---

326   Douglas L. Rathgeb, *The Making of Rebel Without a Cause,* 146-147.

As if to intimidate the moguls, Kefauver had filled the cramped hearing room on the fifth floor of the Federal Building with lurid movie posters, the supposed proof of Hollywood's bad judgment. Kefauver listed twelve current films that he claimed were too violent, too sexually oriented or too pro-criminal. Blackboard Jungle headed a list that included Black Tuesday, Hell's Island, The Prodigal, New Orleans Uncensored and I Died a Thousand Times, a remake of High Sierra. Kefauver's dirty dozen list included the unreleased Rebel Without a Cause. As Warner presented his testimony, the following exchange occurred:

Kefauver: "We've had some calls on Rebel Without a Cause."

Warner: "Whoever called must be working with radar. I haven't seen it myself yet."

Warner suggested jokingly that one of the studio's competitors might have filed the complaint against Rebel. He added, "You shouldn't believe everything you hear, Senator."[327]

Contentions against the film continued in the press, however, as exhibited by Dorothy Kilgallen in her column:

Parents worried about juvenile delinquency will hit the ceiling when they see the bloody switchblade scene between teenagers in "Rebel Without a Cause." One Hollywood citizen who caught the film commented: "'Blackboard Jungle'" was just a mild trailer for this one."[328]

Yet *Rebel Without a Cause* survived while many of its counterparts did not. And in words attributed to William Faulkner, *Rebel Without a Cause* will remain a masterpiece, because it is the American cinema's only Greek tragedy. While leafing through a notebook of articles I collected over the years, I found an unidentified teacher's Greek tragedy unit titled *Rebel Without a Cause: Greek Tragedy in Modern Film.[329]*

---

327   Douglas L. Rathgeb, *The Making of Rebel Without a Cause,* 159.
328   Douglas L. Rathgeb, *The Making of Rebel Without a Cause,* 167.
329   *Rebel Without a Cause: Greek Tragedy in Modern Film.* Date accessed: 29 Mar 2001. Available online at: http://www.geocities.com/Athens/Parthenon/9502/rebel.html

This syllabus is no longer available on the internet, unless it is on a different database. So I will set out its basic precepts. The introduction states:

> There are many films which include elements of Greek Tragedy. Certain western films, like High Noon, Warlock, and Shenandoah incorporate aspects of Tragedy; more recently, Woody Allen has given us Mighty Aphrodite and Husbands and Wives, which redefined Tragedy in terms of Judaism. My favorite for teaching, has always been Rebel Without a Cause.
>
> Perhaps part of the tragic elements of this film are in the tragic irony of its production: the way it created the icon of James Dean, dead before the film's release; the incredible footage of Dean, filmed shortly before his death, advising teenagers to drive carefully—"Remember, the life you save may be mine." More important, perhaps, is the adherence to Aristotles' rules (with an occasional nod to Shakespearian Tragedy).
>
> (Much of this material comes from an excellent article on Tragedy by Douglas Johnston and Brian Grandy. Quoted material is theirs.)
>
> The purpose of Tragedy, as Johnston and Grandy put it is: "to ask questions about the nature of man, his position in the universe, his relation to the powers that govern his life." Jim Stark, the tragic hero of Rebel Without a Cause, is just such a person. He wants to be a man, but if not like his father, then who? He wants to fit in with the other kids, but from the start is an outcast, clearly symbolized by his reprimand for stepping on the school insignia.[330]

The article then identifies the elements of Tragedy:

> The Unities: A Greek tragedy should occur within a 24 hour time period, with all scenes taking place in relatively the same place. Rebel Without a Cause begins in the early morning and ends the following morning. It takes place at several locations in one town.

---

330   *Rebel Without a Cause: Greek Tragedy in Modern Film,* Date Accessed: 3/29/01. Available online at http://www.geocities.com/Athens/ Parthenon/9502/rebel.html

Chorus: "The chorus both commented on the events and partici-pated in them, so that it was both involved in the action and de-tached from it." In Rebel, the gang of kids is involved in the knife fight and the chickie run, and later act as vigilantes (or Erinyes?) judges of Jim's actions.

Hubris: The act of Hubris is the act of questioning the Gods. In Greek Tragedy, the defiance and arrogance of heroes lead to misfortune. Jim Stark defies his father, teachers, the police, and gang members, in his attempt to balance his universe and find the Greek Ideal.

Catharsis: "By participating vicariously in the grief, pain and fear of the tragic hero or heroine, the spectator, in Aristotle's words, experiences pity and fear and is purged." There can be no doubt as to the effect of this film on its audience in 1955. As Joe Hyams, in Little Boy Lost, wrote of James Dean: "..In his acting, he had the intuitive talent for expressing the hopes and fears that are a part of all young people...He managed to dramatize brilliantly the questions every young person in every generation must resolve."[331]

There is a tragic situation. (The author stays with Johnston and Grandy on this as he felt they word it perfectly:)

"In Greek tragedy the tragic situation, in which the characters find themselves, is always a situation in which man seems to be deprived of all outward help and is forced to rely entirely on him-self. It is a situation of extraordinary tension, of utmost conflict. Studying the plots of a number of Greek tragedies, one can find variations of two basic tragic situations:

1. First there is the case of man's miscalculation of reality which brings about the fatal situation.

2. The second kind of tragic situation is that of man between two conflicting principles. The protagonist is suddenly put at the

---

331   *Rebel Without a Cause: Greek Tragedy in Modern Film,* Date Accessed: 3/29/01. Available online at http://www.geocities.com/Athens/Parthenon/9502/rebel.html

crossing point of two duties, both of which claim fulfillment. This is the most compelling tragic situation and is at the same time the one that has most often been chosen by the Greek dramatists."

We can find both elements in the tragic situation of Rebel Without a Cause. Jim miscalculates several times, thinking they can run from their problems or that Ray will be at the police office when he needs him. His final miscalculation occurs when he is trying to protect Plato by disarming him, perhaps finally understanding the helplessness of his own father at the same time.

The second situation is crucial to the story, driving Jim to erupt in frustration when he cannot reconcile the moral obligation of his honor and his legal responsibilities over the chickie run.[332]

In a separate section titled *Some Ideas for Testing and Projects on Tragedy*, the author states:

These are a few Testing/Project ideas I've had for the Rebel/ Tragedy unit. I haven't tried them all out yet, so you might want to use some caution before incorporating them into your own units.

"The Rock" by Harry Chapin: After reading about the elements of tragedy on previous pages, I had the class hear Harry's song while viewing the lyrics. Then, I asked them to write a single paragraph explaining the elements of tragedy that they heard in the story.

I got some interesting results. The kids saw use of a chorus, plenty of hubris, an alienated hero forced to rely on himself, and miscal- culation of reality. I think the kids really did some thinking and were able to recognize classical devices in modern material.

You can find everything you need to do this yourself at The Harry Chapin Fan Page, an excellent site.

---

332 *Rebel Without a Cause: Greek Tragedy in Modern Film,* Date Accessed: 3/29/01. Available online at http://www.geocities.com/Athens/ Parthenon/9502/rebel.html

Library Project: I simply asked the class to read a book and look for examples of Classical Tragedy... [a link is provided with this note] (If you would like a copy of the complete assignment, click here. (You might find some of the books I selected a bit too easy for your own classes.[333]

The unit author also provides a link to Tim Dirk's analysis of *Rebel Without a Cause*. Dirks writes:

It is a film that sympathetically reviews rebellious, American, restless, misunderstood, middle-class youth. The story provides a rich, but styled look at the world of the mid-1950s from the perspective of the main adolescent character. The colorful wide-screen Cinemascope feature affords a classic, semi-glamorized portrait of three troubled, frustrated, anguished, and identity-seeking teenagers, alienated from the world and values of parents and adults. It has also been surmised that Sal Mineo's teen-aged character in the film was gay and troubled by typical problems of in-the-closet homosexuals in the 50s—the film disguises his problems, but hints at the possibility that he is seeking out Dean.[334]

Finding that the film was partly inspired by Shakespeare's melodrama/tragedy *Romeo and Juliet*, Dirks notes that the narrative film is neatly divided into five acts:

- The exposition of the conflict between parents and children

- Interaction between the teenage characters, both befriending and taunting

- The climactic challenge of the daredevil 'chickie run"

- The peaceful and loving, but transitory denouement following the fatal challenge

---

333   *Some Ideas for Testing and Projects on Tragedy.* Date accessed: 3/29/01. Available online at http://www.geocities.com/Athens/Parthenon/9502/tragedytests.html

334   Tim Dirks, *Rebel Without a Cause (1955): A Review by Tim Dirks.* Date Accessed: 3/29/01. Available online at http://www.filmsite.org/rebel.html

- And the final tragedy of the last act when the three young people are brought together and only two survive.[335]

Dirks provides an analysis of the main stages of the film, beginning with Jim Stark's arrest for drunkenness and booking at the police station:

> *The scene in the police station cleverly introduces the three principal characters as they are each separately hauled in for varying reasons on this late Easter night, and their paths cross. Behind wooden-framed, glass partitions off the lobby, two other middle-class, misunderstood, alienated teenagers are also being held for their anti-social behavior: a pretty, unloved girl named Judy (Natalie Wood) in a bright red-outfit with matching red lipstick, and an emotionally-disturbed 'orphan' named John ('Plato') (Sal Mineo). All of them are connected together by their problems – they all suffer from a lack of love and feelings of abandonment, and they all experience difficulties relating to their parents.[336]*

Dirks also incorporates an effective use of dialogue in his analysis:

> *Jim's father tries downplaying his son's drinking. Both his parents argue together in officer Ray's company, while Jim hums and fidgets on the side. Jim is alienated from his conformist, indifferent parents in their Los Angeles suburb. His father also explains background about their family and their parents:*

>> *Jim's father: You see, we just moved here you understand, and uh, the kid hasn't got any friends, you understand, and we moved into a...*

>> *Jim: Tell him why we moved here.*

>> *Jim's father: Will you hold it Jim?*

>> *Jim: ...Tell the man why we moved here.*

---

335   Tim Dirks, *Rebel Without a Cause (1955): A Review by Tim Dirks*. Date Accessed: 3/29/01. Available online at http://www.filmsite.org/rebel.html
336   Tim Dirks, *Rebel Without a Cause (1955): A Review by Tim Dirks*. Date Accessed: 3/29/01. Available online at http://www.filmsite.org/rebel.html

Jim's father: Will you hold it?

Jim: You can't protect me.

Jim's father: Do you mind if I try? Do—do you have to slam the door in my face? I try to get to him. What happens? (To Jim) Don't I buy everything you want? A bicycle, you get a bicycle, a car.

Jim: You buy me many things.

Jim's father: Well, not just buy. We give you love and affection, don't we? Well, then, what is it?

Their love is smothering and artificial. Jim finally can't listen any more and violently cries out to his bickering parents:

You're tearing me apart!...You say one thing, he says another, and everybody changes back again.[337]

Although Jim and Judy first saw one another at the police station hours earlier, their first actual encounter occurred when both were on their way to school. According to Dirks:

For his first day at school, Jim again wears 'adult' clothing—a white shirt and dark sportscoat (and a tie that he immediately removes after walking outside). He joins next-door neighbor Judy on her way to school, recognizing her from the night before in the police station. In an awkward courtship dialogue, Jim tries to make conversation with her. Their simple words to each other reveal both attraction and repulsion, stand-offishness and interest, and juvenile attitudes and peer-pressures:

Jim: Hi. Hi. Wait a minute. (He runs down to her) Hi. I seen you before.

Judy: Well, stop the world.

Jim: Just bein' friendly.

---

337   Tim Dirks, *Rebel Without a Cause (1955): A Review by Tim Dirks*. Date Accessed: 3/29/01. Available online at http://www.filmsite.org/rebel.html

Judy: Well, now that's true. But life is crushing in on me.

Jim: Life can be beautiful. I know where it was.

Judy: Where what was?

Jim: Where I first saw ya. Everything going OK now? (Gesturing toward her house). You live here, don't you?

Judy: Who lives?

Jim: Hey, where's Dawson High?

Judy: At University and 10ᵗʰ.

Jim: Mmm. Thanks.

Judy: You wanna carry my books?

Jim: I got my car. You wanna go with me?

Judy: I go with the kids.

Jim: Yeah, I bet. (The gang's car screeches around the corner). All right.

Judy: You know, I bet you're a real yo-yo.

Jim: (under his breath): I love you too!

After offering her a ride to school, she turns unfriendly, rejecting his request and calling him a name. She runs away to an open carload of other kids in a local gang. Judy kisses leather-jacketed boyfriend Buzz (Corey Allen), the leader of the gang. Judy continues to make fun of him in front of the gang: "That's a new disease." He asks directions to the school from them, receiving deliberately garbled information—but he smiles and turns away, not wishing to provoke hostility. As a newcomer at the school, he is warned about stepping on Dawson High School's insignia on the school's steps and eyed suspiciously by many of the students.[338]

---

338   Tim Dirks, *Rebel Without a Cause (1955): A Review by Tim Dirks.* Date Accessed: 3/29/01. Available online at http://www.filmsite.org/rebel.html

Jim is the only one who calls Judy by name in the film. To everyone else, she is "hey, you!" Buzz does not call her by name and appears somewhat surprised when Jim calls her over to his car by name just before the race to request some dirt, too. Had Buzz not died and remained in the film, the ultimate twist in the story would have been the grand battle between Buzz and Jim for Judy.

In summing up the film's success, Douglas Rathgeb writes:

> *Although Rebel had failed to generate successful imitations during the three decades after its initial success, it stayed alive in other forms. In a 1989 film, Earth Girls Are Easy, a group of aliens watch the "You're tearing me apart!" scene on television. Later, one of the aliens mimics it. A 1991 music video of singer Paula Abdul's song, "Rush, Rush," also paid tribute to Rebel Without a Cause. With Abdul taking the role of Judy, the video featured recreations of the film's major scenes, including the switchblade fight and the chickie run.*

> *Rebel Without a Cause found critical success as well in the long run. It was added to the National film Registry of the Library of Congress in 1990 and placed 56th in a Newsweek poll of the 100 best American films. It still plays frequently on television and in film retrospectives, and was re-released in 1995 to celebrate its fortieth anniversary. Warner Bros. is fiercely protective of it to this day.[339]*

---

339   Douglas L. Rathgeb, *The Making of Rebel Without a Cause,* p. 199.

CHAPTER 19—*GIANT*: THE ENIGMA OF JETT RINK

*L*eslie was already seated in the car, she was rather bored now with the whole business, she thought, *Well, I suppose I've done something again that I shouldn't have. But what? Sight-seeing, driven by a kind of oafish hired man. What's wrong with that!*

"Look," he began truculently, "I didn't know he was buying them like a surprise for you, how would I—"

"It doesn't concern you at all," Leslie said in her best Lynnton manner. "I am rather tired. It has been a long day. Thank you for showing me the little Mexican town. I would like to sit quietly now, and not talk."

Across the little town then, past the mournful steer in his glass case, out to where Reata could be seen hazily like a mirage shimmering in the heat against the flat Texan plain and the searing Texas sky.

I just drove around with this boy—around and around—because I didn't want to go back to the house. And to Luz, I didn't want to go back to my home. But that's terrible, not to want to go home even when you're as tired and hot and thirsty and stiff as I am. You can't go on behaving like this, you know, Leslie my girl, she told herself.

"...girl like you before."

Jett Rink was saying something. She hadn't quite heard. He seemed to be driving very slowly, for him. "What? What did you say?"

*The knuckles of his hands on the wheel showed white. "I says—"
He cleared his throat. "—I says I never seen a girl—a woman—
like you before. You sure are different."*

*She was rigid with resentment. Then she relaxed. Now don't be
silly, this is an ignorant ranch hand, poor kid he's never been
taught anything, he's never known anything but poverty. So now
she laughed a prim little artificial laugh and said, "Yes, the East
and the West are different here in the United States, even though
we say we are one big family."*

*He faced straight ahead. "I ain't talking about no United States
geography. I'm talking about you. I never seen a girl like you. You
ain't afraid of nothing. I've seen a lot of women. I been going with
Cora Dart—the teacher—since she give up hoping she could hook
Bick. She's got education and all, but I never seen anybody like
you, that's for sure."*

*They were nearing the gates now. She'd never need to be with
him again. "Well, that's a very nice compliment, Jett. I'll tell my
husband you said so."*

*Boldly, deliberately, he turned to face her. "No you won't," he
jibed.*

*She turned her head away in disgust. How could Jordan have
dreamed of letting her go about with this dirty little boy. If Jordan
didn't know someone should tell him. She would.[340]*

* * *

On Christmas Day 1907, Glenn McCarthy was born in Beaumont,
Texas to Will McCarthy, a worker in the oil fields, where he would
grow up from rags to riches. He would also become the prototype
for a character in Edna Ferber's novel *Giant* by the name of Jett
Rink. According to the Wikipedia site:

---

340   Edna Ferber, *Giant*, pp. 181-182.

"Diamond Glenn" drew much attention from the national media due to his charismatic personality and his rags-to-riches story. Both loved and scorned by the media, his image formed the cultural mythos of the Texas oil millionaire. A charming, lucky, unabashed businessman. In 1949 McCarthy built the luxurious Shamrock Hotel in Houston, spending $21,000,000 for its construction. He then held what has been cited as "Houston's biggest party" for the hotel's grand opening. Dozens of Hollywood celebrities, many of whom were flown in to Houston Municipal Airport on a Boeing 307 Stratoliner airplane which he had recently acquired from Howard Hughes.

Like most wildcatters, Glenn was an aggressive investor. His multiple ventures led to a series of financial up and downs. In 1952 a life insurance company acquired title to the Shamrock Hotel, which was then sold to the Hilton Hotels Corporation. Glenn restructured his business dealings and persisted. His business holdings included KXYZ radio station in Houston, two banks, a bar, a brand of bourbon called "Wildcatter", the McCarthy Chemical Company, a magazine, 14 "throwaway" newspapers and a movie production company known as Glenn McCarthy Productions. He served as chairman of the former Eastern Airlines and president of the United States Petroleum Association.[341]

Known as "Diamond Glenn" and "King of the Wildcatters", Glenn McCarthy bought land in the area of the future Astrodome—the whole package consisting of 4800 acres. During the 1940s, he opened eleven oilfields while expanding others. At the age of 23, he married Foustine Lee, who was 16-years old at the time. Her father William Lee was a partner in the Yount-Lee Oil Company.[342] McCarthy avoided publicity in his later years and lived with his wife near Galveston. He had four daughters and one son. He died December 26, 1988.

---

341   *Glenn McCarthy*, from Wikipedia. Date Accessed: 13 Feb 2012. Available online at http://en.wikipedia.org/wiki/Glenn_Herbert_McCarthy
342   *Glenn McCarthy*, from Wikipedia. Date Accessed: 13 Feb 2012. Available online at http://en.wikipedia.org/wiki/Glenn_Herbert_McCarthy

Edna Ferber's choice of Glenn McCarthy as a model for Jett Rink was not coincidental. According to her biography on IMDB:

> McCarthy built the Shamrock Hotel at a cost of $21 million. It opened on St. Patrick's Day 1949 with a grand-opening party costing over $1 million. Ferber was one of the guests who stayed in the hotel, and after meeting with him, she decided to write a novel based upon his life. McCarthy sold the hotel to the Hilton family in 1955.[343]

Ferber's book, *Giant*, was a best seller in 1952. And several years later, Hollywood decided to bring the book to screen. As David Dalton notes in *The Mutant King*:

> *Of all Jimmy Dean's films, Giant was closest to the mainstream American fantasies on which Hollywood was built. The movie was more than a look at America through the eyes of Texas, it was a glimpse of Hollywood seen through its own tired lens—a Hollywood fallen victim to the perversions of its own dreams, to its gross delusions of grandeur. "What littleness is all this bigness hiding?" asks a character in the novel, and the movie business answered when it made an unintentional autobiography out of the book.[344]*

It was also a frustrating experience for James Dean.

A number of major actors hoped to be selected for Jett Rink. Warners was looking for someone who could perfectly fulfill the requirements of Jett Rink's Profile, as written by Ivan Moffat:

> *A jack-of-all trades on a Texas ranch, he grew up in the half-world between the animals of the old world and the machines of the new. At Reata, anyhow, he seemed to occupy a small place in the dim conscience of man, and could enjoy the full his bitterness... Perhaps the term 'man' is wrong in describing Jett. The angry boy persisted throughout. And of all the people in our story, the only*

343   Edna Ferber- Biography. From the IMDB Website. Date Accessed: 13 Feb 2012. Available online at http://www.imdb.com/name/nm0272209/bio
344   David Dalton, *James Dean: The Mutant King,* p. 292.

one who did not grow up, or mature, or become reconciled to this earth, was, in purely Texas terms, the most successful one of all—Jett Rink himself.[345]

Casting the role of Jett Rink was not a simple task for Warner Bros., as is described in *Giant: The Making of an Epic Motion Picture:*

> *The most difficult role to cast was that of Jett Rink. Unlike Bick or Leslie, Jett would occupy comparatively little screentime, leaving the burden on the actor rather than the writing. As [George] Stevens noted, "It could be the greatest part of the year, but it's no good unless it's in the hands of a really great actor."*[346]

Robert Mitchum was Stevens' first choice for the part. Mitchum ultimately rejected the role, leaving the studio to draw up a wish list of names, including Cornel Wilde, Ben Gazzara, Anthony Quinn, Richard Basehart, Montgomery Clift, Van Heflin, Jack Palance, John Ireland, Jose Ferrer, Richard Boone, Charles Bronson, Rick Jason, Aldo Ray, Brian Keith, Alex Nichol, Cameron Mitchell, Rod Steiger, Nick Adams and Frank Sinatra.[347] Alan Ladd was ultimately under consideration and ultimately rejected the role at the urging of his wife. That's when a dark horse by the name of James Dean emerged. George Stevens describes their meeting:

> *"Jimmy Dean used to stop by our offices in the bungalow. My secretary, Leona, had a war started with Jimmy Dean because she was afraid of beatniks and he came and sat in her office with those dirty blue jeans on and those boots, itchin' and scratchin' and bothering her an awful lot. But Freddy Guiol and I got a kick out of him. We used to talk to him and got very well acquainted.*

345　*Giant: The Making of an Epic Motion Picture with a Foreword by George Stevens, Jr: Special Collector's Edition,* Warner Bros (1996), p. 17.

346　*Giant: The Making of an Epic Motion Picture with a Foreword by George Stevens, Jr: Special Collector's Edition,* Warner Bros (1996) p. 17

347　*Giant: The Making of an Epic Motion Picture with a Foreword by George Stevens, Jr: Special Collector's Edition,* Warner Bros (1996) p.17

He was a smart guy. Whatever your kind of atmosphere is, he fits into it."348

Giant: The Making of an Epic Motion Picture continues:

Stevens went to great lengths to get hold of a kinescope copy of "The Death of Jesse James" episode of the CBS series You Are There. James Dean played Bob Ford, one of the brothers who notoriously gunned down the outlaw. But as late as November 1954, Dean was still only being thought of for the role of Bob Dace or Jordy, the son who fails to live up to his father's expectations. Sterling Hayden had made his way to the top of the list for Jett (while also appearing halfway down the list for Bick, a not uncommon situation for many of those under consideration). But Stevens' thoughts kept returning to Dean. Perhaps he was reminded of Ferber's suggestion a few months earlier: "I sometimes wonder if Jett mightn't be effectively cast against type, for a kind of sympathy. Smallish, compact, quick on his feet—a sort of Gene Kelly with a quick punch."349

Stevens had James Dean read the part. He said, "After he got by Leona...he stood there, twitched his head about three times and said, 'I can do it.'"350 James Dean got the part, and that's when his period of frustration began.

First of all, because *Rebel* was not completed until nine days after schedule, Jimmy had no break time between the two films. He had planned to go back to Fairmount to see his family and to also attend the Indianapolis 500 before heading out to Texas. According to Val Holley:

His only day off before journeying to Texas was Memorial Day, and the holiday offered him one last, cherished chance to race

348   *Giant: The Making of an Epic Motion Picture with a Foreword by George Stevens, Jr: Special Collector's Edition,* Warner Bros (1996), p. 18.
349   *Giant: The Making of an Epic Motion Picture with a Foreword by George Stevens, Jr: Special Collector's Edition,* Warner Bros (1996), p. 18.
350   *Giant: The Making of an Epic Motion Picture with a Foreword by George Stevens, Jr: Special Collector's Edition,* Warner Bros (1996), p. 18.

REBEL FROM BACK CREEK

before George Steven's prohibition on life- (i.e., picture-) threat-
ening activities went into effect. This time was a Santa Barbara
Event. From an unlucky starting position, he maneuvered his
Speedster up to fourth place by the start of the final lap, and was
working hard to move into third when he overrevved the car's
engine and burned a piston, coasting to a halt at the edge of the
track. According to Sidney Skolsky, "his face was a mask of dejec-
tion." From then until mid-September, the Speedster would be in
the garage, having its engine rebuilt."[351]

The dominant battle in the film from the very beginning centered
upon friction between George Stevens and James Dean. Holley
writes:

...Over the hundred-plus days of filming, there would be at least
three very public confrontations between director and actor. The
first of these happened in Marfa, according to Carroll Baker (the
actress who played the nubile Luz Benedict II). Baker's autobiog-
raphy explains that, despite the stifling Texas heat, Stevens ex-
pected the entire cast, stars included, to stand by on the set in full
makeup and costume at all times. After Dean stood around like
this for three days without being filmed, Baker wrote, he rebelled
and refused to report on the fourth day; consequently Stevens
dressed him down on the fifth, accusing him of costing the com-
pany an entire day of lost production. ..[352]

This and numerous subsequent violations of Stevens' rules prompted
the director to compile a list of delays in filming attributed to James
Dean's tardiness or outright absences. According to Holley:[353]

How Stevens intended to use this list is unknown, but an unfor-
tunate incident the day after its compilation made its existence
somewhat moot. What happened was simply that Dean arrived
late on the set, but his infraction's gravity was exacerbated by a
display of professionalism from actress Mercedes McCambridge
(Luz Benedict in the film). Only a few hours before morning call,

351   Val Holley, *James Dean: The Biography*, p. 269.
352   Val Holley, James Dean: The Biography, p. 270.
353   Val Holley, *James Dean: The Biography*, pp. 271-272.

McCambridge had fallen in her bathroom, hitting her head on a brandy snifter. Even though she had, according to Daily Variety, been "stitched from head to foot," she still managed to arrive on time. When Dean sauntered onto the set, offering no apology or excuse, Stevens blew up, vowing never to direct another film with him in it. Then he walked off the set, leaving the direction to an assistant.[354]

Most of his problems with George Stevens probably stemmed from Stevens' authoritarian nature. Jimmy was treated as an assistant director while working with Nicholas Ray in *Rebel Without a Cause*, and he was granted a great deal of freedom with the role. George Stevens did not allow such liberties. Val Holley states:

...Stevens's exasperation was based solely on professional, not personal, considerations. Throughout filming, and then afterward until Giant was released, Stevens frequently praised Dean's acting in print. "The boy's so preoccupied" he said only days after the last and worst confrontation. "He's the kind that can be late even if he's right there on the set. He gets himself all wound up before going into a scene. But his work is wonderful. Everything went fine Wednesday (August 3, the day after the McCambridge accident) and Jimmy even showed up for his makeup call fifteen minutes early.[355]

In a note, however, Holley adds that he may have transferred his rebellion to *Rebel*:

...On Saturday, August 6, he refused to report for post-recording of dialogue on Rebel, despite a 9:00 A.M. call. To be fair, he may have been suffering from a bad wisdom tooth, which would be pulled on August 12.[356]

Such conflicts did not exist between James Dean and the author of *Giant*. Edna Ferber and James Dean really connected, as described by Holley:

---

354   Val Holley, *James Dean: The Biography*, p. 272.
355   Val Holley, *James Dean: The Biography*, p. 272.
356   Val Holley, *James Dean: The Biography*, p. 272.

She called him a 'genius' and shrugged off his troubles with Stevens as 'success poisoning,' a syndrome she said she knew very well from the days when she had simultaneous hit shows on Broadway. Later she wrote him a letter outlining her conception of Jett Rink's character, explaining that a cruel man can fool the average person by affecting a superficial layer of gentleness—but that she and Dean wouldn't be fooled because they happened to be above average.[357]

More interesting than the conflicts between actor and director on the set of *Giant*, however, is the involvement of the local Marfa citizens with the film. The town of Marfa still retains pleasant memories of the filming of *Giant*, as noted in an article titled "A Texas Town Holds Fast to Its Ties to a Classic". Simon Romero describes the showing of *Giant* in Marfa in 2003:

The filming of "Giant," which cost $5 million to make, left an impression among residents here.

"I'm a little too much of an old lady to say this, but boy did Jimmy Dean have this little sexy giggle," Lucy Garcia, a retired baby sitter who was 15 when the film was made, said in an interview. "We had a 10 p.m. curfew back then, but I'd stay out until 9:59, trying to get me a look at Jimmy."

The crew and nearly the entire cast stayed at the Paisano, recalled Marcos Peña, who as a teenager worked as a porter at the hotel.

"I used to serve Elizabeth Taylor breakfast every morning; she liked a fruit plate," said Mr. Peña, 67, who now works as a serviceman for a gas company. "She had this silver bowl filled with money that she'd stick her hand into and give me tips of $1, $5, whatever was in there."

Leaning on the fence outside his trailer home, Mr. Peña said in an interview that James Dean, who played the role of Jett Rink, the ranch hand turned oil tycoon, was the most amicable of the cast, often shooting pool with townspeople in the basement of

---

357   Val Holley, *James Dean: The Biography*, p. 273.

the hotel. Rock Hudson, Mr. Peña said, was "a little bit more con-servative, kind of like a snob."

"Giant was considered a highwater mark of a certain view of Texas when it was still thought of with some awe as a super-state," said Don B. Graham, a professor of English at the University of Texas and author of "Cowboys and Cadillacs: How Hollywood Looks at Texas."

Nostalgia for the state's ranching ethos permeated the screening of "Giant" on Saturday night, which was sponsored by Warner Brothers. Proceeds from the $50-per-ticket event — organized by Kirby F. Warnock, a part-time rancher and documentary film-maker — went to Marfa's library.

Two actors who appeared in the movie, Jane Withers (Vashti Snythe) and Earl Holliman (Bob Dace), signed autographs.

" Giant' continues to define Texas," said Bill D. Rollins, a San Antonio stockbroker and energy company executive, who attend-ed the fund-raiser wearing cowboy boots with the words "Giant" and "Marfa" tooled into the leather. "It's about the power of the land, both above it for the herds and below it for the mineral rights."

Clay Evans, on whose family ranch "Giant" was filmed, sat quietly for a moment in the cab of his pickup Saturday night after fans of the film made a pilgrimage to the site where the facade of Bick Benedict's mansion has been left to the elements, a few tame an-telope and the occasional jack rabbit.

"My daddy let the Hollywood people on our land and we had some fun," Mr. Evans, 67, said.

While some residents of Marfa reminisce fondly about the filming of "Giant," others say some of the issues raised in the film still persist — even after the population of 3,600 dwindled by more than a third in the mid-1950's, when the debate over segregation gained momentum in Texas and elsewhere.

For example, Ms. Garcia, the former baby sitter, said Hispanics and Anglos in Marfa were at odds over space in the town's cemeteries, which remain almost entirely segregated. Whites in Marfa, she said, were hesitant to sell Hispanics the land they need to enlarge their cemetery.

"A lot of us Mexicans are still pushed around by the gringo like in the time of `Giant,' " Ms. Garcia said. "Some things in Texas take a long time to die." [358]

Ms. Garcia's comments were echoed several years ago in a paper by one of my Latina students after she had watched *Giant*. She noted that her own family (all born in the United States) had been hassled by border guards for one reason or another over the years. One border guard told her father that he could not believe a Mexican would be able to own an SUV! She also noted that her family had been denied service in various diners—similar to the incident at the end of the film, minus the violence.

About the same period of time, another student, also Latina, related to the film differently. Her first cousin was an actor in *Giant*, and he was chosen for his eyes. He was the infant who played Dennis Hopper's son! She told me that for years her family had heard about *Giant*, but none of them had ever seen it! She finally had the opportunity to view the film in my course and was so thankful for that. She also told me that her cousin lived in Los Angeles and that he still talked about *Giant*, even though he was too small during the filming to remember it!

For James Dean, Marfa probably reminded him of his hometown of Fairmount, one of the reasons why he related so well to the residents. He adapted quickly to the dialect and has been noted by some biographers to have had the best dialect of any of the cast members. According to Val Holley:

---

358   Simon Romero, "A Texas Town Holds Fast to its Ties to a Classic," The New York Times Website. 8 Jun 2003. Date Accessed: 13 Feb 2012. Available online at http://www.nytimes.com/2003/06/09/national/09MARF.html?pagewanted=all

The most specific compliment Stevens would pay Dean was that the actor "could mold psychological impediments into his speech and into his movements. This was his finest art. Instinctively he seemed to understand all the impediments people have when they try to communicate." Stevens also admitted that he sometimes underestimated Dean, but "sometimes [Dean] overestimated the effects he thought he was getting—then he might change his approach, do it quick, and if that didn't work, we'd effect a compromise. All in all, it was a hell of a headache to work with him...He developed this cultivated, designed irresponsibility. 'It's tough on you,' he'd seem to imply, 'but I've just got to do it this way.'"[359]

Holley continues:

For all the accounts of discord, there had been times when director and actor worked well together. A reporter who watched the scene of Jett Rink pacing off his inherited property said Stevens took time to explain its significance and mood to Dean, then rehearsed him in it. Dean nailed it on the first take, after which Stevens beamed, "that's just swell, Jimmy." Rock Hudson told an interviewer that it was a common sight to see Stevens and Dean taking long walks together. Although Hudson could never hear what was said, sometimes he could see one or both of them gesticulating as if in heated discussion. The business Stevens needed to take up with Dean was usually done privately, said Hudson, never involving the rest of the cast.

Holley concludes:

The eventual review of Giant in Sight and Sound examined the Dean-Stevens relationship in critical terms: "In the later scenes [i.e., when Dean had cosmetically aged to forty-five], Dean for the first time in his tragically short career had to go beyond the characterization of the young rebel, and his technical resources fail to see him through. His relative failure throws some incidental light

---

359   Val Holley, *James Dean: The Biography,* p. 273.

*on Steven's direction of his players...Putting it very approximately,
one might say that Kazan works through his actors, while Stevens
prefers his actors to work through him."*[360]

360   Val Holley, *James Dean: The Biography*, p. 273.

CHAPTER 20—"DEATH IS MY NEIGHBOR"[361]

"**W**e were with him in California. In his house. Oh, he was on top of the world. He had a new bike covered in the driveway, and he said right away, 'Ey, Marcus, come and see my new bike,' and he uncovered it, and spread the tarpaulin all over the driveway. His new car, Porsch-ey Spyder was in the garage. I didn't see it."...

...it's like taking a hold of a thunderbolt.

"In the house he'd had a Siamese kitten that Elizabeth Taylor gave him. Oh, he was on top of the world. He had a lot of photographic equipment, he was very interested in photography, and was getting quite good at it. He wanted to direct too, which, I am sure, he would have done later on, because he was like that—he couldn't be still, but he was never satisfied with anything once it was done. I think he would have been the best, right among the best, in his profession.

"Just a few days ago, I don't know if you watch TV, but my daughter has seen it, and a few other people—The Allen Show from Indianapolis, and he, Allen, interviewed Jim Bachus, who was in Rebel, and he asked Bachus what was the best film he ever worked in, and he said, 'Oh, Rebel. That was the best.' 'Is it because of Jimmy?' Steve Allen asked. 'Yes,' Bachus replied. And he went on to say that, had he lived, Jimmy would have been the best; even then he was at the very top. And there is no doubt in my mind that he would have been the best.

---

361   "Death is my Neighbor," *Danger*, (CBS), 25 Aug 1953. Cast: James Dean as JB—psychotic janitor. Also Walter Hampden, Betsy Palmer, Frank Marth, Andrew Duggan. Director: John Peyser. Producer: Franklin Heller. Writer: Frank Gregory

"Marcus took a few pictures and the last thing we said to each other, as Marcus and I were leaving, was: I said, 'Now Jimmy, be careful with these races.'

'I will, Mom. I'll be safe there as I am on the road.' And as we were parting, he said, 'I'll be home in October, around the 7th or 8th...' and he kept his word. He came on the 8th, to be buried."[362]

***

When James Dean awoke the morning of September 30, 1955, he had no idea that it would be his last morning. No doubt, he was thinking about the race ahead of him in Salinas, and he was excited because he would be racing his new Porsche Spyder. According to Warren Beath in his *The Death of James Dean,* he was "awakened at 7:20 a.m. by his name being called from downstairs."[363] Beath continues:

Nicco dropped by sometimes to make coffee, clean up, and check on the condition of his property, calling, 'Hallo, Jeemie," from the floor below. When Dean was rested, he delighted in showing visitors how he ascended to his groggy mornings. He staggered to the balcony, threw one leg over the railing, and jumped. He didn't say, "Good morning.' He never spoke until he had had some coffee. He sat blearily at the bottom steps in his pyjama bottoms, beating on his bongos.[364]

Since he planned to be gone, he put his little Siamese cat Marcus in the care of an actress named Janette Miller, and left a set of instructions scrawled on the back of an envelope:

1 teaspoon white Karo
1 big can evaporated milk

---

362   Ortense Winslow, qtd. In D. Mrkick. *Summer Was Only Beginning: A Memoir of James Dean,* pp. 58-59.
363   Warren Beath, *The Death of James Dean,* p. 26.
364   Warren Beath, *The Death of James Dean,* p. 27.

Equal part boiled water or distilled water
1 egg yolk
Mix and chill
Don't feed him meat or formula cold
1 drop vitamin solution per day
Take Marcus to Dr Cooper for shots next week.[365]

His family from Fairmount visited him that day, as did his father Winton. Jimmy was excited to see all of them, including his father, although the air became subdued after his greeting.[366] According to Beath:

Jimmy did not get along well with his father. The obvious root of their mutual unease would be Jimmy's sense of abandonment by his father because of his early consignment back to Indiana after the death of his mother when he was nine years old. Perhaps he had felt unwanted because Winton had not immediately married his mother, Mildred, upon learning she was pregnant. Jimmy had been born five months after the brief ceremony before a Grant County justice of the peace. But time would have smoothed these hurts were it not for something his son found unsatisfying in Winton himself. The man kept himself at a distance that could never be broached, and he maintained a reserve from which he could never be drawn to confront and answer the unspoken accusations.[367]

[Winton Dean and Mildred Wilson were married July 26, 1930 in Marion, Grant Co., Indiana. Their son, James Byron Dean, was born February 8, 1931.][368]

As Bill Bast earlier noted, they had their own way of communicating with one another. Warren Beath describes their method:

---

365   Warren Beath, *The Death of James Dean,* p. 27.
366   Warren Beath, *The Death of James Dean,* p. 27.
367   Warren Beath, *The Death of James Dean,* pp. 32-33.
368   Richard E. Brenneman, "The Ancestry of James Byron Dean (1931-1955), p. 28.

...Like many fathers and sons who cannot talk, they had learned to communicate without talking. College friends visiting the Dean household, hearing Jimmy ask Winton for the car and being answered with a muttered evasion, would be amazed when Jimmy would smile knowingly, 'He'll do it."[369]

James Dean knew better than to ask his father to go for a ride in his new Porsche, so he asked his uncle, Charles Nolan Dean, who finally accepted a drive two or three times around the block. And then it was time for his family to leave:

Winton and Charles sat in the station wagon on the street to talk with Jimmy a while longer. Charles would be leaving that same day to continue his holiday in Mexico, while Ortense and Marcus would be returning to Indiana. It was about 1 p.m. when Weutherich returned, wearing light blue slacks and a red checked sports shirt. Charles threw an arm around Jimmy. 'Be careful,' he said. 'You're riding in a bomb.'

Jimmy giggled. 'That's my baby!

At about 1:30 p.m., Roth wanted to take a picture of Dean and Weutherich in the Spyder. Jimmy grabbed Rolf's hand and raised their arms over their heads in a sign of anticipated victory. Dean clipped a pair of sunglasses over his prescription lenses and tossed his red jacket behind the seat. The safety belt remained unfastened.[370]

Besides Jimmy and his mechanic, Rolf Wutherich, photographer Sandy Roth and stunt driver Bill Hickman were on the trip. Originally, the Spyder was to have been pulled on a trailer, while the men were going to ride in other vehicles. At the last minute, James Dean decided that he would drive the car. He wanted to break it in better and put more mileage on it. Rolf Wutherich, his mechanic, rode with him in the car. The others followed behind. It was James Dean's decision to drive to Salinas through the back country. According to Wikipedia:

---

369   Warren Beath, *The Death of James Dean*, p. 33.
370   Warren Beath, *The Death of James Dean,* pp. 33-34.

On September 30, 1955, Dean and his mechanic Rolf Wütherich *set off from* Competition Motors, *where they had prepared his* Porsche 550 Spyder *that morning for a sports car race at* Salinas, California. *Dean originally intended to trailer the Porsche to the meeting point at Salinas, behind his new* Ford Country Squire *station wagon, crewed by Hickman and photographer* Sanford Roth, *who was planning a photo story of Dean at the races. At the last minute, Dean drove the Spyder, having decided he needed more time to familiarize himself with the car. At 3:30 p.m., Dean was ticketed in* Mettler Station, Kern County, *for driving 65 mph (105 km/h) in a 55 mph (89 km/h) zone. The driver of the Ford was ticketed for driving 20 mph (32 km/h) over the limit, as the speed limit for all vehicles towing a trailer was 45 mph (72 km/h).*[371]

His ticket may have caused him some pause for reflection:

Great, thought Dean. The papers would love this if they picked it up. He had just finished filming a highway safety spot in which he had been interviewed by Gig Young.

'Jimmy,' Gig had asked, 'we probably have a great many young people watching our show tonight, and for their benefit, I'd like your opinion about fast driving on the highway. Do you think it's a good idea?'

Dean had muttered uneasily, 'I used to fly about quite a bit, you know, took a lot of unnecessary chances on the highways. Then I started racing, and, uh, now I drive on the highways, and, uh, extra cautious – no one knows what they're doing, and half the time you don't know what this guy's going to do, or that one – I don't have the urge to speed on the highway. People say racing is dangerous, but I'll take my chances on the track any day, than on the highway.'

Young had seemed relieved. Dean's slightly ridiculing manner at the beginning of the dialogue had intimidated him. He had not been sure Dean was going to co-operate. There was one last

371   *James Dean,* from *Wikipedia,* last modified 8 Feb 2012. Date accessed 22 Feb 2012. Available online at http://en.wikipedia.org/wiki/James_Dean

question. Gig asked, 'Do you have any special advice for the young
people who drive?'

Dean had turned at the door 'Take it easy driving. The life you
save, may be mine.'[372]

Beath continues:

He was aware that his recklessness in cars and on motorcycles
was already legendary. The great actor Alec Guinness had told
Dean he was going to break his neck in the new Spyder. But Dean
curbed his bad-boy road antics around the seasoned race drivers
who were his heroes. The mere fact that you liked to speed did not
qualify you to race competitively in closed events, as had Dean.
The first mistake you made on the course, no matter where, was
duly recorded by an official and relayed to the start-finish line.
If the mistake merited it, the driver would be black-flagged and
sidelined until he explained his action. He might then be allowed
to continue, or he could be suspended for several races. Dean was
qualified, though the opinions of his driving varied. Some thought
him reckless, some thought him over-cautious. Hickman was sure
Dean was going to be a great driver. In any case he had completed or run in several races, and was entered and accepted to
race at Salinas.[373]

Then came a fifteen-minute stop at Blackwell's Corner, located at the
junction of Routes 466 and 33. In a later interview with David Dalton,
Rolf Wutherich said:

When we reached Blackwell's Corners, a sleek, grey Mercedes
was parked in front of the store, another of the racing cars on the
road to Salinas. Jimmy stepped on the brake and we got out. He
took a close look at the Mercedes and chatted with the owner,
Lance Revson, the twenty-one-year-old son of Barbara Hutton.

Jimmy bought a bag full of apples, and hopped back into the car.
He was raring to go. "Non-stop to Paso Robles!" he shouted and

372   Warren Beath, The Death of James Dean, p. 35-36.
373   Warren Beath, The Death of James Dean, p. 36.

jammed down the accelerator without fastening his safety Belt. Blackwell's Corners was our last stop.

We had been on Highway 466 ever since we went through Bakersfield and now it was deserted. No car except our Spyder and the station wagon as far as we could see. Jimmy went faster now—a very natural thing to do when you are all alone on a good road in a racing car. It was just past five in the afternoon. The sun, a ball of fire, shone directly in our eyes. It was still very hot and the heat flickered and danced on the sandy brown road. To the right and left of us was desert; in front of us, an endless ribbon of road.[374]

David Dalton describes the collision:

5:30 P.M.: Twilight. Jimmy had averaged seventy-five miles per hour from the time he'd been ticketed, which meant he must have been doing over one hundred miles per hour in some stretches. The road, growing grey in the dimming light, was empty and flat. Wutherich started to get sleepy:

> *"Everything okay?" Jimmy asked.*

> *"Everything okay," I [Wutherich] answered, half dozing. The monotonous hum of the engine was like a soft cradle song.*

> *We were not talking now—not of Pier Angeli or of Dean's mother or of anything. The only thought on Jimmy's mind was winning that race. There was no doubt of that; that's all he talked about.*

A few minutes later, they approached the intersection of Routes 466 and 41 in Cholame (pronounced shall aim). A Ford sedan going in the opposite direction on Route 466 began to turn left. The driver looked down the road, didn't see anything coming and turned.

---

374   David Dalton, *The Mutant King*, p. 280.

Jimmy said to Wutherich, "That guy up there's gotta stop; he'll see us."

5:45 P.M.: Jimmy Dean was dead.[375]

***

Marcus and Ortense Winslow did not learn of James Dean's death until they returned from their trip to California. Then four days after Jimmy's death, Winton returned to Fairmount with the body of his son. Dalton notes, "Three thousand people, one thousand more than the entire population of Fairmount, attended his funeral on Saturday, October 8, 1955. The funeral, and the memorial services held a year later, were the largest functions ever held in Fairmount, Indiana."[376] Dalton continues:

> *Though the people of Indiana rarely ponder out loud on the nature of fame and death, their poet laureate, James Whitcomb Riley, wrote this verse on the subject:*
>
> *Once in a dream, I saw a man*
>
> *With haggard face and tangled hair*
>
> *And eyes that nursed as wild a care*
>
> *As gaunt Starvation ever can;*
>
> *And in his hand he held a wand*
>
> *Whose magic touch gave life and thought*
>
> *Unto a form his fancy wrought*
>
> *And robed with coloring so grand*
>
> *It seemed the reflex of some child*
>
> *Of heaven, fair and undefiled—*

---

375   David Dalton, *The Mutant King*, pp. 279-280.
376   David Dalton, *The Mutant King*, p. 282.

A face of purity and love—

To woo him into worlds above:

And as I gazed with dazzled eyes,

A gleaming smile lit up his lips

As his bright soul from its eclipse

Went flashing into Paradise.

Then tardy Fame came through the door

And found a picture—nothing more.[377]

---

377   James Whitcomb Riley, qtd. In David Dalton, *The Mutant King*, p. 283.

SECTION FOUR
CONCLUSION

Studio Portrait of James Dean
This photo was used in a Modern Screen
Memorial Edition in 1955/1956.

"**O**kay," Chris said. There were still a dozen cars in the place, all bright and shiny, and as Chris opened the door he knew that they would be looking at him. He turned on the ignition and, door open, he leaned his weight against the cold metal: he strained, and with Hop pushing on the other side the car began to roll forward. He swung the wheel with one hand, pushed harder, and the car picked up speed.

Straining, he saw only the blacktop moving faster beneath his feet, and with a slow swish of white the pile of feathers went past. For no reason at all he thought of the future: although he now silently cursed this car, he really did love it, but he knew that soon he would trade it for something else, something better he hoped, and he imagined through a long succession of cars some distant day when he would be driving down the street in a big station wagon, his wife beside him, kids in the back, a week's groceries in sacks piled around them, and on such a day he wondered what he would do, should he see this car, rising like a mirage, its fire-wall glowing like a bright pink jewel.

"Jump," Hop said, and Chris, looking up from that long black blur of pavement, jumped.[378]

***

September 30, 2012 marks the fifty-seventh anniversary of James Dean's death. And fifty-seven years after his death, people still remember him as though he were still alive today. Fans cannot get enough of him, and many converge on Fairmount, Indiana each year for Fans Weekend and other Dean-related events. His image appears on calendars, mugs, posters, cell phones, key rings, and thimbles. There are James Dean dolls (several varieties), James Dean teddy bears, ducks, and rabbits. Concerning the James Dean doll created by Dakin, Warren Beath writes:

---

378   Albert Drake, *I Remember The Day James Dean Died & other stories*, p. 31.

In 1985, the International Toy Fair in New York saw the unveiling of a James Dean doll which would cost as much as $2000. It was part of the aggressive Curtis Management invasion of the James Dean marketplace. Curtis attorney Mark Roesler announced, "The Dakin people, the largest 'plush' manufacturer in the nation, introduced their new James Dean collectible doll at the toy fair today." "Plush" is the industry designation for stuffed animals.

The basic 18-inch-tall James Dean collectible doll came equipped with an outfit consisting of the red windbreaker, white T-shirt and blue jeans that made up Dean's ensemble in Rebel Without a Cause. This doll would cost $100. The skin would be made of a new porcelain-vinyl material, and Roesler promised it was "the most lifelike doll I've ever seen."

The $2000 version, planned for release three months after the basic doll but never produced, would be dressed in blue jeans, a suede fringe jacket, and a small Stetson cowboy hat. "The expensive version will be a limited numbered edition," the attorney said. "Probably only 500 will be made."

The doll came with a replica of Dean's trademark cigarette. When the American Cancer Society raised hell, Dakin offered a doll without a cigarette.[379]

His image has also appeared in the background of a number of films, such as *Cape Fear*, and on television shows, such as *Happy Days*. A number of actors and singers were inspired by him. In 1996, the U.S. Postal Service dedicated a stamp to him. Numerous psychics claim to have contacted his spirit, and have written books about those encounters. At least two people have claimed to be his offspring in recent years, although proof of his parentage has yet to be presented or verified by anyone. Some people claim that he is still alive, as noted by John Howlett in his biography of James Dean:

379   Warren Beath with Paula Wheeldon. *James Dean in Death: A Popular Encyclopedia of a Celebrity Phenomenon.* Jefferson, North Carolina: McFarland & Company, Inc., Publishers (2005), p. 69.

There are still those who claim that the grave in Fairmount is empty, that Dean was not buried; or if he was buried, that his body was stolen by night soon after the funeral when the earth was still freshly dug. The intention had certainly been expressed, and the local police mounted a night and day guard on the cemetery for several weeks after the funeral. Later, when a memorial was put up to Dean outside the cemetery, the plinth was cut down and stolen. [380]

Articles about James Dean still frequently appear in magazines, including a *Sports Illustrated* issue in 2008. Many people who knew him well and those who knew him slightly have written books about their experiences, providing both truthful and fictional accounts. Teenagers in the 1950s not only wanted to look like him, they wanted to become James Dean. While the teenage look has changed over the years, the Dean motif is still there. The Allsands website summarized this phenomenon in a biography written in 2001. Unfortunately, this article no longer exists on the Web, so I will set out the portion I saved:

When he died, he had Liz Taylor's phone number in his little black book, along with the bug exterminator, proving even rebels must at times lead normal lives. James B. Dean, Hoosier farm boy, alias the universal symbol of adolescent angst and attitude died 40 years ago in September of 1955. It was an abrupt conclusion to a life and a career both revved and cruising in high gear.

Dean was only 24 years old when his Porsche Spyder collided with another vehicle on a California highway. He had just completed filming his third and final motion picture, Giant, with co-stars Rock Hudson and Elizabeth Taylor.

The impact of this collision was felt around the country, but nowhere more than the Indiana farming community of Fairmount, where Dean was born and where he spent much of his childhood. The town would never be the same.

---

380   John Howlett, qtd. In Warren Beath with Paula Wheeldon, *James Dean in Death: A Popular Encyclopedia of a Celebrity Phenomenon.* Jefferson North Carolina: McFarland & Company, Inc., Publishers (2005), p. 100.

In life, Dean preferred the fast-paced life in New York City and Hollywood where he could perform before an audience, but in death he will forever reside in the rural Midwest town he called home. No place could be further from the fast lane, yet he still has his audience and his dedicated fans.

Since that September day, the icon James Dean, has inspired songs (at least 43 recorded about or in tribute to him) hundreds of articles, numerous books, monuments, fan clubs, scandal sheets, movies and plays. The young man given the label, The Rebel Without A Cause, created a sensation not only in the US, but around the world. Fans of all ages still trek to Fairmount from as far away as Australia and Japan. Dean's instantly recognizable image, sporting blue jeans, the dangling cigarette and the characteristic slouch has been deeply etched into our own American culture. But was James Dean really the rebellious, lost youth as he's been typecast?

By all accounts Dean was active in school, playing guard on the basketball team, was a "sub" on the baseball team, and a champion pole vaulter. Even with poor eyesight and a slight build he was considered a well-rounded athlete.

He rode his horse and played ice hockey with his buddies. Although his grades were only average, Dean won a speech contest and an art award. He participated in the drama club, winning yet another award and joined the senior class trip to Washington D.C. It hardly sounds like the description of a tough and aimless young man. His classmates remember him as "just one of the guys."

Not unlike other young men his age, James Dean was enamored with motorcycles and speed. Residents of Fairmount recall seeing teenage Dean bouncing through farm fields and careening about town on his 1947 Czech Whizzer, the first in a line of motorcycles. His antics on the cycle cost him his two front teeth and at least four sets of eyeglasses. He once told columnist Hedda Hopper, "I used to go out for the cows on the motorcycle. Scared the hell out of them. They'd get to running and their udders would start swinging, and they'd lose a quart of milk." Youthful exhuberance and high spirits yes, but hardly unusual for a teenage boy with a set of wheels...[381]

So who was James Dean and why should we remember him?

The truth is James Dean didn't begin his career by hoping to become the symbol of rebellion or of revolution, as noted on the Shortlist Website by Jim Butler:

Speaking exclusively to ShortList, Bill Bast, a friend and former roommate of Dean, who went on to have a successful career as a screenwriter, bridles at the notion of Dean the 'rebel'.

"In life," he says, "his aim wasn't to stir up youth and get them to emulate him, though that appears to be what has happened in fact. He never spoke about changing the world. It wasn't like him to boast so grandiosely. But regarding his own future he had great determination, which I found admirable. If he's known more for rebellion that has to do with the Warner Bros [the studio he was contracted to] PR machine than anything."[382]

Citing Ray Connolly, who directed *James Dean: The First American Teenager* (1975), Butler adds:

Indeed, lest we forget, Rebel Without A Cause, the film that did most to cement Dean's status as this societal outcast, only came out post-death. The power that Dean possessed as an icon and a totem for youth came after his untimely passing. In fact, venerable journalist Ray Connolly, who in 1975 directed the documentary James Dean: The First American Teenager, believes that Dean is iconic for the wrong reasons. "He's remembered as a moody teenage poster boy," Connolly says. "And actually he was an extraordinarily good actor."

---

381   "James Dean Biography," Available on the Allsands website in 2001. Accessed 10 Mar 2001. Wysiwyg://43/http://www.allsands.com/jamesdeanbiogr_rz_gn.htm

382   Jim Butler, "Why Is James Dean a Cultural Icon?" ShortList Website. Dated 2011. Date Accessed: 30 Nov. 2011. Available at http://www.shortlist.com

He's right. Watching Dean's roles today one can't help but marvel at the depth of his talent. His instinctive portrayals of the confused Cal Trask in East Of Eden, the troubled Jim Stark in Rebel... and the proud Jett Rink in Giant mirrored the changes occurring in western society.

In today's cynical information age, it may seem fanciful to think that an actor's onscreen presence could chime with a generation, but back in 1955, this is exactly what happened. Connolly, who was 14 when East Of Eden (the only film released in Dean's lifetime) premiered, remembers what it was about Dean that so captured the imagination.

"It was the reality of his performance," he recalls. "All the films I had seen before then were based around people reading lines, as in a play onstage. Suddenly, these people — James Dean and Julie Harris — seemed to be saying things that they were making up as they went along. Now, I know that's called improv these days, but back then I just thought, 'Gosh, this is so realistic.' It was the first time I'd seen anything like it."[383]

James Dean's style of Method Acting captured the hearts and minds of the 1950s teens. As Connolly notes in his interview with Butler:

"It was a total break," Connolly suggests, "and I suspect that old Hollywood didn't like him much. I know that when they made Giant, Rock Hudson hated him. You see, the main actors of that time — Clark Gable, John Wayne and Kirk Douglas — were straight, wooden men who spoke very clearly. All of a sudden you had this guy who looked little more than an adolescent managing to convey emotions. That scene in East of Eden when he breaks down in tears with Raymond Massey... men just didn't do that then. We all related to him."

This defiance in his acting is mirrored in his personal style. Whether it be slouching around in chinos, pounding the streets

383   Jim Butler, "Why Is James Dean a Cultural Icon?" ShortList Website. Dated 2011. Date Accessed: 30 Nov. 2011. Available at http://www.shortlist. com

of Manhattan with tousled hair and an obligatory cigarette or his classic red jacket, white T-shirt and jeans pose in Rebel..., he was the epitome of cool. Fashion journalist Peter Lyle knows why. "He was very assured in his dress," he says. "If you look at Brando in The Wild One in comparison to Dean in Rebel..., Dean looks more effortless. Plus, you never see a bad photo of him. There are bad pictures of Clint before he became Clint and there are bad pictures of Warren Beatty when he looked clean-cut. You never see bad pictures of Dean."[384]

The line between the characters he portrayed and the reality of James Dean often blurred. While he appeared at times to be cold and calloused on the surface, he was protecting his inner self that had already suffered bruising. As his friend, Lew Bracker, once noted:

"He would be bothered when someone would say he was mean and disrespectful. Because actually, he wasn't. They took silence to mean he cared little or nothing for them. They didn't have the insight, or didn't care to exercise the insight, in knowing that he was a shy boy that just didn't know how to approach them. Instead of making an attempt to approach him, they just, well, they just wrote him off."[385]

But he was more than an excellent actor. On another level, the question of what he could have become enters the discussion. In an article titled "Why is James Dean Worth Remembering?" a friend of his by the name of Melinda, answers this question:

Jimmy was an individual who saw clearly and who had values that were defined and honed through years of thought.

If he had lived Jimmy would have transformed the entertainment industry; injecting the vibrant ideas and values that moved him

384   Jim Butler, "Why Is James Dean a Cultural Icon?" ShortList Website. Dated 2011. Date Accessed: 30 Nov. 2011. Available at http://www.shortlist. com
385   "Biography for James Dean," Available on the IMDb Website. Date Accessed: 5 Mar 2001. http://us.imdb.com/Bio?Dean,+James

originally into acting. Because that industry supplies the memes and cultural content of so much that we, as Americans, live and breathe every day of our lives, and because the world watches us as the edge of cultural change, it is fair to say that James Dean would have changed the world. That was his intention and his aim; to impact the world through the craft of acting.

He understood how it could be used. He intended to use it.

James Dean had confronted such issues and the life of the spirit, mortality, the profound differences between people, and the ideas that drive the world when he was very young. He began life as a Mama's boy, enveloped in maternal attention. He shared with his mother a world of make-believe.; they also talked about ideas. That world was shattered when his mother died and he was relocated to Indiana to live with his aunt and uncle, two people who were decent, kind, hard-working and very different. He was a sensitive child. He did not forget his mother, he continued to remember and to grieve, creating an intense internal life of ideas. Those ideas eventually took him into acting. People who are highly intelligent and creative make their own rules.

I knew James Dean; he was no hormone-driven Hollywood wind up doll. He was insightful, intellectually alive and very aware of the kind of people and motives that confronted him in the reality of Hollywood, 1955. To be successful in Hollywood you had to play the games Hollywood expected. Jimmy understood people; he understood their limitations and their prejudices. He had learned to project what was expected of him.[386]

Melinda was responding to a number of articles written about the time of the fiftieth anniversary of James Dean's death. Some authors of those articles wondered why the public should bother remembering James Dean. Melinda took one such author to task:

---

[386]   The Melinda. "Why is James Dean Worth Remembering?" From Reason to Freedom: Think for Yourself Website. 19 Sept 2005. Date Accessed: 4 Sept 2011. Available online at http://www.reasontofreedom.com/why-james-dean-is-worth-remembering.html

Shelby Legnon, who never knew Jimmy, says that if Jimmy had lived he would have been, "just some old guy, like Brando of Montgomery Clift.' No one could be more wrong. Legnon did not know him.[387]

She describes their first meeting:

The first time I met Jimmy it was over Beanie sandwiches in the kitchen of the family home in West Los Angeles. He was a student; I was a kid. He was the kind of person who listened to children and responded thoughtfully, by which I mean he was able to connect and engage in a real discourse, not talking down to me but exploring the ideas that found their way into our conversation, introducing ideas as part of the text. With Jimmy if there was conversation there were ideas to discuss.

It was on that very first visit that Jimmy and I discussed mortality. It was the first time anyone had mentioned the subject to me. I had been watching a tortoise dissolve back into dust, so to speak. I had discovered the tortoise already very dead behind a bush in the back yard of the house. I was fascinated by the process of its dissolution as ants carried it away and it shrank into itself. I had not told anyone else because I knew how they would react. The tortoise would evoke shrieks and Mom would remove it.

Given a chance I hauled Jimmy back to look, too. Jimmy was delighted. He proceeded to tell me about observing the same process with a cow on a farm back home. Then, squatting down for a closer look, he told me that the essence of the tortoise, the thing that had make it move and live, was gone. The same happened to all that lived, he told me.

From that time on we talked about ideas whenever he showed up for a visit. Towards the end of the visits he had started talking to

---

387   The Melinda. "Why is James Dean Worth Remembering?" From Reason to Freedom: Think for Yourself Website. 19 Sept 2005. Date Accessed: 4 Sept 2011. Available online at http://www.reasontofreedom.com/why-james-dean-is-worth-remembering.html

me about books he was reading and the ideas that excited him in those.[388]

She adds:

Jimmy was looking forward to a career; that career would only begin with acting. He mentioned moving on to directing and other work. He had been unhappy with the way a book he had read was made into a movie. The book was Fountainhead. He wanted to remake it because he thought the characterizations were flat and had failed to evoke the wonderful potential of the human life. I suspect now, looking back through a life time that has afforded me the opportunity to know more than I want about Objectivism, that if he had tried to do the remake he wanted Ayn Rand would have strenuously objected. Jimmy had a strong sense of spirituality that would have offended her. Jimmy would probably have ignored her objections. He was like that. He knew what he wanted and he was determined.

I have many memories of Jimmy; he always found time to talk to me and since we shared a fascination with ideas there was always lots to discuss. The essence of spirit, the past and how we know and understand it; the flow of time. All of these things were subjects we discussed. He did most of the talking, naturally. I listened carefully and asked questions.

Does a shallow, self indulgent kid greedy for fame and the potential for self importance and what fame can buy spend that kind of time with a child? No. Would that kind of discourse slip from the lips of an angst ridden pop tart? Hardly.

If Jimmy had lived he would not have become a fat, self-indulgent has been. He would have taken the capital he had created in name identification and respect and invested it in projects that pushed

---

388   The Melinda. "Why is James Dean Worth Remembering?" From Reason to Freedom: Think for Yourself Website. 19 Sept 2005. Date Accessed: 4 Sept 2011. Available online at http://www.reasontofreedom.com/why-james-dean-is-worth-remembering.html

the edges of thought in new directions. Hollywood would have followed his lead because he was worth following. He would have started projects for kids in Fairmount, Indiana; he would have, perhaps run for office. He would have done good in all directions. He cared about people and he cared about the kind of world his generation would leave behind. [389]

How do modern teens view James Dean? In 2001, a contemporary teenager (name unidentified) wrote an essay for the American Legends website:

Less than five years ago, if someone mentioned the name James Dean, I would have had no clue whom they were talking about. Today, I own calendars, a larger-than-life cardboard cutout, a book, and many videos relating to the actor.

I believe without even knowing it, every teenager in the world has a lot of Jimmy in them. He was a "rebel," and at one point or another we all go against our parents or our teachers. I wonder... if it weren't for him, would we all be goody-goodies? That's a question that will never be answered.)

James Dean wanted to live life to the fullest. He was quoted as saying, "Dream as if you'll live forever. Live as if you'll die today." I think that this is something that everyone should follow. If you want to do something, or say something, then don't let anything get in your way. Things may not turn out the way you want, but at least you'll know. Take chances because you may only get one.

Sadly, Jimmy was killed in a car accident taking a chance. People all over the world mourned his death. Even today people gather at the James Dean Festival (every September) to remember this legend.

---

389   The Melinda. "Why is James Dean Worth Remembering?" From Reason to Freedom: Think for Yourself Website. 19 Sept 2005. Date Accessed: 4 Sept 2011. Available online at http://www.reasontofreedom.com/why-james-dean-is-worth-remembering.html.

There are many great actors today, and I strongly believe that some of them will become legends. But they won't amount to James.[390]

In final analysis, James Dean was the sum total of his ancestors:

* He had the independent spirit of Stephen Bachiler—a spirit that ran down through his Grandmother Dean's Hussey line. He needed the freedom to create and could not tolerate restrictions.

* He had the adventurous spirit of his mother's Cavaliers and his father's pioneering Deans. When he was in his junior or senior year at Fairmount High School, he traveled with a group of classmates to Denver, Colorado. Among the places visited was the Buffalo Bill Museum and Grave on Lookout Mountain above Golden. James Dean was thrilled with that museum and all the excitement surrounding Buffalo Bill and his Wild West Show. He was drawn to bull fighting and auto racing. He rode a motorcycle and while living on the farm in Indiana, he performed acrobatic feats in the barn.

* He also exhibited a Quaker stoicism emanating from his paternal grandmother's family. He didn't complain about his extreme poverty in New York. Once when he and some of his friends were preparing a communal pot for their dinner, his contribution yielded a number of worms floating to the surface. No one said a word. They were all so hungry, they ate it.

* And, yes, he had a mean streak which he hated. No doubt it was handed down to him from Hatevil Nutter and his son-in-law, John Roberts, who brutally persecuted the Quakers. Later descendants of Nutter and Roberts joined the Society of Friends. They were his ancestors as well. He had Stephen Bachiler's temper, something else he hated about himself and something he sought to control. His temper was his worst enemy. He went after David Fox in the classroom when Fox ridiculed his performance. Another alterca-

390   "A Teenager Looks at James Dean," From The American Legends Website.Date accessed: 29 Mar 2011. Available online at http://www.americanlegends.com/actors/james%20dean/teenager.html

tion occurred with someone else on the staircase in the school building. I believe his temper erupted whenever he sensed rejection, and rejection was one of the greatest pains he suffered. Bette McPherson recalled fighting with him. When Jeanetta Lewis talked Bill Bass into abandoning Jimmy, James Dean was completely out of control and sent Jeanetta sprawling on the grass. Barbara Glenn noted a level of violence in their relationship. Some people have speculated that he smacked Pier Angeli. She got tired of it and married Vic Damone. Ursula Andress once said that they fought like wild cats and then made up, only to do it all over again. He recognized his problem because he once said, "I'm trying to get control of the violence in my life...Only the gentle are really strong."

- At the same time, he had a tender, loving nature. Once while traveling with Bill Bast, he either struck and killed a seagull or discovered a seagull along the road that had been killed. Bast said that he burst into tears and wasn't satisfied until the bird was properly buried. He also became quite emotional when his classmates sent him off on the train at the Marion depot for the speech contest in Longmont.

- He related wonderfully with children. In many ways, he was like a child himself—full of curiosity and wonder. Children were drawn to him because he respected them and didn't talk down to them. He always had time for them and was never too busy. He would have made a wonderful scoutmaster! He loved his little cousin Marcus (Markie) Winslow and became like a brother to him.

- He championed the underdog (another inherited spirit.) His ancestor members of The Society of Friends who were persecuted by the Puritan oligarchy did not remain silent about it. They challenged the Puritan power machine and were whipped, fined and imprisoned for their efforts. James Dean once said he hated anything that limited or restricted thought. When the McCarthy hearings focused on Hollywood in a mad search for Communists, James Dean expressed his angry thoughts on the matter. However, no one knows whether he ever voted. He championed the underdog because he knew what it was like to be rejected.

Beverly Wills once wondered whether he wasn't reliving some of the rejection he suffered at the hands of her friends when he made *Rebel Without a Cause.*

- He hated goodbyes. Goodbyes were very hard for him because they meant separation and/or rejection. His mother died when he was a child, and he didn't begin to come to terms with her death until just before he died. I have often thought that he was drawn toward brunettes because his mother was a brunette and in his confusion, he could not separate "mother" from "lover." His father sent him to Indiana to live with relatives, so he was separated from him. He once told James DeWeerd that he thought the reason why his parents left him was because he was terribly evil. His later relationships sometimes ended on a sour note because he demanded an unconditional love from people. He could be withdrawn and moody, only to suddenly spring into action and light up the room, running through a whole stream of emotions in one evening.

- His special place for thought and meditation while growing up was on the bank of Back Creek behind the Back Creek Friends Church. He would sit there to write poetry and draw. It was his place of solitude, providing him a chance to reflect and to dream. He was an excellent artist—a compulsive doodler who often sketched on napkins and other available items. The Fairmount Historical Museum has one of his school papers on which he had sketched a grasshopper in the margin. The grasshopper was drawn so perfectly, it almost looks like real! He was also a gifted photographer.

- Natalie Wood once noted that he kept a scrapbook. She was curious about it and one evening when she and her friend were visiting him, she managed to slip that scrapbook home to look at it and then returned it the next day. (He probably knew that she did that. He wanted her to see it.) She said that it was full of pictures of babies, poetry he had written, and drawings. He also loved classical music, something that surprised Natalie Wood. To date, that scrapbook or his diary have not been found. Several years ago, a book appeared on the market purported to be James

Dean's Diary that had "recently" been discovered and "was now being released to the public." It was available for pre-order on the Barnes & Noble website as well as Amazon. I preordered it—curiosity kills the cat, I suppose. Six months later, I received a cancellation notice from Barnes & Noble. The book was not available and would not be available. I checked the Amazon site and was told the same thing. That's when I decided the whole thing was a hoax, and I forgot about it. Apparently, a few copies made it into print before production was stopped, and it was a hoax—the product of someone's misappropriated mind.

- Elizabeth Taylor became his soul mate during the filming of *Giant*. They spent hours talking and he confided in her. She once said it was so frustrating because they would talk—then he apparently decided he told her too much—and she had to start the friendship process all over again. Both James Dean and Elizabeth Taylor took those conversations to their graves with them, leaving everyone speculating. James Dean had two main confidants: Elizabeth Taylor and Christine White. Elizabeth Taylor kept their conversations private. Christine White has done the same thing.

- He had a playful, teasing spirit. While growing up in Indiana, he teased his cousin, Joan. As she once noted, "He was an only child, and I was an only child. And we fought for position." He annoyed his drama teacher once during a lecture she was giving him over something he had done by withdrawing a cigarette from his shirt pocket and handing it to her. He knew that she was a closet smoker since he scaled through the rafters of the school building and had seen her smoking in the teacher's lounge. He was often his most playful when he was in New York and while he and Dizzy Sheridan were "walking" down the street. Some of his friends have said that he didn't just walk down the street. He zig-zagged everywhere and put on quite a performance. He once put an upholstered chair in the middle of a busy intersection and sat on the chair, smoking and reading the paper. Cars honked loudly while his friends rescued him and the chair just as an angry driver was about to descend on him. He laughed, saying he had given those people on the street something to talk about for the next fifty years! He also had a way of climbing through windows instead of walking through doors, an aggravation Jane Withers put a stop to during the filming of *Giant* by nailing her window shut. After that, he not only entered through the door, but they became close friends. And he was also labeled the most mischievous actor in Hollywood. Reportedly, he once interchanged the door signs on the Men's Room and Jack Warner's Office!

James Dean meant many things to many people since he impacted everyone differently. For me, he is the brother I never had and wanted. Since we are distantly related, we share common ancestors—probably the reason why I have always been attracted to rebels. Their motives intrigue me. Concerning my grandmother's connection with him as suggested by my father—I'm saving that for my next book!

I avoided him for years because of the awful picture I had seen of him taken shortly after death that was shown in the *Death on the Highway* program. Then I rediscovered him while searching for a way to implement film in the courses I taught. In that respect, I feel as though I was a pioneer, blazing the trail for others. Just the other day, I heard a story on the local news channel about a business professor who incorporates Dr. Seuss in his business courses. He believes his use of Dr. Seuss engages the students in what is otherwise boring material! This is currently happening on the same campus where I taught! And since I have retired, a new emphasis on film studies has arisen on that campus. So I view all of that with a sense of satisfaction. After all, my experiment began with a simple question: *how can I implement the use of film in a college composition course?*

James Dean searched for meaning. And in his search, he connected with a fictional character—Antoine De Saint-Exupery's *The Little Prince*. He recognized himself in that character-- as though seeing "through a glass darkly" to "suddenly know!" He was psychic, and I believe that he sensed his time on earth was limited . He realized that his death would come early—hence the reason for his living fast. De Saint-Exupery's final commentary rings a prophetic note:

For me, this is the loveliest and the saddest landscape in the world. It's the same landscape as the one on the preceding page, but I've drawn it one more time in order to be sure you see it clearly. It's here that the little prince appeared on Earth, then disappeared.

Look at this landscape carefully to be sure of recognizing it, if you should travel to Africa someday, in the desert. And if you happen to pass by here, I beg you not to hurry past. Wait a little, just under the star! Then if a child comes to you, if he laughs, if he has golden hair, if he doesn't answer your questions, you'll know who he is. If this should happen, be kind! Don't let me go on being so sad: Send word immediately that he's come back...[391]

---

391   Antoine De Saint-Exupery. *The Little Prince*, New York: Harcourt (1943) p. 85.

SECTION FIVE
EPILOGUE

***James Dean Doll posing in front of Gunther Toody's Restaurant,
Arvada, Colorado during my 60th birthday celebration***
*The celebration was a month late since we were in Fairmount,
Indiana on my birthday. Photo taken June 20, 2003.*

"**W**hy him? Why not pick someone more recent?" my student asked me.

By now the rest of the class had left the room. We were the only two remaining. I began gathering my materials as impatient faces of the arriving class peered through the glass window in the door.

"Because I'm always trying to pound a round peg into a square hole!" I responded.

The young man shrugged and began walking away. Then he stopped.

"Oh, I forgot to tell you. I won't be here next week. I'm going to be gone a few days."

"Where are you going?" I asked.

"I'm going to Las Vegas! Next week is my twenty-first birthday, and I plan to celebrate. But I'll be back the week after next."

I smiled as he walked away, wondering whether I would ever get through to him. And true to his word, he returned to class on schedule!.

"So, how was Las Vegas?" I asked as he passed my desk.

"Oh, you'll read about it in my final self-assessment," he told me.

"I have to wait for your final self-assessment to find out about Las Vegas?"

He walked away with a smile, leaving me swimming in a sea of curiosity.

Curiosity kills the cat, and I had to read his final self- assessment before any of the others. It went something like this:

> "At the beginning of the course, I looked through your course packet. And as I leafed through the pages, I thought, 'So who is James Dean and why is he here?' I may have heard the name, but to be truthful, I didn't know anything about the guy. He lived

too many years ago to have any influence on me. And I didn't like the film 'Rebel Without A Cause.' Some of the scenes were laughable—and I laughed. I was glad I lived in the era of modern film making, where the stories are more believable. Or so I thought! Then I went to Las Vegas to celebrate my twenty-first birthday, glad I was getting away from James Dean for a while!

I couldn't believe it! The moment I entered the casino, the first and the last face I saw was that of James Dean! James Dean was everywhere—on the slot machines—on the wall—behind the bar! Everywhere I looked, I was surrounded!

So I went to another casino, and guess what happened? Everywhere—same as the first casino! I thought I was getting away from him for a while, and it looked like he had followed me here!

I went into a third casino—same story. James Dean everywhere!

So I asked someone, "Why do they have James Dean all over the place! I can't seem to get away from him!"

"Don't you know?" the man responded. "He's only the greatest actor who ever lived! And he's one of the greatest pop culture icons of the twentieth century. Haven't you ever heard of him before?"

"Yeah, sort of," I replied. "I have this weird little lady teacher back in Denver who has him in her course packet."

"I wish I could have had a teacher like that!" the man exclaimed. "I might have learned something!"

I decided there was no escaping James Dean, so I might as well settle down and enjoy myself. After all, what the hell do I know? I sat there, laughing and shaking my head!

James Dean!"

SECTION SIX
PHOTO SECTION

Water Tower, Fairmount, Indiana
Photo taken May 21, 2003.

View of the Main Street, Fairmount, Indiana—May 19, 2003

Close-up of the Bank Building, Fairmount, Indiana, May 19, 2003

Armes-Hunt Funeral Home, Fairmount, Indiana
_Photo taken May 20, 2003. James Dean's body was taken here
after his arrival in Fairmount. According to Phil Zeigler, they
had to re-embalm him because his coffin started leaking._

The Old Fairmount High School Building taken May 20, 2003
I understand they plan to keep this portion of the building.
The rest of it will be torn down. This portion of the building
houses the stage and Adeline Nall's classroom.

Fairmount Historical Museum taken May 20, 2003

James Dean Gallery, Fairmount, Indiana. Photo taken May 20, 2003

Sign at the Loft Inn Bed & Breakfast just outside Fairmount, Indiana
The inn is caddy corner from the cemetery.
Photo taken May 21, 2003.

The Loft Inn Bed & Breakfast
We stayed here during our first trip to Fairmount,
Indiana. Photo Taken May 21, 2003.

Sign at the Park Cemetery, Fairmount, Indiana
Photo taken May 19, 2003.

James Dean Grave, Park Cemetery,
Fairmount, Indiana, May 19, 2003

Photo of James Dean Grave. Photo taken May 19, 2003

James Dean Grave. Photo taken May 19, 2003

James Dean Grave. Photo taken May 17, 2005

Marcus Winslow and Ortense Dean Winslow
Graves, Park Cemetery, Fairmount, Indiana
Photo taken May 19, 2003

Winton Dean and Ethel Case Dean Graves, Park Cemetery,
Fairmount, Indiana. Photo taken May 19, 2003

Mildred Wilson Dean Gravestone, Grant Cemetery, Marion, Indiana. Photo taken May, 2005

Carter Motorcyle Shop Building, Fairmount,
Indiana. Taken May 20, 2003

Back Creek Friends Church, Fairmount, Indiana, May 20, 2003

Winslow Farm House, Fairmount, Indiana.
Photo taken May 20, 2003
The Winslows' dog Elmo appears in the foreground.

Pond at the Winslow Farm, Fairmount,
Indiana. Photo taken May 20, 2003

The Winslow Barn, Fairmount, Indiana. Photo taken May 20, 2003

Basketball hoop in the Winslow Barn. Photo taken May 20, 2003

Trunk in the Winslow Barn
Where the Dennis Stock photo was taken in
February 1955. Photo taken May 20, 2003.

James Dean's hand and footprint in the Winslow Barn
He did this when he was 10 years old in 1941. I think these prints
have been refurbished in recent years. Photo taken May 20, 2003.

Door leading into the barn
James Dean posed here with the pig for the Dennis Stock
photo in February 1955. Photo taken May 20, 2003.

SECTION SEVEN
APPENDIX

"An actor must interpret life, and in order to do so must be willing to accept all the experiences life has to offer. In fact, he must seek out more of life than life puts at his feet."

"Being a good actor isn't easy. Being a man is even harder. I want to be both before I'm done."

"Being an actor is the loneliest thing in the world. You are all alone with your concentration and imagination, and that's all you have."

"But you can't show some far off idyllic conception of behavior if you want the kids to come and see the picture. You've got to show what it's really like, and try to reach them on their own grounds."

"Dream as if you'll live forever. Live as if you'll die today."

"I also became close to nature, and am now able to appreciate the beauty with which this world is endowed."

"I think the one thing this picture shows that's new is the psychological disproportion of the kids' demands on the parents. Parents are often at fault, but the kids have some work to do, too."

"I want to be a Texan 24 hours a day."

"If a man can bridge the gap between life and death, if he can live on after he's dead, then maybe he was a great man."

"Only the gentle are ever really strong."

"Studying cows, pigs and chickens can help an actor develop his character. There are a lot of things I learned from animals. One was that they couldn't hiss or boo me."

"The gratification comes in the doing, not in the results."

"The only greatness for man is immortality."

"There is no way to be truly great in this world. We are all impaled on the crook of conditioning."

"To grasp the full significance of life is the actor's duty; to interpret it his problem; and to express it his dedication."

"To me, acting is the most logical way for people's neuroses to manifest themselves, in this great need we all have to express ourselves."

"To my way of thinking, an actor's course is set even before he's out of the cradle."

"Trust and belief are two prime considerations. You must not allow yourself to be opinionated."

"When an actor plays a scene exactly the way a director orders, it isn't acting. It's following instructions. Anyone with the physical qualifications can do that."

James Dean[392]

392   Brainy Quotes Website: Accessed August 30, 2011. Available at : http://www.brainyquote.com/quotes/authors/j/james_dean.html

BIBLIOGRAPHY—LIST OF WORKS CITED AND PHOTO CREDITS

Works Cited

1 Corinthians 13:12—KJV, *The Holy Bible*.

"A Teenager Looks at James Dean," From The American Legends Website.Date accessed: 29 Mar 2011. Available online at http://www.americanlegends.com/actors/james%20dean/teenager.html

Aquarius Personality Traits—Aquarius Personalities. Accessed September 5, 2011. Available at: http://www.aquarius.arollo.com/personality/

Allen, Jane. *Pier Angeli: A Fragile Life.* Jefferson, North Carolina and London: McFarland & Company, Publishers (2002).

Bachiler, Stephen. World Family Tree at Ancestry.com. Last accessed May 15, 2011. Available at http://www.ancestry.com

Banks, Charles Edwards. The Planters of the Commonwealth. A Study of the Emigrants and Emigration in Colonial Times to Which Are Added Lists of Passengers to Boston and to ... Their Settlement in Massachusetts, 1620-1640. Baltimore: Genealogical Publishing Company (1979)

Barnes, Robert William. *Baltimore County Families, 1659-1757.* Clearfield Co: 1989

Bast, William. *James Dean: A Biography by William Bast.* New York: Ballantine Books (1956)

Batchelder, Hon. Charles, E. "Rev. Stephen Bachiler", *NEGHR* Jan, April, July, Oct, 1892

Beall, Barbara Inman, Ph.D. *The Legacy—A Fifty Year Tribute (1955-2005).* Bloomington, Indiana: Authorhouse (2005).

Beall, Barbara Inman, Ph.D. *The Sum Total: A Search for Levi Clay (1843-1917) and Jesse James (1847-1882).* San Diego, CA: Aventine Press (2010).

Beath, Warren (with Paula Wheeldon). *James Dean in Death: A Popular Encyclopedia of a Celebrity Phenomenon.* Jefferson, North Carolina: McFarland Publishers (2005).

Beath, Warren Newton. *The Death of James Dean.* New York: Grove Press (1986).

Bercovitch, Sacvan. *The Puritan Origins of the American Self.* Yale University Press; Reissue Edition (Mary 31, 2011)

Beverly Wills Biography, IMDb Website. Accessed September 30, 2011. Available at http://www.imdb.com

"Biography for James Dean." IMDb Website. Accessed March 5, 2001. Available at http://us.imdb.com/Bio?Dean,+James

Brainy Quote Website. Accessed August 30, 2011. http://www.brainyquote.com/quotes/authors/j/james_dean.html

Brenneman, Richard E. "Notable Kin: New England in Hollywood, Part Four: The Ancestry of James Byron Dean (1931-1955)." NEHGS *NEXIS*, Vol. X, No. 1 (1993), pp. 28-32.

Brown, Harlene Soper, Find-A-Grave Memorial #37858010, Record Added June 3, 2009. Find-a-Grave.com Website. Accessed September 5, 2011. Available at http://www.findagrave.com

Butler, Jim. "Why Is James Dean a Cultural Icon?" ShortList Website. Dated 2011. Date Accessed: 30 Nov. 2011. Available at http://www.shortlist.com

Byington, Ezra Hoyt. *The Puritan in England and New England.* Burt Franklin, 4th Edition (June 1972).

The Case Against Reverend Stephen Bachiler. Online. Accessed Spring 2002. Available at http://members.aol.com/Lynnash911/guilty.html

Copley, Jennifer, Aquarius Personality Profile. Accessed September 5, 2011. Available at: http://jennifercopley.suite101.com/aquarius-personality-profile-a60945

Cox, Naomi "Amy" Hussey, Story told to her grandchildren. Date unknown. Qtd. In Schoen, Eleanor Campbell. "Our Fascinating Ancestor, Stephen Bachiler." Presentation May 22, 1999. Accessed September 15, 2011. Available at http://www.hampton.lib.nh.us/hampton/biog/bachilerschoen.htm

Dalton, David. *James Dean: The Mutant King*. New York: St. Martin's Press (1974)

De Saint-Exupery, Antoine. *The Little Prince*. New York: Harcourt (1943).

"Death is my Neighbor," *Danger*, (CBS), 25 Aug 1953. Cast: James Dean as JB—psychotic janitor. Also Walter Hampden, Betsy Palmer, Frank Marth, Andrew Duggan. Director: John Peyser. Producer: Franklin Heller. Writer: Frank Gregory

"Dennis Garrett," EDLER, FISHER, REDSECKER, WALD and Related Families. *Notes on some of the ancestors and relatives of Karl & Barbara Edler, Bets & Bruce Wald and Martha & Jim Redsecker.* Person Page 96. Accessed September 14, 2011. Available at: http://www.edlers.org/notes/p96.htm

DeWeerd, James Arthur. Sons of the American Revolution Application for Membership National Number 93009, State Number 1860. Dated June 16, 1965; Accepted June 23, 1965. Ancestry. com. Accessed September 25, 2011. Available at http://www.ancestry.com

DeWeerd, James Alfred. Social Security Death Record. Ancestry.com. Accessed September 25, 2011. Available at http://www.ancestry.com.

Dirks, Tim. *Rebel Without a Cause (1955): Review by Tim Dirks.* Date Accessed 3/29/01. Available online at http://www.filmsite.org/rebel.html

Donne, John. "No Man is an Island." PoemHunter.com website. Accessed October 3, 2011. Available at http://www.poemhunter.com/poem/no-man-is-an-island/

Dow, Joseph. Joseph Dow's History of the Town of Hampton: From Its First Settlement in 1638 to the Autumn of 1892 (History of Hampton New Hampshire 1638-1988). Peter Crandall, Pub (December 1988).

Drake, Albert. I Remember The Day James Dean Died & Other Stories. Adelphi, Maryland: The White Ewe Press (1983).

Edna Ferber- Biography. From the IMDB Website. Date Accessed: 13 Feb 2012. Available online at http://www.imdb.com/name/nm0272209/bio

Epting, Chris. James Dean Died Here: The Locations of America's Pop Culture Landmarks. Santa Monica, California: Santa Monica Press LLC (2003).

Ferber, Edna. Giant. Greenwich, Conn: Fawcett Publications, Inc.—A Fawcett Crest Book (1952).

Frost, Robert, "The Road Not Taken" Mountain Interval (1920). Great Books Online at Bartleby.com. Accessed September 25, 2011. Available at: http://www.bartleby.com/119/1.html

Giant: The Making of an Epic Motion Picture with a Foreword by George Stevens, Jr: Special Collector's Edition, Warner Bros (1996).

Gide, Andre. The Immoralist. Translated by Richard Howard. New York: Vintage International; Vintage Books—A Division of Random House, Inc. (1970—Alfred A. Knopf, Inc.) [Originally published in France as L'Immoralist by Mercure de France, Paris, in 1921. Copyright 1921 by Mercure de France, Paris. This translation originally published by Alfred A. Knopf, Inc., New York, in 1970.

Glenn McCarthy, from Wikipedia. Date Accessed: 13 Feb 2012. Available online at http://en.wikipedia.org/wiki/Glenn_Herbert_McCarthy

Haller, William. The Rise of Puritanism. University of Pennsylvania Press (October 1, 1972).

Hanaford, Mary Elizabeth Neal. *"Family Records of Branches of the Hanaford, Thompson, Huckins, Prescott, Smith, Neal, Haley, Lock, Swift, Plumer, Leavitt, Wilson, Green and Allied Families."* Published Rockford, Illinois; 1915.

Hatevil Nutter Find-a-Grave Memorial. Find-a-Grave Website. Accessed September 8, 2011. Available at http://www.findagrave.com

Hell's Highway—The True story of Highway Safety Films (2003). Actors: Richard Anderson, Sonny Bono, John F. Butler, Hans Conried, Earle Deems. Directors: Bret Wood, Richard Wayman. Writers: Bret Wood. Producers: Earle Deems, Bret Wood, Richard Wayman, Felicia Feaster, Tommy Gibbons. DVD Release Date: November 28, 2003.

The History of Marion and Grant County, Indiana Website. Marion and Grant County Convention & Visitor's Bureau. Accessed September 4, 2011. Available online at http://www.grantcounty.com/discover-grant-county/history

Holley, Val. *James Dean: The Biography.* New York: St. Martin's Griffin (1995)

Howlett, John. *James Dean: A Biography.* London: Plexus (1975, 1997)

Howlett, John. qtd. In Warren Beath with Paula Wheeldon, *James Dean in Death: A Popular Encyclopedia of a Celebrity Phenomenon.* Jefferson North Carolina: McFarland & Company, Inc., Publishers (2005).

Hyams, Joe, with Jay Hyams. *James Dean: Little Boy Lost.* New York: Warner Books (1992)

Ives, J. Moss. *The Ark and the Dove.* Cooper Square Publisher (August 1969)

Jacob Wilson, OneWorld Ancestral Trees, Ancestry.com, Accessed October 9, 2011. Available at http://www.ancestry.com

James Dean, from *Wikipedia,* last modified 8 Feb 2012. Date accessed 22 Feb 2012. Available online at http://en.wikipedia.org/wiki/James_Dean.

"James Dean: A Portrait." WhiteStar Entertainment: A Division of KULTUR. Produced and Directed by Gary Legon. Produced & Edited by Sarah Legon. Written By Gary Legon and David Dalton. Music By Marc Governor. Narrated by Rip Torn. MCMXCV Estate Films Inc. An Estate Films, Inc. Production.

"James Dean Biography," Available on the Allsands website in 2001. Accessed 10 Mar 2001. Wysiwyg://43/http://www.allsands.com/jamesdeanbiogr_rz_gn.htm

James Dean: Hollywood's Rebel, The Picture Show Man 1890-1960 Website: Articles—Personalities: The History of Motion Pictures. Accessed January 5, 2012. Copyright 2004-2012, Key Light Enterprises, L.L.C. Available online at http://www.pictureshowman.com/articles_personalities_dean.cfm

"James Dean's Tombstone Recovered." Mr. Showbiz News Website. Dated July 17, 1998. Accessed 3/9/01. Available at http://mrshowbiz.go.com/archive/news/Todays_Stories/980717/dean071798.html

Jobs, Steve. "You've Got to Find the Job You Love: Text of Steve Jobs Commencement Address, Stanford University, June 12, 2005. Stanford University News Website. Accessed October 7, 2011. Available at: http://news.stanford.edu/news/2005/june15/jobs-061505.html

Lindner, Robert . Rebel Without a Cause: The Hypnoanalysis of a Criminal Psychopath. New York: Grune & Stratton (1944).

Loftin, Patryce, Personal Conversation, Fairmount, Indiana, May 20, 2003.

Love,Robertus (1925). The Rise and Fall of Jesse James. Qtd. In Barbara Inman Beall, The Sum Total—A Search for Levi Clay (1843-1917) and Jesse James (1847-1882), preface.

Main Frame in James Dean Page. James Dean Artifacts Website. Accessed March 10, 2001. Available at http://www.jamesdeanartificats.com/frmain01.html

Marion, Indiana. The Wikipedia Website. Accessed Sept. 4, 2011. http://en.wikipedia.org/wiki/Marion,_Indiana

Martinetti, Ron. *The James Dean Story.* New York: A Birch Lane Press Book—Published by Carol Publishing Group (1975, 1995)

Marston, Philip Mason, *The Reverend Stephen Bachiler—Saint or Sinner?* Published Privately 1961 by the Society of Colonial Wars. Accessed September 15, 2011. Available at http://www.hampton.lib. nh.us/hampton/biog/bachilermarston.htm

Massachusetts Historical Society Collection, 4 Series, Vol. VII, pp. 91-4, notes

Millay, Edna St. Vincent, "Renascence". Archive of Classic Poems. The Poetry of Edna St. Vincent Millay. (Poem originally written in 1912) Everypoet.com Website. Accessed September 23, 2011. Available at: http://www.everypoet.com/Archive/poetry/Edna_St_Vincent_ Millay/edna_st_vincent_millay_renascence.htm

Mrkich, D. *Summer Was Only Beginning.* Ottawa, Ontario, Canada: Commoners Press (2001).

Old Norfolk County records (MS) 8th month, 1st-3rd day, 1651

Pierce, Frederick Clifton, Batchelder,Batcheller Genealogy. Heritage Books (July 1992)

Rathgeb, Douglas L. *The Making of Rebel Without a Cause.* Jefferson, North Carolina, and London: McFarland & Company, Inc., Publishers (2004)

Rebel Without A Cause. James Dean, Natalie Wood with Sal Mineo, Jim Backus, Ann Doran, Corey Allen, Dennis Hopper. Screenplay by Stewart Stern. Produced by David Weisbart. Directed by Nicholas Ray. Music by Leonard Rosenman. Copyright: 1955, Warner Bros. Pictures, Inc. Renewed 1983, Warner Bros, Inc. Package Artwork, Design & Summary 1986, Warner Home Video Inc.

Rebel Without a Cause: Greek Tragedy in Modern Film. Date accessed: 29 Mar 2001. Available online at: http://www.geocities.com/Athens/ Parthenon/9502/rebel.html

Romero, Simon, "A Texas Town Holds Fast to its Ties to a Classic," The New York Times Website. 8 Jun 2003. Date Accessed: 13 Feb 2012. Available online at http://www.nytimes.com/2003/06/09/national/09MARF.html?pagewanted=all

Sanborn, F. B. *The Hard Case of the Founder of Old Hampton.* Accessed September 15, 2011. Accessed September 15, 2011. Available at http://www.hampton.lib.nh.us/hampton/biog/bachilerhardcase.htm

Sanborn, Victor Channing. "Rev. Stephen Bachiler" from *Batchelder, Batcheller Genealogy* by Frederick Clifton Pierce, 1898.

Sanborn, Victor C. "Stephen Bachiller: An Unforgiven Puritan" The New Hampshire Historical Society (1917). Accessed September 15, 2011. Available at: http://www.hampton.lib.nh.us/hampton/biog/bachilerunforgiven.htm

Schoen, Eleanor Campbell. "Our Fascinating Ancestor, Stephen Bachiler." Presentation May 22, 1999. Accessed September 15, 2011. Available at http://www.hampton.lib.nh.us/hampton/biog/bachilerschoen.htm

Scorpio-Rising Ascendant in Scorpio. Always Astrology Website. Accessed September 5, 2011. Available at: http://www.alwaysastrology.com/scorpio-rising.html

Sheridan, Liz. *Dizzy & Jimmy: My Life with James Dean—a Love Story.* New York: ReganBooks—Harper-Collins Publishers (2000)

Some Ideas for Testing and Projects on Tragedy. Date accessed: 3/29/01. Available online at http://www.geocities.com/Athens/Parthenon/9502/tragedytests.html

Spoto, Donald. *Rebel: The Life and Legend of James Dean.* New York: Cooper-Square Press (2000).

Steele, Phillip W. *Jesse and Frank James: The Family History.* Gretna: Pelican Publishing Co.(1997).

Steinbeck, John. *East of Eden:* Penguin Twentieth-Century Classics (With an Introduction by David Wyatt). New York: Penguin Books (1952/1980/1992)

Stiles, T. J. *Jesse James: Last Rebel of the Civil War.* Vintage: (October 28, 2003)

Tarkington, Booth. "Chapter I: A Boy and His Dog," *Penrod.* Classic Reader Website. Accessed September 20, 2011. Available at http://www.classicreader.com/book/1207/1/

The Melinda. "Why is James Dean Worth Remembering?" From Reason to Freedom: Think for Yourself Website. 19 Sept 2005. Date Accessed: 4 Sept 2011. Available online at http://www.reasontofreedom.com/why-james-dean-is-worth-remembering.html

Thompson, Boyce, Jr. "Hatevil Nutter was a Cruel Religious Hypocrite," Thompson Family History Website. Posted April 15, 2011. Accessed September 4, 2011. Available at http://thompsongenealogy.com/2011/04/hatevil-nutter-was-a-cruel-religious-hypocrite/

Trouble Along the Way (1953). Actors: John Wayne, Donna Reed, Charles Coburn. Director: Michael Curtiz. Released April 4, 1953. Warner Bros.

West, Andy. The Back Creek Webspot (2010). Last Updated February 19, 2011. Accessed September 3, 2011. Available at http://www.andywest.org/fm/back_creek.html

"The Whipping of the Quaker Women." From the Dover, New Hampshire Website: http://www.dover.lib.nh.us/Dover%20History/whipping_of_the_quaker_women%20new.htm.   Transcribed   by Amelia Reimer, April 29, 2001. Posted on the Rootsweb Website. Accessed September 4, 2011. Available at: http://archiver.rootsweb.ancestry.com/th/read/HATEVIL/2001-04/0988579425

The Whiskey Rebellion. The Early America Website. Accessed September 6, 2011. Available online at http://www.earlyamerica.com/earlyamerica/milestones/whiskey/

The Wing Family of America Website, Published by The Wing Family of America, Inc., Accessed October 10, 2011, Available at: http://www.wingfamily.org/

Wilson, Leonard. *The Heraldry of the Deane Family*. London, 1938.

Winthrop, John. The Journal of John Winthrop, 1630-1649: Abridged Edition (John Harvard Library) by John Winthrop, James Savage, Richard Dunn and Laetitia Yaendle (Jan 1, 1997)

You are There: The Capture of Jesse James. Director [Sometimes *The Killing of Jesse James*]: Sidney Lumet. Release date: 8 February 1953. Narrator: Walter Cronkite: Cast: James Dean as Bob Ford: John Kerr as Jesse James. CBS Television Network Information available at IMDb website. Accessed September 25, 2010. Available at http://www.imdb.com/title/tt0751918/

Photo Credits

1. Cover Photo—James Dean Walking in the Rain. Original photo taken by Dennis Stock, New York, 1955.

2. Author Photo—Photo Shopped in 2011 by Edward C. Adkins. Original Photo: Senior Picture, Barbara Ann Inman, 1961, Thomas Jefferson Senior High School, Cedar Rapids, Iowa.

3. Frontispiece Photo:--James Dean. Photo purchased in an antique store in Fort Collins, Colorado, January 2004. Original photo taken on the set of *Rebel Without a Cause (1955)*.

4. Prologue Photo: Painting of James Dean and Marilyn Monroe obtained at an antique/collectible store in Georgetown, Colorado. Painting dated 2007, James Dean Foundation under authorization by CMG.

5. Introduction Photo: Marion, Indiana—The Deanfest Headquarters taken May 18, 2005 on our last trip to Fairmount, Indiana.

6. Section 1 Photo: Stephen Bachiler Chair. Photo obtained from Ancestry.com: Available online at http://www.ancestry.com

7. Section 1 Photo: Batchelor Hussey. Photo obtained from Ancestry. com: Available online at http://www.ancestry.com

8. Section 1 Photo: B. F. Kessler Family. Photo obtained from family pictures. Available at Ancestry.com: http://www.ancestry.com

9. Section 2 Photo: Winton Dean Family, date taken—unknown. Photo available at Ancestry.com: http://www.ancestry.com.

10. Section 3 Photo: James Dean's Last Visit to Indiana. Photo taken by Bob Middleton February 1955 in Indianapolis, Indiana. He gave the author a copy of this photo in 2002/2003.

11. Section 3 Photo: Old Longmont High School Building where 1949 Speech Contest was held. Photo taken Fall 2008. The dolls are from the author's website in the Travels with Jim section: http://www. historical-footprints-2010.com

12. Section 4: Conclusion Photo: James Dean. Photo from Modern Screen Magazine's Memorial Issue, dated 1955/1956.

13. Epilogue Photo: James Dean Doll standing in front of Gunther Toody's Restaurant, Arvada, Colorado, June 20, 2003. Taken just before the author's 60th Birthday Celebration. The doll (a Mattel James Dean doll) belongs to the author and appears in Travels with Jim on the author's website: http://www.historical-footprints-2010.com

14. Pictures appearing in Photo Section: All photos were taken by the author during two Fairmount, Indiana trips—one in May 2003 and the other in May 2005.

INDEX

An Apple from Coles County 125
Andre Gide 214
Andre Giide 213
Anglicanism 32
Anna Ewer 88
Annaline Denton 91
Anna Maria Pierangeli 233
Anna Maria Pierangeli (Pier Angeli) 226
Anna or Ann Bachiler 78
Ann Ayers 40, 45
Ann Bates 71, 77
Ann Blount 96
Ann Coleman 41
Ann Cox 82
Anne Arundel County, Maryland 48
Anne Doane 87
Anne Flanders 59
Ann Garretson 82
Ann Hubbard 50
Ann Thigpen 96
Ann, widow of Jeffrey Mingay 81
Ann Wilson 96
Anthony Chamness 53
Anthony Lindsay, Jr. 51
Anthony Quinn 257
Antoinette Perry Award 217
Aquarius 111, 112, 113, 329, 331
Aquarius Personality Profile 112, 331
Archbishop Bancroft 62
Archbishop Grindal 60
Arlene Sachs 110
Armando Trovajoli 232
Arminta Alice Cree 26
Arthur Loew, Jr 239

B

bachelor 57, 58, 169
Bachiler vicar of Wherwell 61
Backboard Jungle 243
Back Creek 105
Back Creek Friends Church 105, 124, 126, 292, 319

C

Lightning Source UK Ltd.
Milton Keynes UK
UKOW050802120712

195862UK00001B/28/P